MESSAGES FROM ABOVE

LOVE KNOWS NO END

A JOURNAL

Also from Mastery Press:

The Blue Island
Beyond Titanic—Voyage into Spirit

Heart's Healing

The Spirit World, Where Love Reigns Supreme

The Hum of Heaven

The Wisdom of Saint Germain

The Gift of Mediumship

Awaken the Sleeping Giant

A Legacy of Love
Volume One: The Return to Mount Shasta and Beyond

To Master Self is to Master Life

A Wanderer in the Spirit Lands

MESSAGES FROM ABOVE

LOVE KNOWS NO END

A JOURNAL

DIANE MACCI

Mastery Press

Phoenix, Arizona

Copyright © 2010 by Adventures in Mastery (AIM), LLC

Published by:

A division of Adventures in Mastery (AIM), LLC

All rights reserved. No part of this book may be reproduced or utilized in any form or by any means, electronic or mechanical, including photocopying, recording, or by any information storage or retrieval system, without permission in writing from the publisher. Inquiries should be addressed to:

Mastery Press
P.O. Box 43548
Phoenix, AZ 85080
PB@PhilipBurley.com
www.PhilipBurley.com

ISBN: 978-1883389-19-2
eISBN: 978-1-883389-34-5

Printed in the United States of America

Cover and interior design
by 1106 Design, Phoenix, Arizona
and Philip Burley

Dedication

For my beloved husband

Angelo

January 25, 1928 ~ November 28, 1986

The Iris
Angelo Macci's favorite flower

Glory to God in the highest, and peace to his people on earth.
—Luke 2:14

Acknowledgments

My deepest thanks go first to my sons, Lee and John Macci, and my daughters, Angela Meade and Sue Zoller. Each one of them gave me constant encouragement, both in my spiritual journey following my husband's death, and in the writing of this book. John constructed a meditation room for me in my garage—assisted by a dust-covered Sue—including a beautiful stained glass window depicting irises, my husband's favorite flower. In that room I wrote the words appearing in this book. Sue's devotion of time and energy to caring for her father during his illness, and for my mother who had come to live with us, made my life much easier. Lee helped me type my original manuscript for the book, and Angela listened with great patience and love. My children are my dearest friends.

Sylvia Norton edited the first draft of this book and gave me confidence that I had something valuable to share, and Grace Kohan did a meticulous job of fine-tuning the manuscript. I thank Marie Wilson for her thoughtful comments, Anne Edwards for her sensitive editing of the introductory and closing pages, and Lynn Mathers for her skillful preparation of the manuscript for publication. Lydia Macci, my daughter-in-law, assisted greatly with many electronic communications. I'm most appreciative of everyone's efforts.

Of course, this book is possible only because of the wonderful meditation classes led by Philip Burley that I attended in the late 1980s. Philip and his wife Vivien opened their home and their hearts to me soon after my husband died, when I most needed support, and they have become my forever friends. Philip encouraged me to begin writing my spiritual journals—the foundation of this book—and to find the love within that each of us has inside. I am eternally grateful for his kindness and for being the best example I know of unequivocal devotion to God.

Contents

Foreword by Philip Burley xi

Preface xv

    1988 1
    1989 41
    1990 89
    1991 149
    1992 187
    1993 235
    1994 275
    1995 321

Epilogue 357

Macci Family Photos 361

Sources 369

Foreword

The inward journey taken through journaling can be life changing, as evidenced by Diane Macci's inspired and faithfully recorded words. She listened so deeply and wrote so directly from her heart that she touched in with the very far reaches of the spirit world to communicate and record directly-spoken, great truths from the realms of celestial light. In doing so, she experienced personal transformation. Through this book, she shares her transforming words with all of us.

As a professional medium who has taught meditation and spiritual development classes for more than two decades, I am delighted that Diane, one of my outstanding students, has written this wonderful book. It will open the way for many others to use journaling to find their inner wisdom. I have had few students to equal Diane's fervor or steadfast, consistent effort in pursuing true spiritual awakening. Through both meditation and journaling, she faithfully and astutely applied what she learned in my classes and from other sources. Her beautiful writings validate what I have been experiencing and teaching for so long, and this is more gratifying than I can say.

Diane was in her late fifties when we first met more than twenty years ago. As she will tell anyone, the single driving force leading her to reach a higher level of spiritual awareness was the death of her beloved husband Angelo Macci.

Diane and Angelo had been so close that she felt a deep need to make contact with him, share ongoing communication, and gain greater closure regarding his death. Diane is not a "poor me" person, and I could see that she did not cling to her husband in a self-centered or obsessive way. She suffered profoundly but accepted the reality of Angelo's death and got on with her life, both through spiritual pursuits and reaching out to others who were suffering too. Having already raised her family, she was ready to start a second life for herself, and that second life consisted of walking the spiritual path.

In the absence of Ang, as she affectionately called her husband, Diane wanted to go on living and growing, knowing in her heart and mind that the two of them would one day meet again. Knowingly or unknowingly, she began to prepare herself to be a more spiritually advanced person than she was when Ang left her to enter the spirit world. After all, he was now on the other side advancing spiritually; why shouldn't she?

The secret to Diane's success on her journey of spiritual growth was obedience to a higher calling. I saw this again and again as I taught the classes she attended. With childlike faith and persistent effort, she would do whatever I suggested to the whole class. When I taught that daily prayer and meditation would open their spiritual senses and deepen their awareness of the spirit world and God, she immediately applied these teachings in her own life. With her family's help, she even turned her garage into a meditation room just for this purpose.

For seven years, every night, all alone, Diane faithfully sat in meditation for spiritual development. This was not a case of blind following or blind ambition, but saint-like faith. She was determined—with the utmost humility—to open her spiritual senses and meet the spirit world face to face. It was with this kind of spirit that she wrote in her journal in an effort to communicate primarily with her husband, but also with others who came in love from the spirit world.

I have my own journaling story: Gifted with second sight and spiritual hearing from early childhood, I heard spirit speak to me in a clearly audible voice, so that anyone in the room with me could have heard it, and I obeyed this direct urging by my trusted spirit guides. Starting in January of 1988 and ending the last week of December, I got up faithfully every Sunday at 4:30 a.m. and prayed for thirty minutes before I took my place to receive dictation from 5:00 to 7:00 a.m. sharp. I experienced these two hours each week as purest communion enveloped in divine love. I didn't care what anyone would think, for I knew my exchanges with the spirit world were as real as any conversation on earth. My notebook filled with messages from spirit, and these words became the basis for the manuscript of my first book, *To Master Self is to Master Life*.

Foreword

Consistent, prayerful journaling made an indelible impression on my spiritual life, and I was never the same. I began urging others to journal, because I knew they too would be greatly rewarded. After hearing about my experience, Diane simply adopted the practice without hesitation. While she did not, as a result, become the kind of medium I am,* she is a genuine medium of another kind. Her inspired words flowed without effort onto page after page of deeply personal communication from her husband and universal wisdom from unidentified loving beings. The results? *Love Knows No End.*

I am humbled and proud to call Diane Macci my friend and spiritual sister. She is a person afire with an unquenchable flame of desire to do God's will and make herself a vessel for his indwelling. She has demonstrated the absolute willingness to give more than one hundred percent in trying to become all that she can become to please the Father and to reach her Angelo. I leave it to the reader to decide if she accomplished her task. From my personal experience with Diane, I know she did.

After Diane had been journaling for a number of years, Angelo came to me, of all places, while I was covered with suds, taking my morning bath! We had never met, though I had seen photographs of him. Filled with surprise and awe, I blurted out, "Angelo! What are you doing here?" He came closer to the tub and said in a clear voice, "Tell Diane that I have appeared to you to urge her to publish her book before she passes over. It is vitally important that she does, though she may not fully understand why until she comes here." With that, he left as suddenly as he had come. I called Diane right away and told her what had happened.

You now hold in your hands the results of Diane's due diligence and Angelo's urging, all filled with eternal love. I know this book will speak to you on many levels; and it may even inspire you, dear Reader, to set special time aside for the sacred and rewarding task of journaling to find your own deeper spirit and awaken you to the reality of the great beyond! I sincerely hope so.

— Philip Burley

---

* Clairvoyant and clairaudient in a literal sense.

Preface

Outwardly, I was acting as if I was okay and everything was fine. But inside I was devastated when my husband Angelo died in 1986. Ang and I had been happy and close. We had been married for thirty-two years, and we couldn't have been more pleased with our four beautiful children and our established teaching careers. We looked forward to a future retirement together where we could relax, travel, and enjoy the laughter of grandchildren. Ang was a supportive, passionate, devoted family man who made everything happen. We shared so many common interests in addition to our family—gardening, music, and vacationing by the St. Lawrence River. He was my life. Now he was gone; a victim of untreatable colon cancer at the age of fifty-eight. What was I going to do—or be—without him?

This book is not about grief, or even about overcoming grief, though my grief did abate as I poured out my heart to God. It is about that outpouring, and the influx of love and wisdom that poured back into me as I took an extraordinary journey to my own inner world of light. In some ways, this book is the story of learning to find joy in little things—like the song of a bird, the touch of a leaf, and the sight of a cloud, but it is more than that.

I received the grace to take the advice of my spiritual teacher, Philip Burley, and sit alone to listen for my husband's voice to speak to me from the spirit world and record what I heard. I allowed myself precious time to do just that. I sat with my journal every night and let my heart flow onto the pages, simply writing down what was coming through. You will find these words in this book. But you will find more than that.

As I listened for Ang, I began to hear higher wisdom, sometimes appearing to come from him, sometimes from unknown others, and sometimes from God, my Heavenly Father. I received words that were to change my life, little by little and day by day, by making me aware of a world that is beyond this world, but no less real. I opened my heart to a love greater than I had ever known, and it is still with me today. My life is now centered on this love, and on the spiritual wisdom within my heart that is always available to me. I can never "un-know" what I have learned—that God is alive at the center of my being, and I am surrounded by a world of loving spirit. I don't have to go to church to find God because he is always with me, inside. My church is my heart, and I can go there anytime. What a privilege!

There are references in my journal to challenging emotions that I experienced in response to certain situations, including a custody battle that affected my family and the opening of my bed and breakfast business.* Though spirit spoke to me directly about my feelings in those particular situations, I found their responses had universal meaning. The messages I received through journaling have been deeply personal, but they are not for me alone.

I'm still the ordinary person I have always been, with typical ups and downs; but now I'm coached, all along the way, to get back on track and re-center my life on God. I'm constantly reminded of the importance of thinking positively, of staying in this moment, and of finding joy in the beauty of nature, in the simple things of life, and in other people, especially my eight grandchildren, who are a constant source of comfort and happiness. It has been a blessing to be a part of their lives.

One theme runs throughout my life and throughout this book—that living with an awareness of God brings constant renewal, relief, and the wonderful fruits of the spirit: love, joy, peace, patience, kindness, goodness, faithfulness, gentleness, and self-control.**

My soul, my heart, and my mind have never been complicated. I'm much like "everyone else." Yet an extraordinary love has come to me, and a brilliant light enfolds me. We can all know this glory because we all carry God within, and we can never be separated from him. I know,

---

* My aunt, Dr. Helen Hosmer, bequeathed her beautiful older home to me where I fulfilled my dream of opening a bed and breakfast business.
** *Galatians 5:22–23*

Preface

beyond any doubt, that these experiences are not only for me. They are for you, and for everyone living on earth and in the spirit world. That's the very reason I want to share them. It is my hope that you will be touched by the light that I know is within you as you read the pages of my spiritual journey.

May you be blessed, now and forever.

— **Diane Macci**

1988

Saturday, July 23, 1988

Spirit:

Strive only for those things of true value; anything less is a waste of time for they do not come from God. The naked truth is full of innocence and is pure. The purer your vision of God, the more you see in your inner sight. God's laws are simple in structure. It is in the interpretation that mankind makes them complicated because one's direct line from God becomes twisted with unkindness and lack of love. As one's ability to seek God and live a life of love returns, so in equal proportion will enlightenment and inner sight return. As your inner sight opens, you will learn many more things, and your life will take on more purpose and meaning.

Your faith must never falter. This is so very important because it is the rudder by which you can sail God's ship in the sea of everlasting life. God alone is sufficient. His direction is all that one needs for he is the source of all things, and all things are connected despite the shortcomings in the doctrine of man-made religion.

You are what you think—so set your sights on God, the Almighty. Jesus is helping you to know love and compassion in the deepest sense, so continue to seek his guidance in daily prayer. Through sheer will of mind learn to concentrate more. Pull your thoughts together. Force them to work for you and then the fragments of inner vision will begin to take more form. These fragments must be assembled together and this is accomplished by inner concentration.

Your ability is growing, so persevere and be patient. Help and guidance will be there at every turn. You are never alone, but you yourself must search for and learn the lesson from each experience. To intellectualize is a fine way to gather knowledge, but not in total. The heart speaks with equal brilliance and should always be listened to with great reverence, for its message comes from God.

Wednesday, July 27, 1988
Spirit:

Melancholy comes because one lacks enough faith to truly see into heaven. Be happy soaking in the beauty and love one encounters in everyday life for this is what accompanies one in his journey into spirit. The problem seems to be a lack of satisfaction with the moment— always with the moment, or is it with the past, or is it truly with what is to come? Examine each more carefully. The past is over; it is finished, and cannot be changed. It must be accepted in your heart for what it is and perhaps used as an important guide and stepping stone so that mistakes are not repeated. Yet, the joy and happiness should always be felt and remembered. The joy comes from the ability to remember the love from the past, for this love will travel into eternity.

What about the future or what is yet to come? It will be molded out of the wisdom and love of this present moment added to the past. What then is the most important? Is it not the present moment? Yes, this is what is so important. One learns from the past, one builds for the future, but one must live each moment now to its fullest because the present contains all three. The future becomes the present which becomes the past, so the present contains all three. Learn from the past, build for the future, but live and love in the present.

Tuesday, August 2, 1988
Ang:

About memory—It is not so important to remember each detail of a memory, but rather the ambiance and feeling of love at the moment. This is what sustains one. The ability to feel the meaning of the spirit is what lasts, not the moment itself. True love is built from these feelings. Think of the end of my illness. Certainly the mundane tasks were not what one remembers but rather the flow of love between us. Love is a great force from God and this force is eternal. This is why you reminisce the feeling rather than the actual sequence of events. The pictures fade, but the true feeling of love can only grow with time. Your insight continues to grow each day also. You amaze me.

Thursday, August 11, 1988
Spirit:

Plateaus are resting places; otherwise the path would be too difficult. Each step must be mastered, and this takes practice, patience and time. Nothing in God's plan happens before it is time. God's plan is flawless; mankind and his free will cause the imperfection. Sometimes one tries too hard, so relax and let things flow naturally. This is especially true when one is tired.

Friday, August 12, 1988
Spirit:

The trouble with earth children is they want, want, want. It is so easy to fall into the pattern of questioning what's next, rather than thanking God for all that one already has. If one would only start to ponder all of the incredible, small wonders in one's immediate grasp, it could happily fill a lifetime.

However, my child, greediness so often steps in the way. Those who have health are truly blessed. Stop to think about the wonders of the five physical senses. That alone is a gift of immeasurable value, and yet, God in his great love and kindness gave each of us five spiritual senses as well. The difference is great, you see, for one is a gift at birth, the other is earned through faith and love toward one's fellow man. Physical senses tend to push one toward wanting, whereas the spiritual senses' inclination is one of giving.

Which of these can bring the most joy? The answer to this question must be pondered very carefully, for you see, my child, the answer will reveal the maturity and development of one's spiritual senses. Desire alone does not open these senses; it is not enough. Desire coupled with prayer will lead one to the right path. Prayer is the spark which ignites desire, not the other way around, for each of God's children has a natural need to pray. It is through this prayer that one desires to find God.

Saturday, August 13, 1988
Spirit:

The answers of your heart, those that live in the deepest realms, will come in God's own time. Patience is perhaps one of your truest friends, my child. You see, within each heart dwells the secrets of God's love and peace, yet secrets are whispered softly in the quietest of moments. Each soul must make time for these quiet moments to hear God. How is this done, you ask? It is accomplished through prayer, love, kindness and peace. When one learns to accept the trials and inconveniences of everyday life and still has love in his heart, then progress is being made.

It is in the small deeds of everyday living that God's voice is heard. You always expect something earth shattering or some larger accomplishment; when instead, each moment lived with love and kindness is what truly matters. This is all God asks—the rest will follow unannounced. It will flow into your life as gently as a flower opens.

Do rainbows not appear instantaneously at a perfect moment of splendor? If you can see all the external beauty of God's world, how much more magnificent is the internal beauty? The correlation is there, but you must put it together with thought; then it becomes action. You, my daughter, are in this thought process.

Tuesday, August 16, 1988
Spirit:

Peace of mind can and will come. World peace must begin within each one of us. The turmoil of daily living is the first battle to be won. Life is not easy, but then it is not as difficult as mankind chooses to make it. Free will is a God-given gift and until man finds the proper use of it, there will be no peace. Free will is part of Divine Order and must be applied within God's rules of the universe. "Free" and "will" are best explained by the following rule—each is free to find the will of God, but until we collectively find God's will, there will be no world peace.

The scope of the world, in general as yet, is so very small. Few in comparison see into the magnitude of God's supreme creation. Each is part of the whole and must submit to God's plan; then all will run smoothly. This is true of everything. Nothing runs smoothly unless each part is assembled properly and works together as a unit. If only mankind would examine more closely the interrelationship between things of creation, rather than how each works separately, so much more progress would be forthcoming.

Everything about life is connected and must be taken in faith, in God's faith, until the answer comes to life. Man tends to ignore this divine connection and wonders why things go awry. God's thinking and ultimate understanding is within the grasp of each of his children, but only when each is willing to listen. Free will must be under God's will, or no will can work. If the word "submit" to God is used, the pride of many becomes involved, yet pride is closely connected with humility or humbleness. When one can learn, and how difficult it is, that humbleness is pride unmasked and stripped of all inadequacies, then true progress can be made.

Thursday, August 18, 1988

Spirit:

This particular message has to do with happiness. What is happiness and how does one achieve it? Happiness is a state of mind and not a result of some physical or material element as you on earth believe it to be. There are, of course, degrees and types of happiness which is perhaps where earthlings become confused. Happiness of the physical body is satisfied by "things," by "doing," and by "touching," but take those away and immediately one is no longer satisfied. There is nothing wrong with this kind of happiness except it is superficial and lasts for a limited time. True happiness comes from God and is a state of mind—an attitude which develops and is nurtured in the deepest depths of the spirit. This kind of happiness must be earned through hard and intense soul-searching. It does not just happen suddenly for it must develop slowly and with patience.

Can you not see that lasting and important attitudes come from thought? How else can they be transmitted into the spirit so that one can take them into eternity? You see, my child, true happiness is brilliant and self-illuminating because its source comes from our Heavenly Father. That is why all the beauties of nature bring such happiness to one. They are God-given gifts, free for each to take and cherish when the spirit has learned their true value.

What will it take to awaken mankind to this simple truth? Love of God is the answer. It is the same thread of truth which weaves itself throughout all things. Happiness comes from one's love of God. It starts deep within as a seed at birth. Each experience in one's life nurtures the seed, or in too many instances, leaves it dormant. So you see again, dear child, that all things come from God, and happiness is no exception.

Wednesday, August 24, 1988
Spirit:

There is nothing more sacred or meaningful in life than holy matrimony. It lives close to God's heart. The bonding of two souls into one is a gift from God, and is so very special. Those who are so honored will find joy in their hearts forever. Far too many on the earth plane fail to take this commitment seriously, and therefore fail in their endeavor to find happiness. The road to oneness is difficult and filled with sacrifice, but how else can true love be found? It is easy to love and be kind when all is going well, but what real merit can be found in this?

Unknown to many, love flourishes the most when the path becomes difficult and filled with the obstacles of life. The reason for this is the need for the spirit to learn the true value and meaning of love. Love comes from the heart of our Heavenly Father and it is given to those who seek its refuge. Love is giving of oneself unconditionally without any expectation of a return. Only then does it come from its true source and uplift the spirit. Ponder the power released when two spirits become as one in a perfected marriage. This is why it is so important for each married couple to seek this union of spirit. The survival of the world is dependent upon love of this intensity.

Thursday, August 25, 1988
Spirit:

"Let there be peace on earth, and let it begin with me," as in the Christian hymn. Peace would reign on our beloved earth if each person could only say "I love you, God." Peace dwelled first in his heart and he meant it for all of his children. Does not each parent wish peace for each of his or her children? Peace comes from love, and thus it follows that peace and love are inseparable or totally entwined, whichever meaning one chooses to use. Is it possible to have love without peace or peace without love? I think not. Peace cannot be bought or bargained for as so many believe. This would seem to be too easy a solution, and has it ever worked? Again, I say, I think not.

Mankind always looks to another for the answer to problems when all he needs to do is look within his own being. This is where the truth dwells, for God placed the answers to all problems deep within each of his children. This is his great gift as our Father, yet many fail to look deeply enough for these answers. Hence, the world is filled with the superficial needs that ultimately cause hate and war, not love and peace. Mankind can reverse this trend quickly and quietly. Each must learn to say "I love you" to another. Each must learn to help another as his brother. Is not God the Father to all of us? Are we not all of the same family? World peace can and must come through the brotherhood of man, and the understanding that comes when love fills the heart. Then, and only then, will world peace be accomplished.

Friday, August 26, 1988
Spirit:

Everything about life is timeless if one really searches for truth. One moment is an eternity for there can be such a drastic change, and yet in reality very little has truly changed. Birth, death, rebirth—what exactly happens? Is it not true that only the physical changes? Everything physical ages in its own time and speed until it eventually no longer exists.

Or does it? Ponder the magnitude of this and perhaps you can catch a glimpse of God in all of his glory. The physical side of life is important only to teach us the existence of its spiritual counterpart—that which lives forever and has no ending. That which one truly loves clings to the spirit and will be there, upon recall, forever. Everything has a physical image and a spiritual image. The physical is there so that the spirit may place a value of recall upon each experience in one's life. The beauty of our ability to recall comes through our ability to love—the love given to each of us by our Heavenly Father. If this beautiful love is wasted, then the spirit has little to recall. This is the fate of many and the reason for so much unhappiness. You, my dear child, must be a channel to educate your fellow man that love is the salvation of the spirit—love of God, love of self, love for one another and love for all of creation.

Saturday, August 27, 1988
Spirit:

Dear child, for Me to enfold you in my arms, you must know My Heart. You must learn to suffer silently, patiently, with love—always with love, knowing that which you seek will be there for you when the time is perfect. Perfection is such a key word, yet taken so for granted. Perfection is the ideal, the dream which lives in the heart of each of My children. The dream is not the difficult task, but finding the true path in which to make it come alive is the struggle of life. The quality of this aspiration is the crux of your life. If the spirit takes command, there is no end to this dream for it then becomes eternal. Make your dream of this quality, my child. Strive daily to find it, never tiring or becoming discouraged. The one who lives in your heart is there at every turn. A love of this quality is made in heaven with "Eternal" stamped upon it, but you must continue to let it grow throughout your remaining life.

As you grow in love for all of my creation, for each of your brothers and sisters, so will love pour into the strength and bond of your marriage.

Never doubt the thoughts which come to you, for they are sent from the highest realms to teach you what you must know to do My Will, which you pray for so often, my child. I hear you always.

Monday, August 29, 1988
Spirit:

Each experience in life, my dear child, offers a lesson to learn, and it is sometimes profound. But more often it teaches equilibrium of the spirit. Nature too, reflects different moods of the spirit, or have you never dwelled upon this? The sun in its beauty corresponds to happiness and rain to sadness, thunderstorms to unrest and glorious sunsets to tranquility. Is this not true? And yet, as one grows spiritually one begins to realize that the spirit needs to know or conquer each of these emotions in his own lifetime. Then and only then can one appreciate and know God's heart.

To understand nature is to see God in all of nature's splendor. Weather corresponds so closely to the moods of each being, but few truly see it. When one is happy in spite of the rain and the thunderstorms in one's life, then sadness or sorrow will always stay in its proper place. It is necessary, yes, but not overwhelming. For you see, the spirit which stays close to God knows that the rainbow will always follow. Nature can teach all the lessons of life if only the children of earth would listen more closely with their spirit senses.

Keep praying, my child, for it helps more than you can see from the earth plane. Salvation will come through prayer and love. Be thou one of its messengers, even when it is difficult to view the end result. Doubt not that only good will come, and it will.

Friday, September 2, 1988
Spirit:

Love is the thread which will link the world together. Too many have strayed away from this lifeline to God and instead have set their sights upon false values. This leads to unrest and emptiness.

Saturday, September 3, 1988
Spirit:

One of the secrets to spiritual growth is being satisfied with one's progress, knowing that more will come at the perfect moment. Unshakable faith in God's plan is a must; otherwise precious energy is wasted on doubt and dissatisfaction. All channels must be open to hear clearly the next important message. Once one learns to listen rather than project his own will, the spiritual climb becomes less difficult. Take time to enjoy each plateau until it is truly understood and accepted.

Nothing new will be revealed until this is accomplished, and it must be done with heartfelt love for God and all of life. To let God control your self-image (defined as one's conception of oneself) until it becomes selfless (having no concern for self) is the most difficult of tasks. It takes untold prayer, meditation and thought, and a true desire to unfold the nine fruits of the spirit into one's life: "love, joy, peace, patience, kindness, goodness, faithfulness, gentleness and self-control." *(Galatians 5:19–23)*

Sunday, September 4, 1988
Spirit:

Trust the Lord God with all of your power and all of your might for he in the end is the beginning. Do you not understand that all things are as one? There is no division. God created each one for the other—to stand as help and support each onto its own but for the other as well. Many sayings come from this, such as, "united we stand, divided we fall." Nothing exists alone. God made everything connected to each other, but it is not always necessary to know the exact reason why each was so carefully created. Man forgets his position in the universe. He places too much value on the physical side of life which is necessary only to find the spirit within. Unfortunately through the mismanagement of God's plan this truth is totally misunderstood, and so many have put the "horse before the cart," so to speak.

God is seeking a way to reverse the trend of this misconception. Many in spirit will come closer to help those who are able to hear. Always write down those thoughts that come to you for there is a purpose and message in each. Let God and his helpers be the judge of what must be said. Pure and clear channels must be available to relay important messages, but as in any dictation, practice and more practice are needed. This is true for you as well so do not get discouraged but try to listen for the words of wisdom which will be forthcoming.

Practice the ability to relax to the point of floating or of being in limbo. Then the message can come through accurately and with precision. Prayer is very important in reaching this state of mind. The vibration of prayer and meditation clears any interference which can distort the words and thoughts being transmitted. You are being trained carefully for this work.

Monday, September 5, 1988
Spirit:

Rainbows of happiness appear as God's light shines upon the beautiful crystal in each of us. The brilliance of this happiness manifests itself through love. The more light one sees from God, the easier the burdens of life will be, for love then becomes the guiding force.

Tuesday, September 6, 1988
Ang:

You must be able to find and give more love even when you think there is none left. When you can do this, new avenues will open for you. One must finish the task at hand before it is time to move on. It is easier to see from spirit how rushing often causes disappointment and unhappiness. Instead, dear, take each day as a present, a gift, and do the most that you can with the circumstances that are presented. Let nothing pull you down spiritually—not problems, not relatives, not people, not any situation. When you learn to do this, you will see many changes in your life, but I shall be there to help you and comfort you always. It must indeed be difficult to learn to know and feel what one cannot physically see. Continue on your path to seek this ability and you will find it. Peace be with you and feel all my love and support. You knew you were special to me when I was in my physical body, but you can't begin to know how special you are to me now. Look at your crystal candlesticks and the beauty all around and you will know. I love you, dear.

Friday, September 9, 1988
Spirit:

There are many such as you on the earth plane, my child. Those of you whose heart is in the right place, but you flounder about not knowing how to help your country, the world and all of mankind. Help for the world must come from the desire of each individual to find peace. If each can find peace from within, there will be peace without; this peace will become visible to all. If each, such as you, could influence but a few others, then the negativity of the earth would slowly begin to reverse itself. The tide of humanity can be changed, but not in a spectacular fashion, but rather as a glimmer of light which comes from the heart of the true believers in God. As these conscientious people, like yourself, begin focusing their attention and efforts in prayer and good deeds, the sleeping giant of love can and will be awakened.

Those of true wisdom must never falter, but instead use the wealth of support they have from the world of spirit. The important work then, my child, is to open the eyes of others to the spirit world. You can and must do this through the credibility of your own life. You must live as a child of God. Never cease to learn and find inspiration from prayer and meditation. Those who can connect themselves to the world of spirit have an untold wealth of information and guidance right at their fingertips. Do not forget this, my child. The support system is already there.

What you on earth must do is learn to tune in and use it properly. Fine-tune your abilities by questioning those coincidences and feelings of intuition to see what message is trying to be conveyed. The touches of love are gentle so you will know that they come from the realm of God. Listen closely, my child, and teach others to listen with you. This is to be your mission. Do not burden yourself with self-doubt. Messages which quietly glide into your thoughts are always helpful, are they not? This is proof enough that they come for a reason. Joy is the result of hearing a message correctly.

Monday, September 12, 1988
Spirit:

Each of us on earth is alone, and yet, not alone. How can this be? One is alone in that each must stand naked before himself and God at some point in his life. Each must prepare for eternal life and this can only be accomplished by soul-searching and looking at the truth which dwells in each of us. How close do you live according to God's law of love? Do you do unto others as you would have them do unto you? Once this evaluation is honestly completed for the first time, the knowing touch from God and his highest realms is felt forever. Then and truly then, one knows he will never be alone again.

To reach the heights one must know the depths. Self-evaluation takes one to the depths of the soul where there is no place to hide from oneself. Whatever one has done against others, one has also done against God. These transgressions must be faced and eliminated through the mercy and love of our Heavenly Father. Jesus was sent by God to show us how to live our lives, and the Bible also tells us how to live our lives. Yet new understanding is being revealed every day. A new age is dawning, and those on earth who have searched their souls and touched this world of spirit will see more of God's truth.

Tuesday, September 13, 1988
Spirit:

Strive to let the light of love always shine upon another and not upon yourself. If you can learn to do this successfully, there will always be joy in your life. It is in giving that one truly receives. Love is the channel through which God can work. Like the drilling of a well, each soul must keep on digging deep inside to find this reservoir of love. It matters not how deep this love is hidden, but rather the intensity with which one tries to find it. Life is like a battleground with peace won through unconditional love for God and all of mankind.

Later, the same day:
How does one help the world find peace? Pass on to another the strength and love you carry in your own heart. If you share your heart with another, then that heart grows in its ability to love more. Think how much more peace there could be in this world if the level of love in each heart would grow just a little. It takes time and patience, this is true, but nothing is impossible with God's help. The vibration of peace through thoughts, prayers and meditation will become stronger and this does make a difference.

Wednesday, September 14, 1988
Ang:
There is never any reason to say goodbye for we are never apart. You knew this innately, dear, because you said you would find me. Little did we both know at the time there would be no need to find one another, because there is no spiritual separation, only a physical separation which lasts just a short while. Continue to have vision. The deeper your love for God and all of mankind, the farther your spirit eyes can see.

Life is the mirror of your spirit; it reflects back whatever image you project through your love. Love becomes light in equal proportion to the energy projected and true love is brilliant. Allow yourself the quiet time needed to restore the calmness to your being. Giving because you must is more draining than giving because you desire to do so. The difference is the merit and value of one's life, for you must judge yourself one day. Try to always give with a happy heart for in serving another you are building energy for yourself. Like all of God's plans for us, his children, what seems simple to understand is difficult to implement in our lives. This is the beginning of faith, hope and love.

Saturday, September 17, 1988

Diane:

The dynamics of the Olympics tend to make one think of the possibility of world peace. Yet, what and from where does peace originate?

Spirit:

Peace dwells within the heart of each of God's children. It lives there safe and protected from all turmoil. How unfortunate that so few on earth are aware of its closeness. Many look elsewhere to find peace, always seeking the answer in some other place. Why can each not see that it lives in one's own spirit?

Diane:

What clouds this vision? Perhaps it is one's lack of humility that is causing the world to fail in its pursuit of peace. Is the ego of man standing in his own way?

Spirit:

If each on earth would only look within to find the answers, peace would not take so long in coming. Peace on earth, good will toward men. Is it really so hard to achieve? God sent his son to show the way and his message is repeated over and over in the Bible, yet so few seem to internalize it. Peace comes when one learns love: the deeper the love, the greater the peace, for one balances the other. Man has not yet learned the importance of this balance within himself. How can the world find peace when its people lack peace in their own lives? Peace can only come to the earth when each truly returns to his focus on God. Peace comes from that God-force within each of us. It was placed there at birth to be nurtured as one's spirit grows in love. What happened to this gift of peace? Continue to seek answers as you search for peace.

Monday, September 19, 1988

Spirit:

Strength of spirit comes through God who is all love. He is selfless and merciful, and so is love. In the book of 1 Corinthians verse 13:4–8, one may put the word "God" in place of the word "love" and it will make perfect sense, for you see, God and love are one and the same. "Love is patient, love is kind. Love is not jealous, it does not put on airs, it is not self-seeking, it is not prone to anger; neither does it brood over injuries. Love does not rejoice in what is wrong but rejoices with the truth. There is no limit to love's forbearance, to its trust, its hope, its power to endure. Love never fails."

Therefore, my child, when you love, you are doing God's will. That is why you find more strength, energy and joy in your heart because with love you can uplift the spirit of mankind. Any positive energy can be used to counter negative energy which takes away the true source of God. Continue to seek spiritual growth because all of mankind will benefit. As yet, man only sees with physical eyes. How much more quickly he will progress when he starts using his spiritual eyes—the eyes which can see into the eternal world of God.

Tuesday, September 20, 1988
Spirit:

It is only when one becomes selfish, that the spirit becomes weakened. One is vulnerable depending upon where he stands between selfish and selfless. The closer one can cling to selflessness, the greater will be his strength from God. This ratio will always be true for God is constant. It is his children who fail to understand this law even though it is explained in the Bible in different ways, for example through the Golden Rule, the Last Supper, the parable of the least of my brothers and in "reap what you sow."

Can you honestly look within yourself and evaluate your motives? Take one day in your life. Do you think of yourself or another first in daily situations? It is then not difficult to know where one stands in relation to selfishness or selflessness. What is difficult is placing more love in your heart, especially under difficult and stressful situations. Each has the potential to be all-loving, but the path is very steep and relentless. Faith, hope and prayer make the journey possible, but only the individual can seek this path of selflessness and love.

Wednesday, September 21, 1988
Spirit:

As love grows, it fills the heart and there is room for nothing else. This is when one feels peace from God. A pure heart is beyond attack from all woes of the physical world and is full of serenity. Love chases away despair and sorrow. It quietly settles into the crevices of unrest and brings calmness. Peace and love form a bond of brotherhood; to call upon one is to find the other, for they live as one. If peace abides, there is love. If love is present, there is peace. Peace of mind emerges as the spirit grows in its ability to love all of God's creation.

Thursday, September 22, 1988
Spirit:

Each time one thinks that an end has come, believe instead it is a new beginning. Since life is eternal, there is no end. Life flourishes on positive thought and action. Eliminate all negativity through prayer and right action. So many on earth think this is impossible, not realizing that it is the thought itself which creates the negativity. Thought precedes every action. One does nothing without thought. Can you not see that positive thoughts come from the spirit where God dwells, and negative thoughts come from the physical realm where evil can hide. For the world to right itself, positive thoughts from the spirit must dominate. This can indeed cause a battleground for turmoil, but each has the ability and power to control action with thought. Positive thought can only produce positive action. Mankind must begin using this positive power from God.

Monday, September 26, 1988
Spirit:

Nothing is as it seems. Everything has a hidden or magical meaning. Only as one becomes closer to God does the hidden meaning become real and thus reveals itself as truth. Look for this truth every moment of your life for it reveals itself at the least expected moment. The Bible tells us two will be sleeping in bed, where one will be taken, the other not. *(Luke 17:34)* Truth does not present itself with force, but rather as a soft, gentle touch of love.

How does one describe a touch of love? Does it not enhance the quality of life with peace and joy? Even the simplest of tasks, regardless of its degree of difficulty becomes easier if there is love in one's heart. The key to happiness and contentment can then be found in love which soon leads one into the beautiful realm of selflessness. To bask in this light, one must talk to God as if talking to oneself, for in reality they are one and the same. God made each in his own image, so to seek this image one must become selfless in order to do his will. Man tends to feel that becoming selfless means one has no identity, when in reality it means, he has found his true self—his reunion with God.

Next perhaps you ask, what can I do to influence my fellow man to this profound truth? Continue on your upward path. Discover for yourself each facet of love in all of its glory. Use God's rainbow as your symbol of truth and love. Its beauty manifests itself in so many ways, yet the white light of God will be the ultimate expression of love. Keep the vision of this pure love and light always in your heart, my dear one, for it will light the lamp of the world. Little rays of light, appearing as flickers of light as in a candle or a firefly, can combine until all may see—whether they choose to or not. This light will one day encompass all and enfold the world into God's arms. Continue to see this vision in your heart, and though you may stumble, the path will be revealed to you as you climb upward. Watch closely and never doubt your ability to see the way. Inspiration can come on the wings of a butterfly, so always be prepared.

Friday, September 30, 1988
Spirit:

Anything that helps someone has value. It matters not what the deed itself is, but rather what was the intent from the heart of the giver. Merit is judged from this intent. Mankind too often thinks he, himself, is in charge of all things instead of giving credit to God, the Almighty, and this turns into being a big disaster in his life. Be sure, my child, that you do not fall into this trap of the mind. God alone is great for he created all things. Man is from his image, so true greatness comes to each only when God wills it and becomes part of it. This is how merit is judged, for it comes from the heart of an individual through the grace of God.

Is not merit but another way of expressing love? Is not love that constant thread of joy which weaves itself into the life of each of God's children? All roads to God must be traveled with love in the heart. This is an absolute, and it is upon this love that merit can be granted. Is the reward for merit greatness, or is greatness, merit itself? Merit and greatness are in the eyes of the beholder, so who is to judge? Perhaps, in truth, merit is to be judged in the realm of spirit and not while we are in our physical bodies.

Wednesday, October 5, 1988
Spirit:

What is the meaning of life? It is the proving ground of the spirit in man. Each spirit has the great need to be released into the physical side of its being. Too many on earth fail in this endeavor. Sacrifice and suffering are looked upon as torture, when in reality they are the doorway to spiritual understanding. One who seeks only the satisfaction of his physical being cannot find lasting peace or joy. Love comes from God, and God and love dwell in the spirit. Until one begins to listen and hear this quiet voice of truth, life has no real meaning or purpose.

As an analogy, think of a switchboard or a computer. The connections and answers are there, but unless one finds the perfect combination, there is confusion. This is true in life as well. Until the physical man finds and listens to his spirit, there is also confusion. This confusion manifests itself in so many ways such as anger, intolerance, lack of patience, hatred and so on. Each one of us could make a list of such actions. Why then can man not conquer these negative reactions?

Perhaps it is because he fails to understand the truth about himself and his connection with God, the creator of all things. Too often man feels life owes him something, when in truth life is a gift from God. Should not man instead give something back to God? Should he not seek the link and understanding of eternal life?

Friday, October 7, 1988
Spirit:

One gains strength of spirit by asking God for help. It is in the questioning that answers are found. Too often mankind lacks the humility to speak and pray to God for his help in solving those problems which arise in daily life. Perfection is accomplished by constantly assessing and changing those imperfections which each finds in oneself. It is easy to ignore these imperfections and excuse oneself, but in the end these imperfections must be faced. Is it not easier to face them now, while it is possible to change the direction of one's life? We, who are in spirit, know this to be true, and will continue to strive to educate those who are still on the earth plane.

Life is for the living, but too many on earth are spiritually dead. Faith, hope and love are not commodities that can be bought and sold, but rather come through the grace of God, our creator. Grace is earned, not through selfish endeavors, but through service to God. As in the Lord's Prayer, "Thy will be done, on earth as it is in heaven" is the key to successful living.

If each on earth would pray to do God's will every day of one's life, heaven on earth would soon begin to emerge. The fruits of the spirit, as stated in Galatians 5, are love, joy, peace, patience, kindness, goodness, faithfulness, gentleness and self-control, and they should be our challenge in daily life. If each incorporated God's law into daily living and loved their neighbor as themselves, strength of spirit would shine forth for all.

Tuesday, October 11, 1988
Spirit:

We, in spirit, can be divided into four equal parts. We can be in four places almost simultaneously, so we can come whenever you call. Be not hesitant to use us in any situation at any time for that is our purpose and also our delight. So many on earth are afraid or reluctant to use this very special service which is a gift from God. Instead, fear or doubt fills their heart and then help is totally shut down during physical life. Your mission, my child, is to try and reverse this misconception. You must not let failure discourage you, dear child, for each on earth wants to believe that such contact is truly there, but due to past fallacies and indoctrination, there is fear of the unknown. You, who believe so strongly with great love in your hearts, are our only hope of changing this situation.

Therefore, you must be strong and always strive to reeducate those that cross your path. It is such a waste that those on earth fail to use this great source of guidance which is always available with only a thought. Pure, selfless type of thoughts will receive priority, for these thoughts come through to spirit the clearest. We know and hear all thoughts, but with any form of transmitting, interference can interrupt a clear response. Lack of love in one's heart for God and his truth is a large stumbling block to success. You, my child, perceive much wisdom and understanding so you must try to influence others.

We, in spirit, will not desert you in this endeavor, but rather will give you insight, encouragement and strength to endure the negative reaction which indeed you must encounter to do this type of work. You are constantly being trained and tested so that you will not fail in this mission. Mankind can and will be saved through contact with God's chosen spirit realm. These special ambassadors will make contact through a planned network until real progress can be seen. Your eyes will be open to this awakening so stay alert and steadfast, for much depends upon those of you who believe in spirit contact through God's love of mankind. To understand or comprehend the immensity of this project is not possible when viewing it from the physical world, so you must take much of it through faith, unfailing faith. We talk to you to give you courage and support that you are indeed treading upon the right path, my child.

Friday, October 14, 1988
Spirit:

Seek your peace from within, my dear one. Try not to be so intent and hard on yourself, but rather let help and guidance float into your being. One cannot demand or dictate calmness—it comes from love and selflessness. As soon as one becomes the least bit agitated or self-serving, true love can slip from one's grasp. God is not judging you for he loves each of his flock, but rather you are dissatisfied and judge yourself. Seek the help that is so available to you from spirit and it will be there. One cannot serve God and self at the same time. There is no room for both and that is where the struggle of discontent arises.

Self is from the physical plane, whereas God dwells in the spirit realm. Of course there is a connection, but it is difficult to grasp the true magnitude as well as the subtleties of spirit life. Many do not even bother, or should we say, most fail to even try. It is the energy behind the feelings of physical life that will be transmitted into spirit life. As one becomes more selfless, this ability becomes easier to perceive, hence, one is elevated in spirit. This is the progression of self-mastery; the ability to project physical experiences into pure fruits of the spirit.

Monday, October 24, 1988
Ang:

Make all songs of love a message of joy to your heart even as the tears stream down your face. You see, dear, our love lives in the beautiful music you hear, in the gentle and trusting eyes of the wild animals you help and feed, in the fragrance and beauty of your flowers, in the hush and quiet of the night and so on into eternity. Our love lives in all of God's creation. Cry, my dearest one, but cry for joy and not for sorrow, for I come in each of God's gifts to bring you comfort and love. Sleep in peace, surrounded by love.

Wednesday, October 26, 1988
Spirit:

The Art of Healing: Each on earth has the ability to heal oneself and many can help in healing another. However, the prerequisite to this gift from God lies in the light of love. How can one heal the imbalances of the body unless the center of one's being, the spirit, is filled with unconditional love. The light of healing comes from this source of pure love. Its color is blue in energy and radiates forth from the mind and the hand of a healer.

Once one has manifested God's love into his being, the next power is that of concentration. Energy running rampant and unfocused cannot be directed to a focal point.

Do you not see that the ability to heal is the direct relationship between the energy and vibration from God's love collected through concentration into a focal beam of light which restores balance to the physical body? Pray to God that you may continue to purify yourself with unconditional love and then the ability to concentrate will develop. You must have faith that each ability will evolve at the perfect moment and it will; this, dear child, is the providence of God and it shall be so. Believe in yourself and in your abilities, and if you remain humble, God will give you great talent to do his work. Be ever mindful and listen to the wisdom of your heart. Nothing is impossible.

Saturday, October, 29 1988
Spirit:

The saying "Love is in the eyes of the beholder" came to you because that is where you will find many answers. Can you not see that love will be returned to you in the same intensity in which you send the love from yourself? Selfless love can always tap into the love of another for there is God's love in each of us. The difficulty is not in another, my child, the truth of the matter is the deficiency is truly within you.

Guilt is not the issue at hand so eradicate the thought and punishment from your mind. Neither will pity be of any use. Instead you must look deeper within to find the unending reservoir of God's love that can heal all things. You must not get so easily discouraged, but rather through prayer and the search for truth, you will find your answer. Words and thoughts can be very enlightening, this is true, but it is in doing that one finds the answers.

The great beauty of love is its healing power. All that seems impossible can be reversed, but only in direct relationship to the intent of love and faith. Faith is knowing without proof that all things will work out, and love is the vehicle through which God can work. If love is selfless, there is no end to its capabilities. The difficult path, my child, is finding the pure love of God. You, and all of God's children, will find it from within through service to others.

As long as discouragement, disappointment or guilt plague your way, you must continue to travel the path. Perseverance, faith, and prayer will be your best allies, for it is a difficult battle to conquer yourself. Keep on keeping on, my child, to find truth. As you bare the imperfections of your spirit, God stands close by to help you. Positive searching and doubt promote progress and this is stimulating. Remember, dear child, love for the sake of loving to serve God. The power of God's love is overwhelming, and you will see this as you progress upward.

Tuesday, November 1, 1988
Spirit:

It is in the thought process that all things evolve. A seedling of an idea is nurtured until it develops as a full-fledged thought. That is one of the reasons quiet contemplation and meditation are so very important. These tiny seedlings get trampled upon by the activities of life. Too many on earth fail to listen to the crossroads of peace and thought, for it is there that one can communicate with God. Thought is the intimate relationship between what we are and what we strive to be.

Wednesday, November 2, 1988
Spirit:

The mystery of growing spiritually is in direct relationship to your ability to love, pray and help other people; only then, can God truly energize your spirit. Thoughts and good intentions are a beginning, but service to others is the real key to God's heart. You must learn this lesson slowly with great patience; otherwise you will falter or stumble at the wrong moment. Can you not see how carefully God prepares you? He will never desert you, but rather stands close while you find your way, much like a child. Look upward, see his challenge of true love and seek its inner beauty. There is no end to love and to its abilities to heal all things because it shines forth from God, our eternal force of love, light and energy.

In your own heart you ponder weakness and the lack of energy in your own being. Is this not true? At these times you must keep on keeping on, for this is the path of truth. You must learn to hurdle the pain, frustration, resentment and all the heartaches of daily living, for in doing so you will touch God. We come to give you encouragement, dear child, for your road is not an easy one, yet the enlightenment you are receiving must light your path for you to continue to climb. Use the help which surrounds you—feel the love, see the beauty. The struggle for your spirit is waged while you are in your physical body, so let it never weaken to all the temptations of fallen man. The greatest merit and reward can only come to a perfected man, one who knows the meaning of love and service.

Judge yourself not by another's accomplishment, but rather by the capacity of your own being. If you examine your own heart, you will see that there is always room for more love to grow and burst forth with endless energy to serve and help others. Thought in the form of prayer and meditation is your greatest source of strength for then you touch God's reservoir of energy. Learn to concentrate your own energies. Refuse to let any situation pull at or tap into your own spirit and pull it down. Give freely of the love generated by your spirit. Each human being is responsible to build the strength of his own spirit and that is universal law. Another may help with love, but there can be no trade-off. Man's destiny is to find and develop his own spirit.

Sunday, November 6, 1988
Spirit:

It is the meaning behind each word that one needs to examine carefully. The dictionary meaning is literal, and of course it is important, but translating the true meaning into one's heart is the most difficult of tasks, and few try to do it. True meaning comes from putting God's wisdom into a word until it becomes a part of one's being as truth. Think of some words such as love, praise, beauty, hope, faith, prayer. Do all these words take on a deeper truth when you tap into the energy of God? There are words of lip service and words of heart. Those words from the heart are the ones which can be heard clearly. Try very hard, my child, to pray with words such as these.

As you can see, it is quality we seek, not quantity. The world truly suffers because quantity has become more important than quality. Is not one act of total commitment more lasting than many deeds which are done poorly or not at all? You see, child, words are similar. Each perhaps has several meanings, but the true quality comes from God. The thoughts which words produce become most important when one serves God. Can you not see this? True expression in the literal sense is doing what one feels, but in truth it is doing God's will which ultimately brings out the best in each of his children. The best is quality not quantity. We bring you this message to help you to focus your energies and concentrate on the tools of healing. What you need will come to you as you grow in spirit and find strength in God.

Tuesday, November 8, 1988
Spirit:

Be humbled by the magnitude of the Lord. It is necessary for each on earth to reflect upon this great truth every day of his life. Too many precious moments are taken for granted, life quickly passes away, and those on earth fail to recognize the magnitude of God and his creation. Many pray, but few in comparison ponder the true meaning of God and desire to do his will. We talk to you often, daughter, so that your awareness will continue to grow and keep you on the path of spiritual growth. It is not necessary to understand God's master plan, but rather pray to do his will on faith alone. Has our Heavenly Father not shown each of you on earth his love by the beauty of his creation? Why is this not enough?

Man fails to humble himself before God. He fails to grasp the simple truth that nothing would exist without God. He barely notices the many intricate wonders of nature, but instead takes them for granted as if each was nothing. This lack of caring and indifferent attitude must begin to change. Many ask how, and we answer with the word, prayer. Prayer is the central thread of consciousness for it connects the thoughts of many hearts together into a powerful energy. Prayer can indeed be selfish, but its source comes from the positive consciousness of a soul. Mankind does not pray for negative reasons, but rather to find answers and help from God. Prayer is powerful and it can change the direction of a negative force. Know this and strive to increase you prayer life.

Sunday, November 13, 1988
Spirit:

Peace of mind is the place where those who love meet God. This special spot is enhanced by everything of love—each kind deed, each thought; the whole of existence is raised by love. Truth about love brings peace of mind for it belongs to God. Everything belongs to God, but mankind is so slow to realize the connection. In its complexity, life is so simple. God's rules are truly few, but man himself has so complicated his own existence.

Let us further examine peace of mind which each tries so hard to find, and yet how elusive it becomes. Peace of mind is nothing more than a calm reservoir of thought. It is that workshop where all rough edges can be made smooth. Like any craftsman, one needs a special tool to perfect his work. How then does one create his own peace of mind?

The answer is praying to God for guidance each day of one's life. Can you not see that each soul must visualize the calmness which comes in knowing the love of God, the creator of all things? Think of the magnitude of this creation—the thought, the work, the love that was needed to create such energy. Once created it is self-perpetuated by man's love for God and his fellow man in the form of a family. One must love God to love himself, and he must love himself to love another, so there must always be give and take in one's life. Peace of mind results when the give and take of each of these relationships is in tune with God's heart.

Tuesday, November 15, 1988
Spirit:

The energy and enthusiasm that you are always so desirous of finding, my dear one, comes from within your own being. Is not enthusiasm, love of life, and energy and vitality, the capacity of doing work you love? If you carefully examined words that are connected to and found in the realm of spirit, you would find that the driving force behind each is love and God, for in reality, they are one and the same. Love is God and God is all love; there is no separation.

In theory, it is simple to those who see with their hearts, but to live your life with all love is most difficult. This, my child, is why you search and scrutinize your own heart so carefully to find the purest form of love which brings you closer to God. To do God's will you must follow his path of love. This is an absolute law, so let nothing block your pathway to unconditional love. It is the key to further development and you know this. You do not climb this path alone. Know that there is help along the way. You shall find it as you continue to seek, and you shall have it. Be at peace, my child.

Thursday, November 17, 1988
Spirit:

Laughter is your best ally, for it releases anguish and frustration so they can float away.

Sunday, November 20, 1988
Spirit:

"Forgive them, Father, for they know not what they do." *(Luke 23:34)* Each Christian knows this magnificent uttering of Christ on the cross, yet few dwell upon its meaning. If Jesus was able to ask forgiveness while being tortured as he physically died, why is it so hard for each of us to forgive our neighbor? It takes so little to love and understand another if we remember that God made us all brothers. Each in God's creation is connected to another. Each, it is true, has its own direction and purpose, but how it fits into the whole is what makes each one of unique value. It is more important how you love; the light which you project, rather than who receives it.

Can you on earth not see that in projecting love, the energy will intensify and then bounce back in much greater magnitude? The gift of love will encircle all things and bring each back to God. It is like water. Each droplet in itself is important, but the total fulfillment comes as each droplet becomes part of the next droplet, and so on, until each is part of the whole. Nothing on earth can stand alone, for each must find its rightful place in God's creation. This is God's absolute law, and it will be done on earth as it is in heaven.

Monday, November 21, 1988
Spirit:

Try not to pass judgment on another, for in doing so you are passing judgment on yourself. You cannot see the inner depths of another, only God can do this. You are responsible to try and help with love in your heart, but one cannot share his deepest spirit with another. Each must earn God's help in doing this. We have sent this message many times to help you. Continue to overcome the hurdle for an important lesson will be learned. Earthly difficulties from the spirit side are viewed so differently. Continue to seek the answer spiritually and remember love is a constant companion.

Friday, November 25, 1988
Spirit:

"In him we live and move and have our being." *(Acts 17:28)* Life must come as it falls, for it is accepting what is placed before you with love that pleases God. Love is the cornerstone from which God can rebuild all that is beautiful and of value. Refrain from "barking up the wrong tree," so to speak. Remain humble, peaceful, loving and kind, knowing that God can accept and work upon this foundation. Be not in a hurry, but always patient and listening for the voice of God within you. Meet in spirit those loving people who have been sent to help you on your upward climb. Happiness comes from doing God's will, but remember there is eternity ahead of you, so listen patiently with faith, hope and love in your heart.

Saturday, November 26, 1988
Spirit:

Child, live each moment in your life with abundant love in your heart and all will work out beyond you greatest hope and imagination. Find joy in the hardest moments, give kindness in the weariest moments, and shine forth with love in every moment. This is the pathway to do God's will, and you must learn to never fail. Live in peace, my little one.

Sunday, November 27, 1988
Diane:

To search one's heart is the beginning of finding God. He lives in each of us, yet how many truly listen to his words of wisdom? Perhaps we outsmart ourselves, always wanting answers that satisfy the physical part of our being. Why is it so hard to believe in what is not seen?

Monday, November 28, 1988
Ang:

Sadness is part of life and you must learn to force your way through to the opposite side where gladness reigns. Sadness finds support in fatigue, self-pity, failing to release pressures which bear upon you, failing to look at the beauty around you, lack of faith, and trying to forge ahead before it is time, and so on, and so on.

Instead, my dearest one, think positively. Feel the vibration of love all around you from me and many others. Those of us in spirit can be successful only through those who listen with love in their hearts for God and for all mankind. You must become more worldly and cosmic in your thinking. To branch out from love within a family level to a much larger level takes a great deal of energy. The vibration of love and light must be built with tedious prayer and meditation which will increase your unconditional and selfless love. You must keep on this path no matter how difficult it becomes. Difficulties are placed there for reasons, so accept them and know that strength, love and patience will help you to overcome.

Ignore any attempts of doubt or discouragement, but rather turn all thoughts to God, love, and blessings—all that is positive and good. When you do this, support from many sources can then help you to do God's will. Input and output will be equal, but not always will it appear to be so. Therefore, you must balance it yourself through positive thinking, prayer, meditation and kind deeds. Always remember, dear, you are in control, and it is your free will and determination which in the end will decide the outcome. God is always there to help and guide you, as am I and others, but the main impetus comes from within your own being. Do not sell yourself short, but always strive for that divine being which dwells within.

Wednesday, November 30, 1988
Spirit:

What is the cause of turmoil and unrest? The answer is not an easy one for it can be one of many reasons or a combination thereof. To name a few: questioning, lack of faith, fatigue through an overload of thought, dissatisfaction with one's progress, lack of meaningful prayer, and a lack of confidence and direction. When this happens in one's life, as it will, the answer is to remain calm and ride out the storm. Problems are an important part of life for they teach each soul the necessary lessons to find God and place him in that rightful position of supreme importance in one's life. Each must find his own salvation and it is the unrest which causes each to continue seeking God within.

Too often unrest is looked upon as a weakness, when in fact, it is truly a strength, if it is not ignored. To be disturbed can cause very positive results. Redirected negativity does bring about productive change. Many theories, inventions and cures have been discovered on this premise and many lives are changed forever. Is this not true in your own life as well? Perhaps the lesson to be learned is this: unrest causes change, but what direction one ultimately chooses, determines the true value of this unrest. Seek and you shall find, my child, for God loves each of his children.

Friday, December 2, 1988
Spirit:

One's innermost being where God dwells is protected and guarded by one's mind in the world of thought. Every action of life is controlled by thought, so to live a life of spiritual value, one must bring his thoughts under control. Too many on earth do not realize the magnitude of this ability to find self-control, but instead flounder in a world of negativism. Every negative thought can be changed into a positive one, but many times it is necessary to tap that innermost place where God dwells. This is where one can find strength, peace and patience.

What is the price to be paid for this help? The answer is written so many times in the Bible. It is faith, hope and love, and the greatest of these is love. Thoughts of love eradicate negative thinking so one can concentrate his thoughts upon helping others. Negative thinking is caused by selfish thoughts, and selfish thoughts do not contain love. Self-control over all thoughts is the key to positive thinking and ultimately to God's world of true, selfless love.

Tuesday, December 6, 1988
Spirit:

God helps all crooked places to become smooth. Pray for his almighty guidance and power to work through difficulties. Think positively and it will be so. Send back to God what you cannot find answers to, and mercy will be given. God will help his children. Remain steady and strong so your vibration may be heard. Pure thought is that which is filled with love. One need never fear the answer to thoughts of this caliber. Love is truth, and since one cannot hide from truth, the answers will ring true.

This is not to say that the answers will always come as one desires them, but they will face one in the right direction. What one must keep away from is doubt, for doubt causes confusion and pain in many forms. Know God will stand firm on his foundation of love, now and throughout eternity. Those who hang on to these expressions of love can always see the spiritual path toward God. Know this and live every moment of your life in the peace of the Lord. In the peace of God's love nothing but good can touch you, for peace comes on the wings of prayer.

Monday, December 12, 1988
Spirit:

Your life will be filled with purpose, dear one. Trust God and those of us guiding you, and all will work out as it should.

Let us discuss the saying: "Everything will work out in God's own time." It is hard for those on earth to accept this because the terminology is interpreted differently depending on which world, physical or spiritual, one is living in. It must be seen as only one world—a continuation from the physical into the spiritual. The dimension of your being and your surroundings change but the central core remains the same.

Try to be flexible and open to many possible pathways and travel. Live your life on earth knowing the unexpected will indeed appear. If there is a detour, so be it. Accept this detour as a challenge, an opportunity to learn a new lesson, to help another, and to explore your own abilities. The possibilities are only stifled by one's lack of faith. Answers come from within where the crossroads or inner sanctums of the physical and spiritual body meet with God. This is where patience and "in God's own time" are one. This is the sacred place where "everything will work out" is formed. Many times the answer is so indistinguishable it takes months and years to be discovered, but it will be so. Life without seeking God's guidance is a crippled life.

Do you not see that the crossroads to eternity can never be found while in the physical body without God's help? You, by yourself, are nothing, but with God you can be everything. The opportunities are available to those who are tuned in to hear.

Tuesday, December 13, 1988
Ang:

Peace comes from within your own being, from deep within your own thoughts, your heart and imagination, and your appreciation of nature and music. As you find peace, even under duress, you are truly learning to find God. Nothing of the physical world can disturb you when you meet with God; all the hurt, all the pressures, all the pain will be dispersed, and you will again find strength.

God's understanding of love knows no bounds, so seek the place of peace where love reigns supreme. To know love is to look into eternity for it too is endless. Love does all things because it comes from God. It uplifts, encircles and protects all who seek its beauty. Pure love never tires, never finds fault, but rather gives strength, peace and patience to its followers. Look to love, my dear one. In its vision you will see the memories of the past, the importance of the present and the glory of the future. We stand together with God in all three, so feel joy in your heart.

One who does not suffer cannot find strength, for it is the suffering which expands the soul to better understand the truth of God's law. Is it not a privilege to begin to understand God's truth? This is your answer to discouragement. Seek all the inner dimensions of love, and joy will be yours. Nothing of love is ever forgotten for it is the bridge to eternal life. I shall always be there to meet you and to encourage you and to bring you love. Happiness lives in the heart.

Wednesday, December 14, 1988
Spirit:

The power to heal evolves out of service to God. Service is the continual desire to do our Heavenly Father's will. It does not happen suddenly, but rather evolves over a period of time. During this period of apprenticeship one learns many important lessons oftentimes through pain, sorrow and trials of many kinds. Doing God's will calls for great discipline, unconditional love, and the ability to see beyond the present moment with great faith. One must not let the difficulties of daily life stand in the way of doing God's work no matter how impossible it may seem. Everything is possible with God, my child, but only if one believes it to be so. Work upon this belief by touching the innermost sanctuary of your own being. Service in its truest form comes through one's ability to love all things without any desire for reciprocity. The difficulty of this task is tremendous, and one only needs to look at the world to see how many fail to hear God's call. Hear this call, and trudge along the pathway with unfailing patience.

It is far easier to follow a light one can see. How much brighter the light will appear if one must stumble and grope in the darkness to find the switch to God's light. Service is the road out of the darkness and love is God's light. Pray for the ability to see in the darkness of physical life with its many difficulties and trials through faith and service to others. Then, when you least expect it, the hand of God will turn the switch to light your way to his power to heal. God bless you, my child.

Saturday, December 17, 1988
Spirit:

Stability comes from understanding the truth. The thought process is very complex for it controls the inner and outward psyche of man. Thoughts come and go but never in the exact same wavelength. Perhaps man patterned a computer to work like a mind, but it does not have thoughts like man. Once a thought is formed, it occupies space as a wavelength. It cannot be erased, therefore it is important to use self-control on one's thoughts at all times. Too often mankind wastes his mind on thoughts of criticism. Better he learns to correct the criticism he holds of himself—then his thoughts would be purer and more worthwhile to mankind.

Did you ever wonder what your thoughts do traveling about in space? Is it not conceivable that it looks for other thoughts on a similar wavelength? Like does indeed attract like.

Look at the properties in many of God's elements. Mercury is a good example. What happens when one piece comes close to another? They join and become bigger. Will mercury do the same with water, sand or any other solid? The answer is no. Look then at thoughts. Do thoughts of hate and envy join those of love and trust? Again the answer is no. What then is the power of thought? Ponder this question as you sleep.

Sunday, December 18, 1988
Spirit:

Negativity is caused by seeing in another what you would like to achieve yourself, but have not been able to accomplish. All negative thoughts and feelings come from this source. To the extent that one is not able to control and reverse these thoughts is the stumbling block to anyone's spiritual growth. You see, you do and you conquer. You must conquer not another, but rather what lives dormant within your own being. The light of each soul glimmers within, yet it must be released by and through the act of love. Pure love holds the key to spiritual growth.

One can mask his life with many fallacies of accomplishments, but in the final analysis of self-evaluation, love will stand in the primary position for it comes from God. In the beginning, love fell because of man's disobedience to God, his creator, but in the end love shall become the new beginning. Few on earth truly examine the power of love for its capabilities are limitless because of its eternal qualities. Again we must emphasize love in its purest sense. True, unconditional love never ends and is self-illuminating. One can always find more to give no matter how dark the pathway becomes.

Can you not see and feel this love in another? What force is it that causes each person to seek an answer to the meaning and purpose of life? The answer, my child, is love. You seek for the privilege to do God's will and the answer always returns to love—pure, unconditional love. The brighter you allow this light of love to shine forth, the greater will be its effect on those around you. You, yourself, are not in a position to see its strength, so leave this decision in the hands of God. Pray to do his will and you shall be answered, dear child—in God's own time. Learn to listen to your own heart, for it knows how to seek and find God's love.

Wednesday, December 21, 1988
Spirit:

Fatigue of the body is very difficult to control and overcome, for it is a strong force and has great power over the actions of man. It is detrimental to the spirit in that the body overrides the needs of the spirit. How easy it becomes to say "I shall pray, meditate and write tomorrow." In your upward climb, pray that you will have strength regardless of what your physical body indicates to you. The difficulties and trials of spiritual growth must be realized and then examined very closely, dear child. You do have the strength and power to overcome fatigue and pressure upon your spirit. Each time you overcome this feeling, you walk a step closer to God, and you will feel his hand upon your shoulder.

Repeat the 23rd Psalm, pray for others, put yourself and your life in the proper perspective. Pray to love more deeply, to have more compassion for your fellow man and to know God's will. Life is all the more difficult if you fail to see beyond earth's shadows, so pray to do our Father's will. Take the time to ponder, to seek inner peace, to love another—these are the treasures you will bring with you into eternal life. We do not say to ignore the tasks of daily life on earth, but rather strive to let each task enhance your spirit as well.

The priority of life is to help your inner and outer beings to become as one. Let them not be divided for then, my child, you will not find the peace you so desire. Life is in the eyes of the beholder, so let faith, hope and love shine brightly in yours. Take each day as it comes, and make it the best that you can. Love surrounds you; feel its strength and all will be well. Rest in peace.

Tuesday, December 27, 1988
Spirit:

The greatest joys of life come from the spirit of man. God placed each of these joys in proper order, but it is man, himself, who fails to seek and find them. You, on earth, see with such limited vision. So much importance is placed upon material and physical pleasures, because many, even religious people, think life is short and something of the physical world will be missed. One with this belief understands so little of the magnitude of his own being in relationship to all of God's creation. The true purpose of life is to love—to do unto others as you would have them do unto you. As you look about, what do you really see? Look closely at yourself. Why do you not feel joy each morning upon waking? Perhaps your spiritual vision becomes clouded by your physical eyes. You must continue to strive to see and to feel more with your spiritual senses.

1989

Tuesday, January 3, 1989
Spirit:

Spiritual merit comes from the flow of surplus love from one's heart. It is measured by the world of spirit, so one really does not know its true value while living in the physical body. If one lives trying to collect merit, it will elude him. Merit is that selfless love which comes with self-mastery. Too many lack the desire to develop such love. Through clouded vision, their eyes fail to see God's wisdom and truth. The ability to see or feel what appears not to be present, but really is, becomes the new dimension for that person. You see, therefore, the ability to sense and to know is the most important. It is a form of radar, a personal radar which can perceive God. You, my child, are beginning to tap into this source of knowledge. This awakening is closely connected to one's ability to love—love that has earned merit.

Do you not see, to teach others the meaning of spiritual love, you must first experience and live in its sorrow and beauty? As one searches for the beauty in each of God's fruits of the spirit, there is great pain and suffering as well. One must feel and learn the opposites in order to find the importance of life itself, and the importance of giving back to creation more than you take. This, my child, is merit. Can you not see it more clearly? What you give, over and above what you take, goes into eternity as merit. When each soul on earth can learn this lesson, heaven on earth will be established. Merit is a great gift from God, and it is the key to opening the door to life's true meaning. This desire to find merit is what you seek.

Monday, January 9, 1989
Spirit:

Life is perceived by the sum total of one's thoughts plus the love flowing from one's heart. If the thoughts and love flow together in unison, one finds happiness and peace. This unison is a treasure of the soul. It cannot be bought, borrowed or stolen; it must be earned.

Sunday, January 15, 1989
Spirit:

The more resentment one builds in himself, the less love he feels for another. This is a discussion on the balance between all things. Many times it may appear uneven, or perhaps unfair, but those with faith know in their heart that there is a purpose behind all things. Many times it seems that the more you give, the more is needed, and yet, where is the return? Do you not see that many times the return is invisible in your physical life, but no amount of love in the form of giving is ever, and do underline ever, lost. This love is what will build the planet earth to beauty and glory. God so loved the world that he gave his only begotten son—how much is your love? Is not a kind thought, a good deed, or a touch of love well within reach?

It is time for action instead of reaction. Perhaps a major problem with those on earth comes with the action. How much easier it is to react to someone else's action than to initiate action oneself. The problems of earth will begin to change in direct proportion to the number of people who take action. What is the driving force behind this positive action? Is it not a form of love or caring? The more love one feels for God and life in general, the better will be the balance in one's own life. True love promotes positive action and dissolves fear. In looking at the planet earth, more love is needed.

Wednesday, January 18, 1989
Spirit:

Find in tomorrow those lovely moments which passed by unnoticed today.

Thursday, January 26, 1989
Ang:

Dear, always remember the greatest gift of life is love in your heart, and of this you have an abundance. Let everything else pass by unnoticed, or at least try to let aggravations affect you as little as possible. In the end, they will mean nothing. Try to see the long-range plan and know that at the right time all things will fit into place. Tests are sent to find your true values; this makes the road harder to travel, but there is a purpose even if you cannot see the reason. This is where faith and hope enter to help you over the humps. Deal with your own responsibilities, but each must be in control and account for his own life. This is the purpose of free will.

Saturday, January 28, 1989
Spirit:

To be a healer you must learn to harness the powers of concentration which lay hidden in the ability to love. You must love God and all of his creation with unconditional love. This is not an easy task for it takes great self-control to suppress the selfish part of oneself. Control of one's thoughts is the first step. You see, child, if you direct these thoughts to always come from the positive side, what is negative will continue to lessen in strength and frequency. Do you not find this to be true? Your ability to love must come from within this negative place, and it must be conquered through diligent effort and work.

Prayer is your best ally, for it brings you closer to the source of love, strength and patience. Love is planted and experienced as a child, grows with friendship, flourishes in marriage, buds in the years of raising children, but it does not burst into full bloom until there is unconditional love in one's heart. This is God's law, and all must work to abide by it. Love has many facets; but to learn the secrets in each brings one closer and closer to God. This desire to be near to God is the original driving force behind each human being.

Positive thinking brings one closer to the light of love, but negativity diffuses the light and many lose their way. If you choose to help your fellow man, you must learn to brighten your own light until it shines true.

Again, it is not an easy task, so hardships must be presented and placed in your path. Love, as you continue to learn, clears the way for healing to take place. Learn this lesson well, for it is the bridge to further development as a healer.

Monday, January 30, 1989
Ang:

You're welcome, dear. I find a great deal of peace knowing that you are taken care of, for it is my gift of love and concern for you. Everything you feel, I feel as well. We are truly one. Did we not have it all right from the very beginning? How happy and good you always made me feel. Life is bittersweet, dear, so savor the happy moments for they shall always be there. I share all the beauty and love around you. Suffering enhances one's growth and God spares those who love by giving them wisdom. You know many things and we are able to touch although we are separated. The prayer room is so lovely. We watch and give you encouragement from spirit, and we know that you feel this. It has taken lots of hard work—a work of love—and you will see great results. The energies will build slowly. The window is such a lovely tribute. I shall end our meeting with thanks to you and a heart full of love. Sleep in peace.

Tuesday, January 31, 1989
Spirit:

Each human being is important for he is a child of God, but his true importance is his relationship to the whole of existence. Each is a link in the chain of creation, but the chain is only as strong as its weakest link. When more on earth become aware of the interconnection of all things and the need for auras to touch, then perhaps heaven on earth will become more of a reality. Each is important as an individual, but true value emerges with the ability to become part of the whole.

Friday, February 3, 1989
Spirit:

How much do I love you? Let me count the ways. This can hold true in any situation. The more love that can turn into positive and constructive energy, the sooner mankind can be freed from negative forces. Negativity is always present, but when it becomes the dominant force, then mankind is no longer in control. The beauty of love is its ability to make one aware of what is right and of true value. Once this path is found, the energy keeps one striving to climb closer to God's heart. Life is like a giant magnet enabling each of us the opportunity to draw experiences of love into our own aura to find peace and purpose. Reinvestment of this energy is of great importance. If one feels blessed by God's touch, he must feel obligated to pass it along to others. This is the path of salvation for all of us. We are connected—each a living form drawing strength from another through caring and love.

Wednesday, February 8, 1989
Spirit:

In true reality, Diane, you can only heal another when you are able to see clearly into his heart and find where love dwells. Healing can happen only on a pure vibration. Can you not see the result of resentment, fatigue or annoyance? Try harder to strive for that unconditional love you seek. When you desire a return or predetermine how another should react or behave, then the communication is not pure, for you have already judged, and that is not healing. Pure love gives the greatest results. As you progress, this will become clearer. Use empathy more; try to feel what another is feeling and this will help you to understand. I come to encourage you to continue striving along this spiritual path. Wisdom will come to those who seek, and a new world will open before you, but only as God finds you ready. This is the test of patience to do God's will.

Saturday, February 11, 1989
Spirit:

You must continue to be strong, so pray for added strength in your daily life and it will be there. Love seeps out of your inner being and fuels your spirit with energy. There are many goals for you to seek, but first master the weaknesses which stand as stumbling blocks. Purity comes from the constant cleansing of the spirit of all its flaws.

Sunday, February 19, 1989
Spirit:

Always strive to look up and see the rainbows of life. Look for what can be and will be. You see, my child, the human spirit is so easily discouraged and stifled, or so it seems by the lack of vision. Earthly problems and the drudges of mundane tasks slowly begin to erode and tarnish the brilliance of the spirit. In order to see clearly, you must wash away all impurities with prayer. Faith, hope, strength and love are always there; it is you who fail to see them. Vision is easily clouded by doubt. Can you not see this?

God's touch allows you to know that dreams will come true, but only at the right moment. Lessons are learned through hardship and pain for this awakens the unending capacity of love. All roads in life lead back to love for it is the link to God and eternity. You already know the formula, dear child. Now you must strive to solve the problems which lead to the solution. Vision makes this road to God and eternity possible, so keep it close to your heart and always in your sight, and you shall find what you seek. God be with you.

Thursday, February 23, 1989
Spirit:

Love for another is a manifestation of one's love for God. The deeper the love, the closer one feels to his creator. Understanding which brings peace is an outcropping, a special reward for this love. Love, once felt and shared, is never forgotten. In his ignorance and lack of understanding man tries to suppress the one true link to the world of spirit through sorrow and sadness. Love is not lost when one physically dies, but instead joins the God force which keeps the universe in perpetual motion. Energy is needed to maintain life. Is this not true? God created each form of life whether animal, vegetable or mineral to interact with each other, to join forces for the good of all. What then is the driving force behind this complicated network of creation? Is it not love?

Think more deeply about this profound thought, my child. Life is an empty shell without love. Yet, it is the quality and depth of love which builds God's world. The most important and lasting love is that of the spirit. Physical love, or love of material things, is short-lived because of predetermined limitations. Physical life is but a chapter in the book of eternal life; spiritual love is that which moves on into eternity. We come to you to help you further understand those difficulties which enter your life. These tests are necessary for you to develop more in your desire to be a healer. One must continually seek the depth and breadth of love. True love once felt is there forever and brings peace to one's inner being.

Ang:

Yes, dear, this is a message from me too. As our love grows it expands outward and helps everything we touch. It brings new life and energy to the universe. Continue to learn, to seek and above all, continue to love. I am there with you, for we are as one. Rest in peace and love.

Saturday, February 25, 1989
Spirit:

You must develop images through the energy of your thought process. The energy is very powerful, and you will feel the intensity throughout your body as you develop your ability to collect this energy. Intensify your concentration; let the images develop through space and try not to see them as though looking at a picture. It takes practice, patience and a true desire to touch the lenses of love, and ultimately God. We give you this message to encourage you to develop your abilities. Every ability has the potential to grow; it only needs to be nurtured in the right way. As you progress, the path will become clearer. Can you not see this? Follow the lead of your heart and love, for within are the answers.

Sunday, February 26, 1989
Spirit:

My child, you must carefully examine the importance of unconditional love in your life. Love of this kind is the channel where energy from God flows unobstructedly. It is necessary for one to open this passageway. As one gives unconditionally from oneself, an equal amount of energy may then be returned. As one proves his worth, extra energy can be stored. It is this extra energy which can be used to do God's will. It is an energy of merit, so to speak. Strive to give more love, to be more patient, to become more pure in God's eyes, for then and only then will you be worthy to do his will. The foundation must be built with pure love, and this, my child, as you well know, is the difficult task.

Monday, February 27, 1989
Spirit:

Have faith in God's will. Believe, and it shall be so. Doubt brings weakness and despair, so do not allow yourself to see any result which is not positive. Energy which can be used to help in healing must be collected from only positive thoughts filled with love.

Saturday, March 4, 1989
Ang:

Life is a process of constant change ruled by exact laws of balance and give and take. Everything has a positive and negative side, and love is the primary force which keeps this balance. Faith and hope are also great allies placed there for added strength and courage. Keep busy with kindness; those activities which make the spirit reach out to touch eternity. Each thought and act of love touches God, so it therefore touches me for our love is part of God. Thought is the true act of love. While on earth, the physical side of love becomes emphasized and many lose the opportunity to find the real meaning. We were blessed with my illness, because it forced us to search for the true meaning of love, and we found God to be the core.

My dearest one, look beyond today, tomorrow or years from now, and see the love shining in my eyes and heart for you. It will be there forever. There is so much for you to learn, to experience and to accomplish. I shall be there to help and encourage you every step of the way. Each difficulty or hardship you hurdle brings you closer to that purpose. Keep doubt away with faith; keep despair away with hope, and always know love surrounds you. Our love is blessed by God and it shall never cease. Hold close to your two favorite passages from the Bible: "Ask and it will be given to you; seek and you will find; knock and the door will be opened to you." *(Matthew 7:7)* and "There are in the end three things that last: faith, hope and love—and the greatest of these is love." *(1 Corinthians 13:13)*

Sunday, March 12, 1989
Spirit:

How does one find the path to God's heart? There is no perfect map to show the way. Each must chart his own way through sweat, toil and tears. Just as one feels the despair of reaching a dead end, miraculously a new path appears into view. This is the beauty of God's love. One must always have faith this new path will appear, for those who doubt will surely miss the turn. Listen, my child, to the song of love in your heart. Follow the dreams which emerge and place them into your vision even when you cannot see them clearly. Mist often covers the beauty one is to behold, but those with patient endurance wait for the perfect moment to behold God's grace.

Thursday, March 16, 1989
Spirit:

It is through struggle and duress that one learns. Can you not see this, my child? Precious energy is wasted when one tries to hurry or interfere with God's divine order. Life unfolds, much like an exquisite flower, in God's own time. Those who have faith and endurance await the perfect moment. Growth of the spirit is never rushed, for in rushing one loses the lesson to be taught. Joy must emerge from every trial of life. It is easy to find joy when all is progressing well in one's life, but there is little, true growth in spirit or in one's love for God. Truer meaning emerges when one is faced with a loss or a change in one's life. How soon can the waves and turmoil of your own life return to ripples and ultimately to calm.

Seek the calm by commanding control over the turmoil of your own mind. Listen to the strength, love and patience of God. Listen and see and feel with your spiritual senses. This, my child, is what you seek, but finding them takes faith, hope and love. Hear the music of Heaven in your own heart. See the light no matter how dark the night. Feel the touches of love sent from above. Slay all the foes of love for there are many, and master daily life by finding the joy in mundane tasks. Much can be learned by this but few hear the message. Continue to search and you will find what you seek. Many are coming to help you find the way, so reach out your hand for their guidance and help. Peace be with you.

Sunday, March 19, 1989
Diane:

My frame of mind is not really one of being troubled, but somehow I am unsettled and lacking my usual calm, philosophical self. In trying to find peace, I feel I must pull back and again enjoy life for the sake of living. What is to be, will be, and I must wait patiently for it to happen. Grabbing the bull by the horns was never my style, so it is detrimental to me to seek so hard. I'd rather open naturally like a flower of God.

Spirit:

Your thinking is indeed right, dear Diane. God made each of you in his own special way, out of a unique mold which will never again be duplicated. Each is connected to another through his love, but each must find his own path into God's heart. How easily you, on earth, displace those lessons that you learn. Rules of universal law must be used in all things. By all things, I mean, in every moment of your daily life. Does not breathing in meditation teach you this? Slowly, in and out, with special concentration and gratitude on the beauty of God's gift, which *is* you.

Life is the school, so to speak, that teaches the lessons each must learn to do God's will. Be careful to learn in progression and try not to hurry ahead in hopes of early admission to the next level. Take time to enjoy and love each moment. Find the purpose and God force in each, and carry it along with you as you face the next lesson. Patience and love will smile upon you, dear child, but as you seek God within yourself, take time to savor the view. This is the secret to spiritual development. In the deep heart of one's being, there is great joy and fulfillment waiting to escape and do God's will. Your talents and abilities will develop, but in God's own time.

Has this not been a most difficult lesson for you to learn? Confront it with prayer and love. You are the instrument through which God may better the world, so let him show you the technique and choose the music. Your task is to practice and turn his gift into something of beauty for all to hear. This is unconditional love. Peace be with you.

Thursday, March 23, 1989

Spirit:

This is the perfect day, Maundy Thursday, to address the topic of pain, Diane. There are three kinds of pain: physical, mental and spiritual, and each in its own way takes its toll. Physical pain is felt by the body, emotional pain is felt by one's mind, but spiritual pain is felt by God. Physical pain in most instances is short-lived, and can last no longer than one's lifetime. Mental pain delves deeper into one's being and can thwart the development of the spirit. Spiritual pain is unrelenting because it follows one into eternity. God, in his mercy, tries to teach and guide his children away from this pain, but each is responsible for his own path.

You must let go of the pain you watched and put it in proper perspective. The suffering is indeed over, and through this suffering, Ang is on a higher level and closer to God as a result. This you know, but the pain coupled with the loss is difficult to overcome, for with physical death comes a new pain. Do not hide this pain from yourself, but rather pray to God for help in understanding the magnitude of such suffering.

Mental pain is slower to heal, and it takes much diligent thought and a positive outlook. It is in this mental pain that ultimately the spirit can become stunted in its growth. Spiritual pain is suffered for God and the growth of all of mankind. Christ understood this truth, and freely gave of himself. Pain, in itself, is not so important, but faith in knowing there is a purpose makes the pain bearable.

How often God must cry as he watches his children. Tears are indeed beautiful for they cleanse and heal the wounds of the heart. A broken heart learns of suffering, and as it heals under God's guidance, others may be healed as well. Empathy, not pity, is the key to healing. To feel and understand the pain of another is the secret to helping others. First, you must understand and heal the pain within your own being. Call upon God and those of us in spirit who stand so close. Peace be with you, child.

Monday, March 27, 1989
Spirit:

How deep must one search the soul to find answers and to find peace? Sometimes the answer cannot be found—it just is. Perhaps God must try to find a purpose worth salvaging from a situation which just is. Patience is the key ingredient to making this situation tolerable. To blame oneself for failing in such a situation causes guilt, and perhaps this guilt is unearned. If this is the case, try detaching oneself and look from afar. If you truly love, there is no guilt, for one gives all he has to give, and God can ask no more than this. It is good to search, but it is also good to be satisfied. When search and satisfy become one with each other, peace will be yours.

Saturday, April 1, 1989

Ang:

There is no need to long for me; you know I am right there beside you. Instead, believe and work toward our touching each other more. New ideas, new dimensions, new techniques take time, energy, study and love—more love than those on earth are even aware they have buried in their hearts. Your great gift, my dearest one, is your pursuit of love. You continue to find bridges across pain built upon this love. As this network of bridges becomes stronger and very secure, we, in spirit, can meet you. Think of the joy of such a gift. You must keep your feet planted firmly on the earth, for this too is necessary. If only I could share the knowledge I have learned since passing into spirit, but that is a path you will one day travel, and I shall be there to meet you.

Let the pain go and remember the love which is ours forever. The light of true love is beautiful so try hard to visualize it. It will never diminish but only becomes brighter. Do the mundane daily tasks with joy in your heart. A capacity for joy, even in the darkest of times, is the gift of enlightenment. That is where we can meet, and I'll always be there for you.

Sunday, April 2, 1989

Spirit:

You are right, for we do come close. Pure, simple and sincere thoughts give the finer vibrations which can bring us into your aura. Simplicity brings such beauty and love. It cleans the mind of debris so that thoughts may be connected with oneness to God. Peace is total oneness with God for with peace comes the realization that all things belong to God and to each other. Who on earth can claim the beauty of nature to be his own? Does it not belong to each one? The difficulties arise in how each perceives the truth in his own mind. Life is given as a gift to learn this truth from God. Love is the core of our being. To love God, to love each other and to love our earth is the purpose of life.

The path to this realization is a difficult one. Plowing through the pain of life releases the joy which becomes trapped in the intrigues of daily life.

Many times it is necessary to come very close to distress and despair before one realizes the value of what he indeed, already possesses. Loss should bring growth of one's ability to love. God gave us love to fill all the voids of life. One never loses that which he loves, for love is eternal and it goes before us into eternity. Man's perception encompasses a limited vision and if only he would learn to see further, the world could rapidly find peace. Work to help enlighten those who come into your life. Work simply, quietly, persistently with love in your heart, and you shall find help in abundance.

Tuesday, April 4, 1989
Spirit:

The greatest joys in life are the unseen ones. Lack of imagination stunts the spirit because spirit knows it can soar to great heights. It is negative, limited vision which stunts growth. The more one opens his sight to the unknown, the more he can see. Fear is present only when one does not love enough. To love is to chase away the fears, anxieties and negativity. Peace floats on the wings of love.

Make a list of those things that you most enjoy watching in nature. Many will be peaceful and calming. Return to the basics, and find their true essence. From there, one can find his true value and what he must accomplish. Those who wait patiently with an abundance of love will not wait in vain. Do quietly what you must and wait for God and his guides to show you the way. Search for the strength to persevere the trials of life, for the love to bring you joy and for the patience to make all things possible. Peace be with you.

Wednesday, April 5, 1989
Spirit:

The energies are there, but you must learn to concentrate and focus these energies. It will take time and patience. Continue to call artists to come and familiarize themselves with your energies. So few try or believe that they can do this, so many in spirit will come to help. Ang will be especially helpful for you, so seek often to find him. He cheers you in all endeavors. His link to you is very strong and this will be important as energies grow. Keep on keeping on. A great deal of perseverance is needed. Call on all of us when you work as you have been doing.

Friday, April 7, 1989
Diane:

Where am I headed, dear Spirit Guides?

Spirit:

Where do you want to be headed? Search yourself in depth and understand those special desires and talents you wish to pursue. We can help only after you choose the direction you wish to travel. We can try to influence you to seek out those paths in which we see you are gifted, but in the end, you must make the decision and commitment. Too many on earth are either totally uninformed or choose to make a semi-commitment to spiritual growth. Can you not see that the desire to do God's will with your special abilities is the most important factor? The blueprints of the soul are written with life. The rough draft must come first and slowly the details evolve. We help as this process unfolds and we see the necessity. Each must be worthy of further development. Have faith in God, in yourself and in our ability to help you.

Saturday, April 8, 1989
Diane:

What is the secret to finding unconditional love?

Spirit:

Unconditional love is like standing in the presence of God. The true desire of each on earth is to seek such love, and one spends his life trying to find it. Love cannot be bought, borrowed or stolen. It must be earned by each unselfish deed done, not for any reason except that you care. If there is a motive or a desire for something back in return, it simply does not count. This is not to say that kindness given because you should is not right, it is simply not as pure as unconditional love. The purer the love, the brighter the light will shine. Keep knocking on the door of love, my child, and it shall be opened to you. Be true and honest with love of yourself, and it shall be given unto others. The path will become clear to them who do God's will. Peace be with you.

Wednesday, April 12, 1989
Spirit:

Take this day as it comes and find the special jewel that it has to offer. Often in one's rush toward accomplishment, the true purpose of the day is lost. What travels far into eternity, manifests itself slowly with great care. Remember this as you travel life's path for the best is yet to come for those who love others as God does. Try to do this each moment, my child, no matter how hard it seems. Peace be with you.

Sunday, April 16, 1989
Spirit:

Many times it seems as if life fails to give us exactly what we wish. Beware of the danger in thinking the grass is always greener somewhere else. Instead, dear child, work to make it greener right where you stand. The time spent on solving difficulties is never wasted, but rather it brings out the best in one. Can you not see this? The problems become magnified by the lack of a solution which then clouds the pathway between the heart and mind. The balance between the two is a necessity. Ponder this thought and see if it rings true.

Monday, April 17, 1989
Spirit:

Dear child, the key is the ability to think of another before you think of yourself. When one can do this graciously with love in his heart, mastery is beginning to come into focus. The rough corners of unperfected love are abrasive to the spirit, and cause wounds which take on many forms. How one deals with and ultimately heals them is the core of life. Send out kind thoughts, love and prayers to those who hurt you and release the pressure within yourself. Anger, resentment and emotions such as these are like a double-edged sword for they harm your own being as well. Find other outlets for such feelings and let God be your guide. Let go and let God. Search for the true meaning and find peace.

Tuesday, April 18, 1989
Spirit:

When you can live and do for others with peace in your heart, you will be ready to do God's will. This is a very difficult task, so as you always strive for patience with others, learn to be patient with yourself. Try to set some of your goals to synchronize with eternal time, for earth time will one day be of much less importance to you. The physical body puts such limitations upon the mind of man. Try to exercise your mind far beyond the realm of physical things for this is where true happiness will one day be found. This is not to say that your physical life and duties are not of utmost importance. Rather to help you see more of the divine plan and wisdom to know you are part of something far beyond what you can now understand. What you love will never be lost to you and this you now understand.

Sunday, April 23, 1989

Diane:

I arose early to see the sunrise—what I've been trying to do to enjoy the early morning. Each day I try to remind myself to be patient and await the purpose of my life—in God's own time.

Spirit:

Faith in God and oneself is the key to love, but as the door opens one must come to grips with other emotions as well. It takes time to only see love in all things. Prayer helps immensely because it focuses and gives purpose to one's thoughts. To do deeds of worth and value one must add prayer and love to this thought. This, dear child, takes time and great patience. The right moment for action will come, but be not in a hurry. Nurture and care for the bud of purpose growing in your heart. At the right moment it will burst forth into full bloom, and you shall do God's will. Continue to seek and you will find joy in everything.

Thursday, April 27, 1989

Spirit:

Did you ever ponder the idea that perhaps you tend to put too much pressure on yourself? With the exception of an occasional bout with laziness, why can you not be satisfied with what you do accomplish? That area between what you do and what you think you should do causes unrest and eventually negativity. This undermines your peace of mind. Is this not true? Take each day as God gives it to you with love. You, my child, tend to forget to take one day at a time and make it a masterpiece when dealing with your personal life. If another becomes involved, you tend to forget yourself. This is admirable, but not at the risk of failing to look closely at yourself.

Why do you love? Where does love come from? What is its true purpose? Love is the core of your being and it is connected to all things. If you think you can separate yourself, you must reevaluate your priorities. God is in all things, so you, dear child, are part of God. God gives each of his children his unconditional love; it is you that complicates this precious gift. Some answers become clearer with patient endurance. Live and enjoy this day. Find value and worth in each task you undertake. Let life unfold with a free spirit, one which is open to all of life's treasures. Relax from those pressures which you alone create. God's love is abundant and eternal, so there is time to do his will. Be patient and send forth vibrations of love.

Friday, April 28, 1989
Spirit:

Can you not see that resentment is nourished and kept active by your own act of judgment upon another? It is in God's hands to speak, not yours, my child. The heart of your spirit is pure love, and to allow yourself to feel anything less causes many other emotions, which then cause you pain. Pray for those who pull at your happiness and judge them not, for in judging them you live in your own flaws. Correct in yourself what you see in others; and this, dear child, is done through prayer, love and perseverance. Two wrongs do not make a right, so refrain from making judgments. Peace follows love everywhere, so live with love in your heart. Be grateful that God has given you wisdom to hear his words, and pray that you may grow in love. Become worthy to do God's will, and the way will be shown to you. Grow within yourself.

Remember the words of Matthew 7:1–5, 7–8: "If you want to avoid judgment, stop passing judgment. Your verdict on others will be used to measure you. Why look at the speck in your brother's eye when you miss the plank in your own. How can you say to your brother, let me take the speck out of your eye, while all the time the plank remains in your own? You hypocrite. Remove the plank from your own eye first, then you will see clearly to take the speck from your brother's eye..." "Ask and it will be given to you; seek and you will find; knock and the door will be opened to you. For the one who asks receives; the one who seeks finds; and the one who knocks enters." May you find peace, child.

Thursday, May 11, 1989
Spirit:

The answer to most of the hurt and truth of our lives lies buried deep within our heart. Life has little meaning without this truth, but few try to find it. The path is not easy to tread, but well worth the effort. Those who dwell on earth fail to see the importance of finding a true path of love. Instead of concentrating on this higher meaning of values, the effort is placed upon material things, those pleasures which satisfy only the physical side of their lives. How short-sighted a view this becomes, for spiritual desires are those which last for eternity. What in truth, my child, can be taken into death of the physical body? Name one such item.

What then is the purpose, if any, of collecting so many physical possessions? Life must have more of a balance, and we hear your prayer to do God's will. Continue to climb the path of spiritual endeavors and you shall find them. Let not disappointment and discouragement be your focus, but rather be led by your dreams and visions. To go or to do must first be born as a thought, and this is where a dream begins its formation. Dreams do become reality, and one must believe in one's own potential to make this happen. Do you not see what love can do? It changes despair into destiny, but how many take time to listen to the call of one's spirit? The physical need usually takes precedence, and at times it must, but you, dear child, must guard against this.

Find a way to let others hear your message. Live your conviction and love of spiritual pursuit in every aspect of your life. Perhaps the saddest part of physical life is the regret which one takes into the spiritual side of life when he dies. Regret does not die, but travels along as a constant companion. Be careful, my child, to eliminate this unwanted companion. Many on earth feel it as guilt, the silent ally of regret. Love destroys both, so use it abundantly as a wellspring to renewed life. Love never fails those who put God first. Peace be with you.

Saturday, May 20, 1989
Spirit:

One keeps love alive by constantly using it. Love grows through use, and it cannot remain the same. It can endure all of life's trials for this is God's plan. Love is not short-sighted for it knows the meaning of eternity. It has the power to heal all things if given the opportunity. Love is honest and sincere for in it lies the truth of creation. It never fails, for only those who abuse its principles fail. Love is gentle in the hands of those who understand its potential. Joy is the result for those who learn its secrets through communion with God, nature, family and spouse. Love does not find fault with another, but instead tries to understand. It stands not in judgment, for it sees only good. Love seeks not revenge, but instead eases the pain of those filled with anger. It shines forth forever.

Sunday, June 4, 1989
Spirit:

Losing the one you love is but a stepping stone into eternity. Look at the whole with vision, for this teaches the importance of each part no matter how small. Can a house stay standing if its foundation is weak? Try to always see beyond what appears to be. Seek the purpose of all of God's creation. Live in his love and there will be no fear.

Monday, June 5, 1989
Spirit:

Be still, my child, and build your foundation in seeing the greatness of God. The road is tedious, long and filled with many obstacles, but there is always love and beauty to ease the burden. Fear not, for there are many to guide and help you. Take time to feel their presence, for God sends them in time of need.

Wednesday, June 7, 1989
Spirit:

Where does one find unconditional love? In the beauty of God's heart which manifests itself in all that you love. It lives in the peace of your inner being and in the depths of your mind, where all spiritual life begins. The physical existence tends to dull the many opportunities which shine forth from spirit, but God is an eternal light and his patience and love never fail. Continue to seek the answers to your question. Be not discouraged by others for love conquers all negativity as it grows stronger. This is universal law, my child.

Sunday, June 11, 1989
Spirit:

One must find tranquility in one's own heart before he can help another. To be tranquil, one cannot judge another; he may only judge himself and his own purpose. How near can one approach God's love? Are moments being wasted by lack of discipline and faith? Pray and ask for God's guidance and love to shine brighter in daily tasks. Pray to do his will and it will be so. Answers come in many ways, so listen closely and be aware of the subtle signs.

Friday, June 16, 1989
Ang and Spirit:

To find meaning in life one must constantly search. It is in this search that peace comes. Turmoil and unrest causes one's soul to seek prayer. Prayer, my child, is the pathway to God's great wisdom. How else is he able to communicate in such a busy world? God talks to you in the quiet peace of your own inner thoughts, so take time to listen. Place yourself in an ideal atmosphere so you are attuned to his message. Continue to fill your heart with love and good deeds. Let not opportunities of good will pass by unnoticed, yet take time to bask in the joy of living as you give to others.

Life passes quickly, and yet, deeds of love live into eternity. Prepare for this eternity in each moment of physical life. If only more of mankind were aware of the truth of God's spirit world, though this awareness is awakening like a sleeping giant. Continue to see this new dawning; watch as the rays of awareness light the minds of mankind. Be a part of this triumph through your positive attitude and love of life. It is through this projection of positive thinking that change comes to be. Prayer is thought and thought can be prayer if there is love in one's heart. Can you not see, hear, and feel the connection of all things, my dearest one?

This camp is so beautiful and peaceful, not only because it is a lovely spot, for there are many lovely spots, but because of the love that permeates here. Ponder this point. What in fact makes the heart and soul happy? Which is of more importance, or do they enhance each other until they become one? There is in the heart beauty of thought as well, and this is where unconditional love lives. It is that special place where beautiful thoughts become energized with love and sparkle forth to light the dark side of humanity. Continue to send forth thoughts such as these to cleanse the world.

Sunday, June 18, 1989
Spirit:

Everything belongs to God and in his mercy he shares his wealth with each of us. Through this example, we too should learn to share. Physical life is short, and there is so very much to accomplish, so it is wise to share all knowledge and wisdom. Spiritually open persons will hear the call. Seek the fruits of the spirit, and by this I mean, those deeds by which your capacity to love are manifested in each moment of daily life. Live as if each breath were your last. Waste not one breath on idle deeds, but rather look to God for guidance. See the kindness and potential in each of God's human treasures, and take care not to judge them with your eyes, for in truth mankind has developed little vision in matters of the spirit.

I want you to know that help is coming, so continue to pray and be open to all change by continually listening to your heart. As love grows within, so shall your ability to perceive messages become stronger. Learn to hear the call of God's will rather than your own. Abilities appear in proportion to one's intent on spiritual growth. This message comes to encourage you to be faithful to your nightly routine of prayer and meditation. Only through this path can you reach your own potential to help others. We come close to guide and help you. Hear us in your thoughts and trust your intuition for it guides you well. Find peace through the gift of love.

Monday, June 26, 1989
Spirit:

Am I better than any other man? No, my child, each is equal in the eyes of God which shine forth with abundant love. Each has the potential of accomplishing great things, but at every crossroad be very careful to hear the voice of your inner self who belongs to God. Opportunities knock at one's door in strange ways, and unexpected events in life are those which teach the greatest lessons. Ponder the enfoldment of any life and see the truth of this. The reaction of each to this truth is the beginning of joy. Joy is God's reward for love. Without love there is little joy and it fades quickly. Continue to love God with strength and depth, and his light shall shine about you, my little one. Never doubt, but always seek that purpose which seems so often to be buried. At that perfect moment, your calling will surface. Peace be with you always.

Tuesday, June 27, 1989
Spirit:

The trail must end and each can say when it is enough, so death will come quietly when it is time. Ponder not what you have done is enough; for in the end love is all that truly counts. Peace from within is won through acts of love, but few understand the magnitude of kindness. This message comes to encourage you and bring you support and love. The road can be lonely, yet you are never alone. Strive harder to touch the companionship that is always there. Seek to see with your inner eyes the love that surrounds you to comfort and support you always. What you seek you will find, but the pathway of service is tedious and must be walked with courage and dedication. Self-mastery is a gift from God to those who learn to love selflessly. The two are inseparable, for they travel together through eternity.

Sunday, July 2, 1989
Spirit:

Beauty comes through the eyes of love. It can not be hurried, but rather ripens with the warmth of each new day. Beauty is in the eyes of the beholder, for each must perceive the truth as love continually unfolds before him. The key to happiness is being able to unlock the source of love deep within regardless of the pressures from without. As one awakens from sleep, and again must face the problems of life, it is necessary to take a few moments and reflect upon the beauty of life itself. God gives to each of us the ability to see this beauty, but many are blinded by selfishness and negativity. Life is not easy, but God gave each of us the power to find faith, hope, peace, joy, and most of all love, in our daily lives. Take the necessary time to touch into this power upon awakening. It can permeate any negative force and reset the mood of the day. Peace can then reign within your heart.

Tuesday, July 4, 1989
Diane's prayer:

Happy Birthday America! What a perfect day to start my week of special prayer. God bless this country and help her to become loving and strong once again. May all those in spirit come to the earth plane and influence each and every citizen to respect and cherish his freedom to live, pray, and love in such a great land. America the beautiful, may God continue to bless her. May all people wake up to the truth and see beyond earth's shadow. Thank you, God, for your many blessings.

Saturday, July 8, 1989

Diane:

Where does love come from, Dear God?

Spirit:

Love abides in all that is beautiful, caring and kind. It is a gift won by service, dedication and yes, my child, sacrifice. Love cannot be taken for granted, for then its growth is stifled. Love reaches out to connect with the light of all that is true and good. The strength of one's spirit comes from this light of truth. Love hides not from this light, but rather grows stronger in its presence. Good deeds and kindness, given without reward, are the cornerstones of love. The struggle in life is won by learning to give for the simple joy of giving; this is selfless love. Each time one can overcome the selfish desires of the physical body, love from within the spirit is released to do God's will.

All things must balance in the end. Each is meant to feel the pain for all things come from God and are connected. Love is the ingredient which holds us all together. Without love, we would shrivel and perish. Love does bring both sorrow and joy, but one must know the pangs of sorrow to truly feel the ecstasy of joy. To praise God with gratitude in one's heart no matter what the circumstance, miraculously returns as love. This is the beauty of God's love.

Tuesday, July 11, 1989

Spirit:

Travel the road of life lit by the light of God's love. The brightness of this light depends on the love shining forth through unconditional love. Light from this source is brilliant, for it is found through dedication, prayer and sacrifice. Do you not see, child, the necessity of suffering? Enlightenment is the answer to suffering. Love is suffering and suffering is love. They must travel hand in hand otherwise enlightenment cannot follow. God alone knows the perfect moment to give encouragement. Always look to his mercy with gratitude, for his love will never fail to bring you peace.

Saturday, July 15, 1989
Ang:

The reservoir of love knows no end, so you must dig deeper. Growth comes by standing upon the brink of disaster and not giving in to either doubt or discouragement. One must always look within in times of distress or despair. The hardest of all emotions is helplessness—what to do next after many so-called failures. There really are no failures, but rather situations in which one has learned another lesson in finding the true condition of his spirit. Spirits can be down, but never out.

The control of your physical life, its desires and weaknesses, is the key to spiritual growth. Trudge through the difficult moments for in hindsight, they will appear as only a blink of the eye. My advice to you, my dearest one, is always strive to put these difficulties in their proper perspective. Let the moments of despair be forgotten, and for those feelings which cause bitterness and pain, refuse to let them take control again. Each has the power through the strength of God's love to rise above the emotions of the physical side of the body. Once one recognizes the inroad of this emotion, take another route which is filled with more love and understanding. I'll be there always to help you. The road is difficult, but the destination is worth all the hardship. How happy it makes me to know you can hear me. I love you, dear.

Wednesday, July 19, 1989
Spirit:

Each life has a distinct purpose. The key to finding happiness is to link one's thoughts to this purpose. One must be quiet and calm to hear and receive these inner messages, thus prayer and meditation become very important in opening the channel to such messages. Those who help from the other side are not chosen haphazardly, but rather great care and thought is given to every life and its purpose. The "new age" is the slow awakening to the realization that God's plan is far-reaching and interconnected. In fact, it is so vast, infinite and eternal that those on earth cannot comprehend the immensity of his plan, nor do many see the purpose of their own life.

Each is God's child, and like any loving parent, he tries to guide, teach and influence our lives to have purpose. The nine fruits of the spirit are proof that help comes to us. They are "love, joy, peace, patience, kindness, goodness, faithfulness, gentleness and self-control." *(Galatians 5:22–23)*

Those in the spirit realm can only communicate through thought, so one must make time to listen each day. Prayer opens a pure channel and all the energy of truth can be used to further good works. Nothing in God's world of spirit is ever wasted. It is in the physical plane that man is slowly destroying his own environment in countless ways. There is great need for awakening the spiritually blind so this can be corrected. You, my child, are beginning to sense the enormity of this project and to realize the need to be alert to your intuition. Keep on this path to seek guidance and help, and above all, pray to love all mankind with an unconditional love. Love will save the world, when all can learn its path.

Sunday, July 23, 1989
Spirit:

God created each of us in his own image. Each of God's creations is meant to bring love, peace and joy to every other of his creations. We are connected and important to one another for the survival of all. To love and nurture the smallest of God's creations is necessary to balance the universe. Thought in the form of prayer equalizes and gives energy to balance the negative forces. That which the mind of man cannot understand must be taken in faith—this is where earth needs much healing.

The human being too often fails to humble himself before God, instead placing too much importance on himself, finding pleasure in material things and pleasing the physical body. The ability "to take" slowly erodes the desire "to give," and the spirit becomes stunted and disfigured. Love is the healer of all things, my little one, and there are so many facets to love. Love has the ability to turn each pain into a form of joy and beauty if used as God meant it to be. Seek the ability to do this. Pray each day that you might be worthy to do God's will. Find the truth and beauty of God in everything that you do. Be patient with all of life, helping each to find peace within oneself. To do less will block the view of eternity, and you must catch a glimpse of God's masterpiece to do his will. Continue seeking, my child. We come close to help.

Monday, July 24, 1989
Spirit:

One cannot blame others, either friends or relatives, for those misfortunes which befall us in our lifetime. This, my child, is karma or destiny. To accept this is not always easy, but it brings strength into one's life and often is accompanied by a new and greater purpose. Rebel not, but rather accept hardship as a gift of learning, for with it comes the gift of greater wisdom. Life is often difficult and hard to accept, but love eases the burden. The beauty of nature lightens the disappointments and gives new meaning to each day. The start of each new sunrise brings hope, and sunset soon follows with peace and tranquility.

See all of life as part of this picture painted with love, hope and peace. God in his mercy gives each of his flock the tools to carve a life of beauty, but it is the responsibility of each to find his own inner strength through prayer and thankfulness. How easy it is to become lazy and join the monotony of daily routine, failing to see the spark of vitality in all that surrounds one in the wonder of God's creation. How endless they are. Live in these wonders and as life unfolds, be prepared to accept its vicissitudes with a loving heart. We do not say this will be an easy task, but continue to look for that divine being within the self. This search can help to lift the consciousness of all of mankind. Love perpetuates an energy which is powerful and beyond earth's understanding, so send it forth with great abundance and faith.

Thursday, July 27, 1989
Spirit:

It is a difficult task to equate the value of any particular life, for each is important in its own chosen way. Let nature be a lesson to each as life unfolds at the perfect moment. Dissatisfaction is the result of too little faith, hope, love and patience. Free will must be kept in balance and always attuned to the finer vibration of God's will. To do less allows weakness and negativity to seep into one's daily life. Strength comes from God through prayer. Never underestimate the power of prayer. It has the ability to align one's thoughts closer to God and the true purpose of life. Questioning and searching has great value, but be sure to put each lesson into practical use. By this we mean, find the joy in every situation no matter how difficult it seems to be at that moment. It is these small pieces of hardship which build one's joy for eternity.

Life is only a stepping stone, but few take the time to ponder the importance of physical life. Take time to pray, my child. It will change your life, and it will help to change the vibration for all life. It is like a beautiful sandy beach; each grain of sand is important to the whole and has purpose for being there. To know you are important is the basis for a fulfilling life. To pray to do God's will can lead to a blessed life. Stay ever on this path and seek a life of true love.

Monday, August 7, 1989
Spirit:

Count your blessings, and count your blessings again and be grateful. Everything one experiences is a gift from God, but your reaction to these experiences decides the joy and peace in life. No one owes you anything. If you can learn to give of your heart to another, the channel or gift for helping is opened wider. Pray harder, little one, and trudge forward with courage. If only at this moment you could see the love and help coming your way in the form of encouragement. Look with love at the beauty and wonder of God's world and nature in all of its splendor. Continue to give of yourself in kindness, and a new world of purpose will unfold before you at that perfect moment. God watches each of his children carefully and none will be forsaken. It is in the trying that wisdom grows. Pray, meditate, read and listen closely, my child, and joy will indeed follow you. Peace be with you.

Friday, August 11, 1989
Spirit:

Live with peace and love in your heart, and the road of life will be smoother. Center your thoughts upon the fruits of the spirit wherein seeds of love grow into eternal happiness. Physical possessions fill the needs of physical life, but they are short-lived and of little value in the world of spirit. Love is the most precious of jewels in the eyes of God for it can indeed change the world. Continue to see the vision of eternity, my dearest one, and you will forge through any turmoil that life can bring. You must conquer your own thoughts and live a life of true love before God can use you as a channel of truth and healing.

Try to understand others and their special situations and struggles with empathy, and not with judgment, as a mirror from which true reflections may be seen. To see oneself clearly, all emotions must be accepted and dealt with honestly. Examine the motives behind the purpose—are they selfish or selfless? One's heart will lead the way if you will listen. In the final judgment, each will judge himself, so take time to live your convictions. Everyone sees flaws in another, but is it not possible one possesses in himself that very same flaw? Try to love, at least in your thoughts, more in the framework of eternal time rather than in physical time.

Saturday, August 12, 1989
Spirit:

Joy is one's ability to accept with love the gift of life, and send this love forth to all mankind. Think with universal love, and expand your ability to love in every experience and deed. It is the continual and constant love which one projects that changes into light and energy. This light can be used to change the earth. Energy is never wasted in spirit, but selfishness and greed cause the light of earth to slowly dim. Only a change in attitude can regenerate this light. Love recharges all things, but a toll must be paid to use this energy. Love that is given freely to God, even under sacrifice, is pure love, and this can be used to influence others.

You on earth have no conception of the forces of energy yet to be discovered, or even conceive of how it works, or how all things are interconnected. It is through the proper use of love that spiritual abilities unfold. This is why hard, loyal work and sacrifice must be given unconditionally. Love, with merit, can be used to do great work for God. Always place love of God before all else, for then life will have more meaning and purpose. Live today with love and vision in your heart, and tomorrow will follow with a purpose that you will see.

Tuesday, August 15, 1989
Ang:

Dearie, continue to concentrate on your ability to focus your thoughts. Thought is the key to our drawing closer. Love and all of its feeling are recorded in thought. To recall and love in the feeling of these moments is not an easy task. The more relaxed and at peace one becomes, the easier it is to do. To detach oneself from the physical world is hard and takes much practice. I too must learn to tune into the same vibration and it must be done simultaneously, so you see, dear, it will take much work and patience.

Love is a feeling, is it not? It is the feeling behind the experience which becomes important, not the experience itself. The mind grows in love by recording these feelings and that is what makes love so powerful. You and Sue [our daughter] were talking about finding it harder to feel connected, but this is necessary, otherwise you would become stunted in your spiritual growth. Change, and one's ability to accept change, is vital to finding one's purpose in life.

What appears to seem as a failure is often the stepping stone to a new discovery about oneself and often life itself. It is good to seek new levels, but let them unfold with patience, for love is earned with service to God through other people. One never truly fails, but through perseverance turns these experiences into something of value. If only you could see the purpose behind the suffering, dear, then you would know the value of such anguish. Be happy today, on our thirty-fifth anniversary, for I am with you now and forever. Dream, for we are together more than you know. I love you.

Wednesday, August 16, 1989
Spirit:

Learn to accomplish above and beyond interruptions. Concentrate your efforts in what must be done; then listen closely for guidance. Lack of energy can result from lack of purpose. You must find time to read more. Set a time apart from other activities and be faithful in fulfilling it, as you do with prayer. We can work with this form of energy to revitalize your effort. Cast away discouragement and those activities which pull at your spirit. Heal thyself with purpose and less self-doubt, for there is much ability and talent hidden in each of God's children. Finding the right path to tread becomes the answer, my child. How can one find this path, you ask? Seek counsel with your inner self and listen closely to its quiet and peaceful message. Agitation shuts down communication while love reopens the door. Love more, give more, pray more and read more. These activities will help you do God's will.

Saturday, August 19, 1989
Spirit:

Let not one's own pride and ego stand in the way of spiritual growth. Are we not all brothers destined to the same place after death—that glorious world of spirit? How short-sighted we are as we live our lives. Complications in life are often self-made, but how easy it is to blame another for problems which arise. Life is a gift, and how blessed is that person who sees love clearly as he lives. How easily one bears the yoke of life depends upon his ability to love, which is the most positive of all thoughts. Loving thoughts which turn into loving deeds do change the forces around a person. Positive thinking, love, and acts of kindness banish fear and negativity from one's life, but it takes discipline, prayer, and daily soul-searching. Unconditional love, my child, is found in the core of one's being where God dwells. Continue to search within for this love. The world can change more quickly if those in the physical world will work together for tolerance and peace.

Moments spent in prayer for peace and for a more loving world are never wasted. Faith, hope and love are the tools one must use to find God, so remember to use them with abundant patience. The timetable of eternity is beyond your comprehension at this moment, but trust in your ability to imagine the beauty of such a world. We come close to guide and protect you with abundant love. Try never to feel lonely, but rather reach up with thoughts of love and contentment which we will feel and then return with even greater intensity. Take the time to feel this energy. Build upon it for this is what you will need to do God's work: concentrated energy which comes from your ability to love unconditionally. This, my child, is the secret you are beginning to know. Peace be with you.

Monday, August 21, 1989
Diane:
I am trying hard to overcome my lack of enthusiasm. Ever so often, I fall into a slump expecting outside forces to cure the lack from within.

Ang:
One must shoulder his own listlessness. Others' negativity can make the task more difficult, but blame cannot be placed upon them, for one must dig deeper and find the spark of joy in his own blessings. Practice what you preach. Think of the many blessings your life holds.

What is it that causes such discouragement? Is it not the feeling of being trapped with little freedom to come and go as you please? Find solutions to this problem and go more. Are you not learning that each is responsible for his own happiness? You cannot buy or give another happiness for it is a feeling from within. The best one can do is place another in a setting of love and caring; the rest is up to them. Relax, dear, and enjoy life. Accept what you cannot change, and go forth with love in your heart and sparkle in your eyes. We work together always.

Monday, August 28, 1989
Spirit:

Find joy in nothingness and you will surmount a large hurdle of life. God, love and life owe you nothing, but rather the joy found in each day is what makes life become filled with love. Mankind always wants, but it is in the giving that joy emerges. You, my little one, get discouraged too easily. To live life with peace and patience takes strength, courage and much self-discipline. As each step is mastered, you understand more of the larger purpose of God's plan. Free yourself of anxieties for you *can* guide and help others. But free will is a God-given right, thus making each one responsible in the end for himself.

Love yourself and your life, and for those problems which loom larger than you can handle, ask God for guidance and help. Ponder and think in solitude, and then listen for the answers in your heart. Do not blame others or find fault, but instead pray that they may be comforted and eventually find joy in nothingness as well. Peace be with you, child.

Thursday, August 31, 1989

"I lift up my eyes toward the mountains;
whence shall help come to me?
My help is from the Lord,
who made heaven and earth.

"May he not suffer your foot to slip;
may he slumber not who guards you;
Indeed he neither slumbers nor sleeps
the guardian of Israel.

"The Lord is your guardian; the Lord is your shade;
He is beside you at your right hand.
The sun shall not harm you by day,
nor the moon by night.

"The Lord will guard you from all evil;
He will guard your life.

The Lord will guard your coming and your going,
both now and forever." *(Psalm 121)*

Diane:

Each day I experience peace in my mind,
peace in my heart, peace in my body,
peace in my soul...
I am blessed, and I am a blessing.

Spirit:

Find your peace within, and enjoy your daily tasks regardless of how menial and boring they appear. You add pressure always seeking for God's will when it is necessary to build your foundation by finding joy in every task. Let time become less important in your life. It is not how much you accomplish but rather the *quality* with which you work. Savor the beauty of the outside world for this adds to the beauty from within. Many feel working hard for money is all important, but working to find unconditional love is more important than gold. Money buys material things which perish in time; love can change all things and endures forever. We remind you of this only to comfort you through this difficult time. Torture yourself not on what you do not accomplish for that erodes one's peace of mind. Pray often for guidance and for others who are less fortunate than you. Find joy through love, my little one, and always listen to the cry of your heart.

Friday, September 1, 1989

"The fruit of the spirit is love, joy, peace, patience, kindness, goodness, gentleness, faithfulness and self-control." *(Galatians 5:22–23)*

Spirit:

Learn them and live them well for herein lies the road to doing God's will. One must be tested beyond a doubt before further knowledge and assignments can be given. Strength of spirit takes much more work than strength of body for one cannot see the progress physically; it is manifested by one's faith. Falter not in your ability to see beyond, even if you think you see little. Hope and imagination is always available and must be used until one is worthy of God's trust to do his will. Many feel seeing is believing, but you, my child, are learning the true path; that believing is seeing. Many help you with love and support. Feel us near. Peace be with you, and shower yourself with patience. Life is eternal so there is no rush.

Saturday, September 2, 1989
Spirit:

What brings sorrow and pain was once the very thing that brought you joy. They are truly the same, but at opposite ends. Most prefer joy, but to grow spiritually, one must experience and accept the extreme opposite, which is sorrow. This is how one learns the lessons of life. Joy and sorrow are both in the realm of spirit and feelings, are they not?

The ability to recall the feeling of a special occasion is the true value of that event. Faith, hope and love are all a part of one's ability to grasp the sensitivity of feeling. Experiences of life are the testing ground of the spirit; it is a showdown, so to speak, between the physical and spiritual aspect of man. If the spiritual man becomes dominant, there is more joy in one's life. Why should this be so, you may ask? If one ponders the meaning of life, the plan of life, it becomes clearer, does it not?

Physical life is short when compared to life in spirit. One is an average of eighty years, while the other lasts forever. The physical body returns to earth from whence it came, and the spirit returns to the realm of God where it lives forever. Is it not important then, to work upon those things which pertain to the spirit and spend less time on pleasing the body? Unfortunately, many on earth fail to see the connection between the physical and spiritual aspects of themselves. Their view is very limited and this becomes harmful to all. Plant the seed of love at every opportunity, my child. This is to be a life-long mission and you must never underestimate its importance. It takes a long time from seed to blossom, but the end result is worth the effort. So it *is* with the fruits of the spirit.

Saturday, September 9, 1989
Spirit:

Each prayer and deed done for God lifts the vibration of the whole earth. Make no mistake about this universal law. Faith, hope and love travel through eternity and they connect the two worlds together. It is man and his limited sight that fails to see the importance of love and the golden rule. How simple the rule is: "Do unto others as you would have them do unto you." *(Matthew 7:12)*

Be strong in your beliefs, my child, for it is important to live what is in your heart. This is true of even the smallest of deeds. If it feels right, do it. Nothing is lost if you try, but everything can be lost if opportunity passes by unnoticed. Pray for awareness. "Grant me, God, the serenity to accept the things that I cannot change, courage to change the things that I can, and the wisdom to know the difference." *(Serenity Prayer)*

Monday, September 11, 1989
Spirit:

Waste not today by yearning for tomorrow. When, dear child, will you begin to see the wonder, beauty, and love which abide in every moment of life? God's grace is finding the good, the positive side to every situation. Growth comes with solving the problems which confront you now. Look deeper within your heart for the sound of joy, that note of peace which can calm all unrest. "Ask and it will be given to you; seek and you will find; knock and the door will be opened to you. For he who asks receives; he who seeks finds; and he who knocks enters." *(Matthew 7:7–8)*

The foundation of the future is built today. Dreams are helpful if they encourage you to pursue the tasks of today. Energy is generated by a delicate balance between the past, present and future, but it must be activated by the action of your daily life. The concern for the future tends to sap your energies for today, so be on guard to keep this from happening in your life. Live today with pure love and truth, and tomorrow will unfold and bloom in full glory.

Thursday, September 14, 1989
Spirit:

The plight of the world will reverse itself as peace and love enter the heart of each individual, each family, and each nation. What then is peace? Peace is the tranquility of the soul—that special place where eternity can be seen and each moment of life becomes important for its ability to create positive action. All positive thoughts and action can be transformed into positive energy. This positive energy is the force which can be used to wash the world with love. Find this peace, my child, in all that you do. Force it to rise to the surface by praying for God's help. It is not for you to judge what is important, but rather to find the peace to handle each situation as it presents itself. It is in this tranquility that the answers to problems unfold. It is the calm beneath the turmoil that one must seek to find the peace of God's will. Peace is the gift of a loving heart; it is that simple.

Peace is found in each act of kindness to another. Peace is found in the joys and wonder of nature to those who see its beauty. Peace is found by those who can give for the sake of giving, expecting nothing in return. Peace is found in prayers of thanksgiving. World peace will be found when each can see the love and good in himself, his family, and his neighbor. Peace be with you.

Sunday, September 17, 1989
Spirit:

Love God first. Feel his presence around you always, for his love is manifested through the love that radiates around you. It takes great faith, hope and fine-tuning to hear the message. This is the reason for prayer and meditation. You are fine-tuning the transmitter and receiver to and from God and his magnificent realm of spirit. Be faithful and strong in your endeavor to seek guidance and it shall be there in great abundance.

Tears make the journey all the more meaningful, so welcome them as a sign of deeper involvement. God must test love, endurance, and patience before one is ready to do his will. The value of life is based upon one's ability to love even in the most difficult of situations, for then you see a glimmer of the magnitude of God's love for us. He cries, but never with despair, for each of us has the ability to change and do what is right. He laughs, for each of us has the ability to love, and love always brings joy and laughter. Yet, dear child, the greatest joy comes when difficulties cloud this love and joy, but faith lifts one's spirit to see beyond that moment of darkness.

Saturday, September 23, 1989
Spirit:

To serve God, one must love every moment of life, knowing that each experience teaches an important lesson. One must learn to differentiate between the physical and spiritual aspects of life and seek the true value of each.

Monday, September 25, 1989
Diane:

I'm annoyed with myself for a lack of enthusiasm and desire to become involved with any chores or projects…questioning myself as to the reason. Where have I misplaced the sparkle and joy? It is a glorious day outside, so bright and sunny.

Ang:

Recharge your battery by plugging into the vitality and beauty of what surrounds you. Everyone feels the drudgery of life, so forgive yourself for this and move on into more joy. How lucky to have a beautiful grandbaby you are about to help care for, our house is paid for and spiritually alive, a new kitten to love and play with—activities confront you everywhere. The pluses are many, so rejoice, my dearest one.

Love your life to the fullest and continue to help each person you meet, for giving is the answer to curing the pitfalls of responsibilities which pull at one's own energy. Some of these pitfalls are caused by others, but in truth it is one's inability to deal with this overload that causes the "dead battery." All you need to do, dearie, is recharge. You have done this successfully many times. I am always there to help you, and I'll be holding Melissa [our granddaughter] right along with you—for I can do that. Many things are beyond your understanding, but believe, and wonders will unfold for you. Be happy!

Monday, October 2, 1989
Diane:

What is the lesson that I am to learn? I pray that an answer will soon come my way. It seems I go one step forward and two steps backward.

Spirit:

Try to reevaluate your concept of time, and place it more in the realm of eternity. Life is divided into segments and each has importance in relationship to the whole spectrum of God's plan. This is the reason for patience. One must have faith that all of the segments will fit together perfectly, but in God's own time—not as you desire—for he knows best. Physical life trains and helps each to find one's own path and purpose. Think and live only positive thoughts, and joy in your heart will be God's blessing.

Tuesday, October 3, 1989
Spirit:

The lesson of love and patience is a hard task, but the rewards are many if one continues to be strong and persevere. The storms of life can be difficult, but peace can be restored by prayer. The connection to God is always open; it is closed by one's doubt and negative thinking. Fear not, anguish not over problems, but instead have strong faith that answers and solutions will come, and it will be so. Peace is the reward, my child, for those who believe.

Wednesday, October 4, 1989
Spirit:

Dig deeper. The attitude of "when is it enough?" stifles one's growth; for in reality, it is never enough. Each on earth is here to serve God and his brother, for a fulfilling life comes naturally just like the dawn of a new day. Lack of energy and luster is nothing more than self-pity, no matter how small the degree. Life is what one decides to make of it. Give abundantly of the love which dwells inside, and purpose will continue to grow and shine forth. God must test those who desire to serve him, so remember this well when discouraged and low in energy.

The battle of life is won in the mind—that part of one's body which transcends so-called death. Death is the transition to new life, but, dear child, that new life will have its beginnings in the pattern set by physical life. The more knowledge one gathers about the true meaning of faith, hope, love and patience in this life, the closer one will be to God throughout eternity. Too few look beyond the moment and beyond their selfish desires, allowing many opportunities to serve and help others slip away unnoticed. This is what ails the world. Be one who is destined to try and reverse this trend and to open the eyes of the unbelievers to the world of spirit. However, one must first, dear child, learn to concentrate and control his own life. Peace be with you.

Sunday, October 8, 1989
Spirit:

Man has to learn to seek first the Kingdom of Heaven, the place of stillness and quiet at the highest level of which he is capable. Then the heavenly influences can pour into him, recreate him and use him for the salvation of mankind. Be proud of yourself, dear child, for you are progressing upward in your climb to do God's will. It is in this seeking that answers will come. The important and most meaningful solutions come from that small voice within, the one that you know is right, in spite of what others may recommend and advise.

Monday, October 16, 1989
Spirit:

In living, one must learn to turn off or tune out the agony. Concentrate only on what is positive. The loving side of life can always pull one through the tedious drudge and mire of daily routine. Look for the small signs which can be missed so easily. God beckons those who watch closely and appreciate his gifts of the spirit. See life as it truly presents itself, dear child, and God will help you do his will. Love and joy come in equal proportion to one's ability to give of oneself.

Where is your first priority: with yourself or with the need of another? Search and pray hard for the latter so that the limited sight of physical life can be the vision of what is to come tomorrow. Service, given with joy in one's heart, is the stepping stone to enlightened and true purpose—what one has been born to accomplish. The master plan is beyond comprehension at this moment in life, but know it is there, and your purpose will unfold at the perfect moment. Trust your heart fully, your intuition, and your imagination, for they guide you always in the right direction. Life must be lived with only positive vibrations.

Tuesday, October 24, 1989
Spirit:

Pray to have your heart filled with nothing but love, patience and compassion for all of mankind. Those in spirit can address those who find this path of universal love. All ego, all concern for oneself, must be pushed aside so that love may prevail. It looks easy in theory, but in reality the road of the spirit takes total commitment to God and his royal realm. Dedicate yourself to love and service, and knowledge of what to do will be forthcoming. Pray, pray, pray, for it is the key to unlocking the wonders of God's plan. Stay ever alert as you seek to do God's will. Think about all you have learned in such a short time. Prepare for much more to come your way.

Wednesday, October 25, 1989
Spirit:

Stay attuned to God through prayer. Find the calm beneath the storm of aggravation and turmoil. Forgive the world and those who have not found the peace and light from God. You, yourself, create unrest because you fail to see the goodness which lies beyond the surface of a given situation. Pray for this ability to know the good and help others to find it. Calmness comes with true understanding.

Know this and seek to find the heart of God which in turn will show you the way to your own reservoir of love. This reservoir of love is endless. Do you not see that the more one taps into it, the deeper it becomes? Spend little time agonizing, but instead lift your heart up in prayer to find equilibrium once again. "Never fear the storms of life, the Master stands by looking on. He will protect you and will give you your heart's desire." Remember well, your message from Saint Germain. Continue to learn to control you own emotions in every situation so that you will be ready to do God's will.

Saturday, October 28, 1989
Spirit:

Feel the love and vibration, and relax and let your imagination fly like the wind. Let it be free and at peace. The pressures of life are only as severe as you, yourself, allow them to be. When one turns his face to the warmth of the sun, it just *is*. One does not have to find the warmth; it is there for the taking. So it is with peace and love. It is there for those who know its true value. This is the beauty of God's truth.

Tuesday, October 31, 1989
Spirit:

Patiently walk the path of faith, my child. Trust and know that at the perfect moment, when you are ready, the answers will come in close succession. Ponder the importance and magnitude of the work started. Remember this through the trials, fatigue and hardships of daily living, when it would be easier to overlook the life of prayer and meditation. Results happen with dedication to the truth of God.

Saturday, November 11, 1989
Spirit:

Take time to think, and take time to contemplate *what* you think. Thought is too often taken for granted as if each thought only comes by chance. Mankind must change its understanding about thoughts. Those in spirit who wish to help must be heard and understood through the thinking process. Many times random thoughts are placed there with a true purpose, perhaps to change the direction in which one travels. Listen, my child, for these very important threads of thought which mingle amongst your own thoughts. Conquer the desire to always rationalize or understand each thought immediately. Sometimes they will return to haunt you for more must be done to settle these reoccurring thoughts.

You see, dear child, all action begins as a thought. What you wish and what lies hidden in your heart must surface as a thought. Nothing could be accomplished without thought. Life is thought in action; waste not one in idleness. We come to guide you and to help you build a strong foundation to follow God's will. May peace follow you, my child.

Thursday, December 7, 1989
Spirit:

Faith is *believing*, my child, even when one does not understand how it can be so. Doubt is the imposter, so send it flying into space where it will be lost. All things *are* possible with God. Run the tape and hold the basket, and one day your loving faith will be returned. We relentlessly remind you to give for that is the purpose of life. When giving becomes as joyful as receiving in everything that you do, your true purpose will shine forth. Work even harder to find the calm and peace within, for this releases bountiful love; with this love, one can see visions of eternity.

Monday, December 11, 1989
Spirit:

The purpose of life is to love all things and all situations that are sent forth for each to handle. Life is a gift, yet the ability to handle its trials becomes the pathway to God. Each must find his own way, but knowing through faith that guidance is always there keeps one going in the right direction. Take time to appreciate the view along the way. Storms of the soul are needed to wash away the debris of futility.

Thursday, December 28, 1989
Spirit:

Truth is not written down—it just *is*—for it abides deep down in every heart. It is the light of the soul. It can be diminished to seeming darkness, but it can never be extinguished. Truth is knowing without doubt what is and what will be. As one climbs closer to God, seeking the path of unconditional love, more truth about spirit becomes evident and pieces of life and truth fall into place. To grasp the truth takes honest and sincere soul-searching. One must dig deep into those special places where despair, pain, frustration, resentment and fear dwell.

Each must be faced with honesty, for it is often easier to blame than to forgive. One need not look far to find this to be true. Look in your own life, dear child, and what do you see? Life is given freely by God; what you make out of this life is your gift to God. If you listen closely, he will guide you to do his will. Fill your heart with endless love and be patient. Many stand close to help. Pray, meditate, learn to concentrate and listen carefully, for this is how truth evolves in your being.

1990

Monday, January 1, 1990

Spirit:

Look up the meaning of "to serve." The first meaning is "to be a servant"; another meaning, "contribution to the welfare of others." As with so many things in physical life, it is the connotation that one places on a word which then can become a way of life. Clear your mind of past associations and begin anew. Look with an open mind where time becomes unimportant. See through problems and solve them with love. Erase resentment, even if justified, for forgiveness brings one closer to God and unconditional love.

Dear one, to become an instrument of God's will, you must find forgiveness in your heart for yourself as well as for others. Truth is uncompromising; it stands as a pillar of God and a refuge which each must try to find. Be relentless in your search, but walk with love and forgiveness as your guide, for without them you will become blinded to the true path.

For you see, love must prevail to find lasting peace, and this peace begins in the center or heart of each individual born into the world. Touch each that you meet with this pure love. Take time to recharge this light with prayer and meditation. Strength is measured by the quality of love you ignite in another. It is that simple. Love sees love; love seeks love; love finds love. Peace be with you.

Thursday January 4, 1990

Diane:

At night I decided to try the Angel Cards that my friend Mimi brought me. I need to spend more time in prayer and meditation. The Angel Card that I drew was *Purification*. On it, it said "to make perfect without faults." I must ponder the choosing of this card.

Spirit:

You must follow the path of Jesus and learn purity of love. Be hard on yourself and strive to love without any desire for a return. This, dear child, is purity of love. You are on the path, but conquer the desire to be selfish and thinking of yourself. To do God's will, you must shine forth with love for all of God's creation. Follow the song of your heart for it will guide you well, but remember that love knows no boundaries.

Thursday, January 7, 1990
Ang:

We are one and the distance between us, in earthly time and space, causes greater longing and increases our determination to close the gap as much and as quickly as possible. It is through thought vibration that you and I make contact and it makes communication between us possible and bring us into oneness.

Love is the energy which transcends the separation of so-called death and binds us into one. Death is of the physical body and that is all. Your spiritual attainments go with you into the spirit world. Everything else is left behind. Here thought is everything. On earth you have time and space due to distances between people and things. In spirit no such a thing exists. The body and other earthly realities are not here to encumber; thought moves instantly to its object faster than the speed of light. Therefore, in the afterlife there is no such thing as time as you experience it on earth. It is through your mind and its thoughts that you are able to perceive our presence and reality. By thought you are able to discern our presence, so pay close attention to it in order to receive our messages. With close attention to your thoughts you are able to pick up the reality of our presence. Think you can, see it happen in your mind, and with intense prayer and desire, it shall be so.

Doubt and discouragement hinder the result, so eliminate their effect through positive action. There is a fine border line between the right and wrong use of imagination. With the right use you can experience our reality. Develop the right use of your imagination, combined with prayer and love of God and your spiritual senses can't help but be opened. If you do this you will be successful in contacting and communicating with me even more than you are now. You are getting better at this as the energy from accumulative experience is increasing and that helps greatly. Persevere and know that your efforts to spiritual awakening will be met with success. Rest in peace, my dear one.

Thursday, January 11, 1990
Spirit:

Rest your weary mind. Thoughts become locked within if too much pressure is exerted. One can force flowers to bloom perhaps sooner, but it will happen, dear one, in God's own time. Try to enjoy what you must do, but leave time for what you want to do. Let life flow more gently with less pressure and effort pondering what shall be. Let not the present moment become lost in what might not even come to be. This, my child, is faith. Patiently plodding through difficult times knowing good will eventually come out of sincere efforts. Relax and enjoy. We see you becoming too methodical in your existence. Where is the spontaneity in your life? Rediscover this joy! We watch, we love, we guide. Remember, you do not trudge alone toward God and your true purpose.

Sunday January 21, 1990
Spirit:

Be patient, my child, and have great faith. Life is the testing ground. Be prepared to meet many obstacles for it is the surmounting of these problems with the hope of answers that gains merit. Merit contains no falsehoods or lies, nor can it be bought and sold. Merit dwells in the inner being where God with his truth and love are the strongest. Submit yourself willingly to these trials and learn more about the depth of your own being. Can the love of Ang ever be diminished? In fact, does not the joy of this love give you greater strength to undergo more of life's unexpected happenings—like being snowed in halfway to Potsdam? Find the beauty of the snow, and the unexpected opportunity to walk up and visit Ang's Aunt Mildred. Do you understand the issue at hand?

Learn well, my child, and your deepest desires shall come to be. We encourage you to continue seeking through acts of love, prayer, meditation, reading and further study. Ask, seek and you shall find, for so it is written in God's words. Yet, to gain this insight and knowledge, each must pay the price of learning life's many lessons.

Continue to seek joy in everything you see and do; for light, no matter how dim, can always be seen by those who train their eyes to see. Stand alone, if need be, to prove the truth of this fact. Resentment, anger and all such emotions are easy to express, but love, my child, is the path to always seeing this divine light. May peace, endurance and patience follow you everywhere. We stand close to help you. Can you feel the presence and touch of our love coming your way? God bless you.

Saturday, January 27, 1990
Spirit:

The word for today is *enjoy*. Remember, child, God meant for each to experience the joy of living, and soaking into their spirit all those great attributes which come from faith, hope and love. To enjoy, one must release oneself from the burdens and the small aggravations of daily living, for in the light of God, each becomes dissipated and of small value. Love is made of this everlasting light, so make room in your heart and enjoy those bountiful gifts presented to you each day from God. Miss not one of them, but rather gain strength and energy from their existence. Always take that extra moment, regardless of fatigue, and go within to find the answers to concerns which rest upon you too heavily. God hears those sincere calls of despair and he answers you subtly, thus ultimately releasing them through joy. Joy takes on many forms and the breadth of its ability depends upon you, my child.

Ask, seek and knock; repeat again, and remember its message. "Ask and it will be given to you; seek and you will find; knock and the door will be opened to you." *(Matthew 7:7)*

Continue to climb, for you are indeed upon the right path. Those of us who love are many, and we are always there to protect you; and by *you*, I mean everyone. Pray for the world and for each and every person, my child, for herein lies heaven on earth. May peace be with you always.

Thursday, February 8, 1990
Spirit:

Pray for strength and fortitude to do all that must be done. Take one chore at a time and complete it without worrying. Practice what you preach! What difference will it make in a hundred years? Relax and enjoy life for that is the secret to growing rich in spiritual values. To take time to savor the gift of life and its many experiences teaches one the value of life itself. Profound experiences come as one gains the ability to appreciate them. To find, one must always seek. Dear child, falter not in your climb for spiritual awakening.

Sunday, February 11, 1990
Ang:

Darling, have heart for you are finding the solace of thought. Each day brings you closer to the truth about thought—for you see, joy *is* a state of mind. That is why you can think yourself into a happier state. Positive thinking works, but let's break down exactly what specifically works: memories bring back happy moments; beauty of nature touches the soul; prayer abates loneliness and despair; and productivity of any kind focuses the mind outward to positive thoughts. Is it not possible for me to join you in each of these special gifts of the mind?

As you learn more, dear, you will see that thoughts are not as personal as you once thought them to be. They can be shared to bring happiness to many depending on how you use your own free will. As you continue to clear away the debris of selfish thinking, you become more aware of universal thinking. Universal thinking is pure thought and the ability to connect thoughts of all things. You will reach out far beyond daily schedules, extending outward to touch the infinite world of eternity. This is where the two worlds, the physical and the spiritual, can meet and become one. Can you not see how blessed we are to begin to understand this great truth while we are each in a different dimension?

Fine tune your ability to think beyond life itself. Grasp control of your thoughts and let them hear the voices of the world of spirit. Dear, your talents are so many and you have the help of countless souls because you are beginning to understand more about the world of spirit. So few at this point do, therefore many want to work with you to release more energy to do God's will.

Thought holds the universe together. Conscious connection in a way falls under the category of thought. Each living thing can communicate but it happens differently, so ponder and imagine these things and more understanding will come. Remember, all things begin with thought, connect together with thought, transcend time and space with thought. Learning to fine tune and how to key into the proper vibration is what the world needs much help in accomplishing.

You must learn to do this in order to help more people. Pray for God's help—add this to your prayer to do God's will—that he will give you the gift of tuning into various vibrations of thought. Become more aware of others' auras for this is the manifestation of their thought pattern. It will come, but it is time to see clearer. Work harder to see my image for this will help in all you do. My thoughts and love follow you everywhere and you know this. We are truly blessed. Peace be with you always, my dear one.

Sunday, February 18, 1990
Diane:

Thank you, God, for the resilience of the spirit.

Spirit:

Be thankful for the knowledge that positive thinking and joy are only the next thought away. Make captive any discouraging or negative thoughts and send them out of your mind. Life, dear one, is what you choose to make it. Adversity should always be looked upon as a challenge from God to teach you an important lesson so that his will can be found. To give oneself to God means to trust him completely, knowing the best is yet to come, and with patient endurance it will be so.

Have confidence in yourself that you hear correctly from spirit; then even more can come through. The only power that limits your abilities is you, yourself. Think success, and it will follow as the night follows the day. Take nothing for granted, but rather praise God for the many gifts presented to you each moment of every day. Look, find and collect them, placing them deep in your heart as a remembrance of God's love.

Do you not try to find ways to please those you love? See and know that God does the same for his children. Ask yourself; how then may I please God? What do I feel will make him filled with joy? The heart answers—to love everything and to take the time to find the joy that may lie hidden within.

The success of life is the ability to turn each experience into a positive action and an outcome in which you can feel pride. Joy is the result of God's approval, for to know God, you must truly know yourself as well. God wants to speak through your actions. Will you let his love shine through? Meet today with love. Peace be with you.

Saturday, February 22, 1990
Spirit:

Love life, for in doing so, one shows his love for God. The superficial world is what one can only see on the surface. Continue to pray for the inner world, and for that place of deeper beauty to surface and make inroads on the visible side of physical life. Dwelling on the negative side, the negative emotions of man just digs society that much deeper into despair. Refuse, my child, to dwell upon this, but rather see beauty and it will one day be so. Visualize good, and only good will come.

While still in the physical plane, one does not have the ability to clearly see the influence of positive thinking, but much energy comes from such thought. It is energy which can be used to accomplish much more than the earth plane can imagine. We speak this way so each will know his prayers are never in vain nor wasted. Pure love and thought knows this to be a truth, so continue seeking its path. We come close to help; trust your own ability to feel us. Peace abide with thee, dear child.

Sunday, February 25, 1990
Spirit:

Dear child, the ingredient you fail to remember is patience—in God's own time. What confuses you is that area between what you wish to accomplish, that dream which you perceive and know can come true, versus where you are in your development at this moment. Rather than ponder this problem of the proper route to take, spend more time on faith.

Know you can believe and have faith in yourself, child, and all will come to be. No one mistake, misjudgment or wrong decision will alter this course; rather it will teach you more. Sincere intent is what can be seen clearly from spirit; the brilliance of a selfless desire pulls to itself many ideas and help from those in spirit. You wonder how sacrifice enters into the road of advancement toward spiritual growth and the desire to do God's will. The truth of this, dear child, is you will never know. Sacrifice is a sacrifice only if it is accepted with love and faith. When you see it as a sacrifice, then no lesson is truly learned. Does this not make sense to you? Sacrifice must be judged through the eyes of God for he alone knows the truth within a pure heart.

Giving, because you think you should, is not the same as unconditionally. Love for a gain is not the same as selfless love. Deep within each heart is built selfless love, but this love gets hidden by physical life and the influences of negativity. Trying to release this love is the most difficult of tasks and takes all that one has to give; for true, selfless love has no beginning and no end.

Strive to be honest with yourself always. Find the faults and pray to correct them, for life has flexibility and free will. Forgive yourself for poor judgment, and you then learn to forgive others. Chastise yourself, but then move on, and learn from each decision in life. Find peace in all that you do.

Monday, February 26, 1990
Spirit:

Life is beset with moments of floundering, but it is through these very moments one grows the most. Understand this and flow with it, increasing your faith and desire to be worthy to do God's will. You know how quickly life can change. To remain stationary stunts the possibility of further growth. Learn to accept the unknown with true faith. This is the key to accomplishment. Trying and experiencing new challenges is the only way one can truly know oneself. Steady as she goes. You know the nine fruits of the spirit: love, joy, peace, patience, kindness, goodness, faithfulness, gentleness and self-control. *(Galatians 5:22–23)* Work hard to bring them forth in any endeavor you choose or one that is placed before you.

Saturday, March 3, 1990
Spirit:

Today will be filled with many fun experiences, so go and enjoy. The intricate workings of thought will become clearer in time. Keep the channel open through prayer, meditation and pure thought. Find more self-control as you discipline yourself daily in all that you do. Remember where you put things; remember names and become more aware of all that you see; increase your ability to concentrate; plan your time and what you desire to accomplish more carefully, and then do it. With greater ease God can help those who learn how to train themselves to do his will. Try hard, but always with joy and love in your heart for then you are calm and relaxed. You cannot force yourself into the world of love; entry must be earned.

Tuesday, March 6, 1990
Spirit:

Dear child, what you term "floundering" is simply the pathway to God's heart. Love is not learned easily for there is much sacrifice along the way. Accepting with love all the circumstances in one's life is never easy.

Ask always with joy in your heart, knowing that all that is supposed to happen will come to be at that perfect moment. Many things are beyond your understanding at this time, so accept it in faith. Self-discipline is an important lesson, but again we emphasize it must be accompanied with joy. Having to sacrifice is made much easier when love and joy are present. Remember, you are a child of God and he wants you to be happy.

There are times when you push too hard, my child. The most beautiful of things happen with spontaneity, or so it appears. The seed of thought, that special moment of planting, may not bloom forth into being as quickly as those of you on earth may desire. Remember that time is not the only factor involved. Use each moment and cherish it as you might a picture, for it will not come again exactly the same.

You *are* what you think, what you cherish, what you love, and what you do. Take the time to mentally absorb all the gifts from God into your being, for then only joy can follow. Memories contain joy, experiencing each moment brings joy, and imagining brings joy. Past, present and future all contain joy for those who see through the eyes of love. Peace be with you, my child. We come close to help you.

Monday, March 12, 1990
Spirit:

"Not my will, but Thine, be done." *(Luke 22:41–43)*

You must find the peace within, which is God's gift to each of his children. In striving to do his will, be careful to wait for the perfect unfolding of your talents. Ability grows out of the love and experience which comes before. This is an exacting law and one must wait with great patience for fulfillment. Perhaps you prepare the way for another. There is a simple rule to remember, child—in spite of all the books and advice that you read, peace must accompany every step of your pathway to God. Know this and absorb its message into your being.

To open one's mind to knowledge is good, but follow only those ideas which guide you from within. That inner and higher self knows what you need, so do as it bids. Each develops in his own special way, and each is different, so remember to give your self space in which to grow.

Individuality is derived because of free will, not in spite of it. To grow, the spirit must overcome the temptations of physical life. This is done by the uniqueness of each inner being and no one, let me repeat, no one, can totally tell you how this is to be accomplished. Trial and error is the only way to find truth. Let peace be your guide, let love be your compass, and let God gently blow the vessel of your spirit to its perfect enfoldment. Strive and work hard to learn, but we urge you to be patient with the outcome.

Prayer, peace and love are all that is needed. Prayer strengthens faith, peace encourages strength, and love connects with the power of all things. We encourage you to ask, seek, and knock, but always do this with peace and patience in your heart. We come close always to help you dream your dreams. Worry not if you remember them as you awaken; the message is received within and recorded. Peace be with you, my child.

Thursday, March 15, 1990
Spirit:

Charity of the heart, my child, should not be compared with charity of money. They are not the same, and it is beneficial if you will ponder the difference within yourself and come to peace. Money is of the physical world, and charity of the heart is from the spirit world. Let fairness not be the issue, but rather turn your thoughts to what can be done with what you have. Continue to realize that you shall indeed judge yourself one day, not on what you accomplished, but instead upon the intent and love that was in your heart. Do good deeds for the pure joy of giving. When you place material value upon it, part of the goodness is already lost. Look to God when confused, for his truth will fill the anguish so you can again move forward with faith and patience.

Physical life is short compared with eternity, but think as though you are already in eternity, for truly you are. Let love lead you where it must, always having faith in what happens, for there is a plan. Help from those already in spirit is close at hand. Strive for peace in all that you do, remembering that good always finds good, even though patience is needed to see beyond the moment. Joy is the reward for finding wisdom through the pain of life. God bless you, dear child.

Saturday, March 17, 1990
Spirit:

Continue to study and ponder always using your ability to imagine what you desire. Those in spirit will come close to fill in the details and intricacies of your masterpiece. Can you think of anything that can be done totally alone? Even thoughts which everyone thinks to be so private, includes a multitude of outside experiences, feelings and people. The selfish person thinks of self first, and then moves out to others. We ask you to first think of the whole—others and their needs—and this will bring you into the deeper part of yourself where love truly dwells. Continue to strive for this perfect love, for through it, you will find the keys of heaven.

Sunday, March 18, 1990
Spirit:

Dearest child, look to the wider spectrum and do not get caught in lesser emotions. It will be time soon, and think of the happiness your mother is yet to find. Many will help her because she is a good person; you always felt this even through the difficult moments. Forgive her, love her, bless her and pray for her. Think of all the positive thoughts you think about; write a list as you have done before when you became sad. This helps both of you. Thank God for the opportunity to find peace in such a situation. Let your love run deeply and this will cleanse away the hurt and anguish. Let not failure enter into your being, but instead make all situations a stepping stone to greater awareness and love. Keep the pain of selfish thinking out of the picture, for the masters create their masterpieces in life through selfless love and compassion and faith.

Faith, dear one, can glide you across any pain, for you know it is necessary even when understanding fails. Seek the white light which contains all healing and look to the rainbow of God. Happiness lies at the end of this rainbow, so continue to follow it all the days of your life, my child. Do not forget to smile and find joy in *everything*. This ability is a true gift from God; use it abundantly as you paint your own masterpiece of life.

Wednesday, March 21, 1990
Spirit:

Remember, child, to keep peace within yourself. Ride out the storms with faith and love, never doubting the perfect solution will be the outcome. Continue to realize and convince yourself that each is responsible for himself. As a man thinks, so he is. Prayers, support and love you have to give, but your mind belongs solely unto yourself, and this is true of all.

Is your mother wanting of care, kindness and love? We think not. Accept the solution which is set before you for it is helping many others as well. Look deeper into the motives behind the hurt and ache. It doesn't matter what others think, dear child, do what you feel. Truth is the essence of life for as you line your sorrows and joys next to it, the answers become apparent. Joy and sorrow balance one another for this gives one equilibrium to walk the cutting edge of life. Neither one should dominate for it is the balance which brings happiness. One should not love only the good, the beautiful and the easy road, for it is the bad, the ugly and the difficult road that teaches faith, hope and patience. Look at your life—is this not true?

Your mother loves you in her own way and finds comfort in knowing you tried to comfort her. Be glad that she has found peace, accept the help with love and move on. Life is filled with wonder, find your next mountain to climb with peace and love in your heart. Listen within for guidance for many come close to help, especially your beloved Ang. He talks to you in your thoughts and helps with decisions more than you know. Your daddy thanks you for your love and caring. Weep for others if it can be of help to them or for your own spiritual growth, otherwise it is wasted effort. See God's love in all the beauty which surrounds you. We come close to you. Peace be with you.

Tuesday, March 27, 1990
Ang:

Be patient, my dearest one, for good things often take time to work out as they should. Nothing of true value happens without a firm foundation, and you must be patient while this is being established. While you are waiting, ponder the art of forgiveness, for you must learn the ability to totally forgive, no matter how difficult it might seem. One cannot love unconditionally without first forgiving the trespasses of others. The energies from God can only pass into a pure channel, so continue to strive for this purity of heart. Positive thoughts and positive action must prevail. See in your mind the encompassing light of pure love—no strings attached, no criticisms, no judgments. "Do unto others as you would have them do unto you." *(Matthew 7:12)* Only good can follow such action. Be at peace—I'm with you always and you know this. Such a blessing!

Thursday, March 29, 1990
Spirit:

Learn to organize your time, dear child, and be very consistent. This will gain merit and help you greatly to achieve your goal. Take time to enjoy the beauty of nature, especially early in the morn. The stillness of the day as it just begins refreshes the soul and gives meaning to all of creation. Take care not to waste this most precious time, for spiritual growth arises from moments of attunement. How can one ever be lonely with so much life and beauty surrounding them? It is the finding of such joy that makes physical life so worthwhile. Continue seeking for the inner beauty, dear child, even if you are misunderstood, for in truth you are following the pathway to God. We can only guide; you must follow your heart and intuition. Strength comes through the mind so find this strength each day of your life. We come close to help you. Peace be with you. (Paused for a little and then continued).

Life will be what you, yourself, make it to be. Too often mankind has the false impression that others influence their life and are to blame for events and feelings which occur. This is simply not true. It is one's own personal reaction which makes one happy, sad, hurt, angry, etc. How each sorts through these problems truly shows the time spent on spiritual growth. Love is the barometer of stability. Peace occurs when one is truly balanced in his life, and this happens through one's ability to love and to accept love.

Love brings security and disperses fear. Love becomes courageous in times of peril and gentle in times of despair. The facets of love are many, and the depths of the soul see the needed image as it examines itself in the mirror of the subconscious mind. If that mirror sees only love of self, life will have many problems; if instead one sees himself connected to universal love, the spirit springs forth with solutions to those problems which appear.

So you see, dear child, the ability to love is the most compelling force of all life. It is the motivator of all things and must be brought to the surface of one's own being and into the consciousness of one's life to be faced with the truth of what you are. One cannot hide behind falsehood for long for it destroys the energy of spiritual growth. Life becomes filled with the darkness of hate, fatigue and despair. You begin to understand the cause of such problems in the world, yet wonder how to go about correcting them. Is this not true? Remember the power of a caring smile, a cheerful note or phone call to a friend, a prayer sent with concern and love. Life is the sum total of the whole. Each kind gesture, no matter how small, given with true love is all that is needed to help the world. Love radiates light and truth; those things which thrive on darkness and falsehood cannot tolerate the light of love.

Therefore, dear child, shine forth with the light of God and love, and it will make a difference. Teach these to all you meet by the brightness of happiness for it can and does affect others. Continue searching for what you seek, and it shall be there at the perfect time. This you know, so move forward in peace and love. We come close to guide and help you.

Saturday, March 31, 1990

Spirit:

Your mission, my child, has always been that of the silent partner. Is this not true? Your forte has been in the field of guidance; not so much for what you say, but rather for what you are and what you stand for. You are there with strength and love when needed, so have faith it will continue. The world will be saved by many like you who stand ready with love and prayers to do what is asked of them without complaint and doubt.

Strive for perfection, but do not chastise yourself in the process. Be grateful always for the many blessings which are set before you, and remember, most of all, to be patient. Patience is the key to success in any endeavor, but the time must be right. You, my child, know all of these profound things, but at times you fail to apply them to your own situation. Of all of the virtues, perhaps patience is the hardest to discern.

Waiting for action in any given endeavor takes great self-control, but look and see from the perspective of eternity rather than in terms of physical life. This lack of understanding causes misery for mankind. The vision is distorted by narrow beliefs for many only see with their physical eyes. The time will come when you will help many to understand more, but for now be patient and diligently work to perfect your own temple with love, faith and prayer. Feel us coming close to help you. May peace follow you everywhere.

Monday, April 2, 1990
Spirit:

Hang on tightly to your dreams, to your aspirations and to that high ideal of doing God's will. Life will be exactly what you, dear child, want it to be. Prayer and meditation guide you on the path, but it is your thoughts and actions which ultimately lead the way to goodness. Strength comes from within your own being because you *are* a child and temple of God. You are capable of doing all things in essence, but the reality of earthly life puts limits on these accomplishments. Begin thinking in the realm of no limits, that all things are possible, and live the remainder of your physical life with this belief.

You limit yourself because of past programming. Believe in your ideals, know that they will be fulfilled in eternity if not now. Man's present state on earth cannot stop the advancement of a soul who is determined and centered on God. Find purity of heart in all that you do and let nothing interfere with your heart's pure desires. "Do unto others as you would have them do unto you" *(Matthew 7:12)* must ring true always. To do less is not living up to the beauty of God's love.

Be not content with excuses for yourself; face the truth as it is with honesty and little compromise, for negativity often appears in the guise of compromise. Guard yourself well against such intrusion, my child. Honesty shines like a beacon in the darkness of man's primitive soul. Each needs enlightenment to release this beautiful light. Take the time to enlighten yourself as you walk the path of life. You do not walk alone and you know this. Feel the help and guidance from those who watch and guide you. Peace be with you.

Saturday, April 7, 1990
Spirit:

Child, be ever mindful of positive thinking. Mankind destroys many good things by allowing doubt and negative thinking to enter into otherwise pure thoughts. Learn to accept special moments as a gift for your own faith, and do not become an intellectual picking apart every detail and question until the beauty of contact is destroyed. Love cannot be pondered, for you see, dear child, it just *is*. That is why Jesus said that one must become like a child to enter the kingdom of God. Do you not see that it is the simplicity of faith and love, a trusting attitude which frees the soul from fear? Fear arouses all the negative feelings, and there are many. Continue to believe in your dreamlike world, for much truth is to be found in this inner world where thought rules supreme.

Perhaps we have all been taught or trained to believe that thought is like an illusion, or something to be questioned and put on trial. But inner thought is truth and should be accepted as such. It is doubt which pushes away this truth. Many tend to use the word *naïve* in explaining one such as you, dear child, but could it not be that their faith and love are lacking? Fear makes one question, and questioning pulls one away from seeking the truth.

Look up the word *illusion*. The definition is (1) something that deceives or misleads intellectually, or (2) a perception of something objectively existing in such a way to cause misinterpretation of its actual nature. Another word of importance is *vision*, which is the actual power of imagination. Learn to accept your vision and illusion with more trust, and more will be revealed.

There is no end and no beginning to universal laws and truths, dear child. This is the importance of a circle which represents the cycle of all things. Life, physical life, is the illusion for the perfect mind. That mind where God dwells in our inner self would not have created life on earth as it is today. We come to reawaken this truth in your thoughts, so that you will continue to climb spiritually and be ready when the perfect moment arrives. Remember, dear child, your must change those around you with *your* vision, so be not affected by theirs. Believe in yourself for you are wise and more knowing than you realize. We come close to help. Peace be with you.

Tuesday, April 10, 1990
Diane:

I have much I want to do, but first I must send away the bonds of fatigue. How often one says, "the spirit is ready, but the body is tired"? If ever I can arise each morn with boundless energy, yet not have to work through the fatigue of my body, then will I have arrived in the Kingdom of Heaven?

Spirit:

Love, dear child, is that boundless energy that you seek. Surround your being with unconditional love, and fatigue quickly dissipates from whence it came. Do you not see that despair or lack of purpose feeds the fires of fatigue? This is why purpose, no matter how small, leads you into the light of truth. Fight through this desire to do nothing, for each time this is accomplished, your spirit shines brighter. Life is meaningful for those who learn to praise God, for those who learn to find their true purpose, and for those who seek the beauty of unconditional love.

To see these truths you must earn the right through prayer and good deeds. Happiness is not a gift, my child; it is earned through acts of love guided by the experience of faith, hope and patience. Where does energy come from? Is it not true that sometimes the more you do, the more energy you have? What is the secret of such energy? You seek at deeper levels, my child, and this shows growth. Continue to strive for control of your own being and find joy in each task—no matter how small that task may seem. Peace be with you.

Wednesday, April 11, 1990

Diane:

Why is it in life that one often realizes his own faults when perhaps it is too late to rectify the mistakes toward a certain person? What is guilt?

Spirit:

Guilt, simply put, my child, is lack of love. Love, you see, must be learned and worked upon, perhaps harder than any other fruit of the spirit. Man takes so much for granted in his physical life. He thinks love will fill his being upon command. But many emotions, and most of all, pride, jump in the way of this unconditional love for all things. Guilt is that area in life which tells him more love should be found, for indeed it is there. Guilt tries hard to tell him that the body is out of sync with itself. If he does not cover up the truth of this problem, real progress and wisdom is disclosed. Always look beyond the problem or see it from a loftier perspective.

Love, true unconditional love, sees beyond the faults and into the true spirit of another. True love always forgives and helps. Sometimes this help appears hard and even cruel, but only the giver knows the true purpose of his giving. This is the seed of guilt feelings.

In striving for more perfection, dear child, judge and then forgive yourself, and move on. Each experience of your life teaches deeper meaning; use this knowledge to love more in the next experience. What you couldn't do for one person, perhaps you can do for the next. Life is a continual progression, an unending puzzle, for each piece must fit into place. Peace be with you.

Friday, April 20, 1990

Spirit:

Does not each difficult experience teach you something new, dear child? "Thy will be done" from the Lord's Prayer—that ability to succumb to trusting God's will completely is not an easy road. But it is a necessary one to be an *instrument* of God's will. Servitude and obedience with love, given unconditionally, will only shine through more clearly as one learns to accept, with faith, the frustration of decisions out of one's control. Enter the Kingdom of God by *knowing* that the proper decision will be forthcoming. Remember, dear child, what looms so large and important at this moment will fall into proper perspective if one waits with patience, knowing that prayers are heard. Look beyond the moment; be open to changes and opportunities which are placed before you. Find that place of peace within where all storms of physical life are calmed. The tempest is often one's own free will taking command. *You* want something, *you* think it should happen a certain way, *you, you, you*. God will show the perfect way, if one will be patient and wait.

> Our Father, who art in Heaven, hallowed be thy name.
> Thy kingdom come, thy will be done on earth as it is in heaven.
> Give us this day, our daily bread, and forgive us our trespasses
> as we forgive those who trespass against us,
> and lead us not into temptation, but deliver us from evil.
> For thine is the kingdom, and the power and the glory, forever
> and ever. *(Matthew 6:9–13)*

Doubt not for one moment that your prayers, deepest feelings, and emotions are being heard. Move onward and upward toward that goal of doing God's will. Training in spiritual values is learned through much pain and sorrow, and you know this. Love always emerges the victor, so keep this love strong and pure for others to see. Can you not feel us coming close to comfort and guide you? Find peace, my dear child, you walk with many.

Tuesday, April 24, 1990
Spirit:

Patience is a key word in the path of life. Without the ability to wait, sometimes for only a short period of time, one misses that "after" vision which reveals so much. As you stare at the red in the stained glass window, it appears to be only red, yet, if you take a moment to meditate and remove yourself into a trance-like state, the "after" image is one of lovely turquoise. Use this little exercise in all that you do, for it is in this "after" image that so much can be revealed.

Do you not see, child, that the world of spirit reveals itself almost like a mirage. Look up the word *mirage*. It is similar to the word *coincidence*, is it not? Your love of fairy tales and books of imagination only enhances your desire to see what others believe not to be true. Have faith that perhaps you see and know more than you think you do.

Life is a journey of experiences felt by both the physical and spiritual being. The line between the two is very *fine*; sometimes they overlap into the other as growth is experienced. Doubt not your imagination, my child, for it holds the key to a whole new world. All things are possible with God, so deepen your beliefs and convictions. No other human being can influence you to believe differently if you stand firmly upon your faith, hope and love.

Faith is trusting God, hope is using your imagination for what can be, and love is the vehicle through which one accomplishes these things. Have confidence and be positive at all times. Dreams do materialize for one who has strong faith. We come close to encourage you to be unaffected by the trials of life. They come as a test to further teach you God's laws. May peace remain with you, my child, in all that you do. God does work through those who love him.

Wednesday, April 25, 1990

Diane:

My mind feels scattered, or should I say, thoughts. Therefore my usual calmness is being disturbed. I must pull positive thoughts together so there is less area for doubt, indecision and negativity. I know I am learning new lessons, and problems will be solved with patience and perseverance.

Spirit:

Learn this lesson well for it is so important. The circumstances of life are there and change very little. Do you not see that it is your *reaction* to these circumstances which makes it seem so difficult? What has truly changed? Your desire for the bed & breakfast is the same; the amount of money is the same. Be patient and meet the next obstacle with peace, knowing that help is there. If it is not meant to be, have faith in your decision at that moment. Refuse to let others' emotions erode your own peace of mind.

Enjoy today, and let not unrest destroy your ability to help others. Go about doing what must be done with joy in your heart. You *are* in control of your own being. Honor this gift and give thanks to God for your many blessings. Just take the time to see the beauty of springtime and all of life for it is there for the taking. Pray that God will guide you, and he will. "Ask and it will be given to you; seek and you will find; knock and the door will be opened to you." *(Matthew 7:7)* This passage we continually place before you. It is the pathway to finding God.

Tuesday, May 1, 1990
Spirit:

Sometimes life with its ability and inclination for right prevails, and the path to follow shines forth with a bright, steady light. Have faith that such ideas will burst forth from within the temple of God. Those who love with a pure heart are not deserted, but instead find strength in that which is right in the eyes of God. To love is inspired by those from spirit, yet the source of love is the universal power of our Heavenly Father. Remember, dear child, that in judgment of another, one must first judge himself, for the ability to judge is done through the eyes of God within your own being.

This physical life is made most difficult because of the struggle we all have in choosing to do what is right as opposed to what is wrong. As instilled in man by God, we innately know what is right. It is called conscience. Contradictory to this reality is all the wrong that we do. Right thinking leads to right action and negative to wrong action. This arouses negative emotions, such as hate, greed and envy. Wipe clean thy slate, dear child, and joy shall again be restored. Think through the eyes of love, feel through the eyes of spirit, and live through the eyes of God. Only there will you find peace!

Bless you, child of love, for we come in peace to guide and help you heal yourself. To be an instrument of God's will, one must believe in his own ability to hear the instructions of the God force within. Knowledge and wisdom appear through the force and power of faith. He who believes he knows much, in fact, knows very little, for spiritual wisdom comes on the wings of faith. The secrets of healing come to be through faith in the ability to heal. Touch only hastens the pathway for concentrated thoughts of perfection. Belief in the ability to accomplish such feats makes success possible. Believe it shall be so, and it shall be so. Pray with a knowing heart, my child.

Wednesday, May 2, 1990
Ang:

Go inward, dear, and find that sanctuary of peace. Continue to find that pathway of pure love, and at the perfect moment, your true calling will appear. Do you not see your own steady and continual growth to higher consciousness? Be patient with yourself. Perhaps you expect too much, too soon. Each soul must be born into a spiritual life, so let the nurturing and growth period be one of happy and joyous awakening. Seek for control of your physical being, but let this experience enhance your life, not hinder it. We continue to repeat your motto: "Ask and you will receive; seek and you will find; knock and the door will be opened to you." *(Matthew 7:7)*

Look upon tears as a touch from those of us in spirit who love you and come close to guide you. The heart of love is endless and goes on as does eternity, so find joy in this journey. Pray, meditate and visit that lovely place within where peace and love always dwell. At the perfect moment, your rose will bloom, and your true purpose revealed.

Sunday, May 6, 1990
Diane:

I do not like this empty feeling which seems to press down upon me at this time. Little joy and sparkle seem to fill my being, and yet, I know not why. There is beauty in springtime and in the lovely music which I hear, yet my heart feels heavy, lacking my usual sparkle. Why is this so?

Spirit:

Fly up into the world of eternity through the gift of imagination, dear one, and view life from a higher perspective. What happens this moment or the next, or even into tomorrow and beyond, is not as important as you think it to be. One day or even a few days is a mere blink in the life of eternity. Mankind places too much emphasis on the present moment. Let it roll in and out as the waves of the ocean, being important for only a brief interlude. Instead, focus on the whole of creation and marvel at its existence. What is most important is the energy of the moment and those thoughts which are sent out into the universe to be gathered and used to create harmony.

Pray to God with praise in your heart for guidance and perseverance. Anyone can be happy when life is filled with sunshine, but fewer can see joy through the mist of the clouds. Walk your chosen path in spite of the storms, my child, for the warmth of love and peace lie beyond the mist, perhaps but one step further. Strength of this kind can only be found within. Look more deeply and it will be there.

Thursday, May 10, 1990
Spirit:

Life can be beautiful, if only you would let it pass by naturally. Do you not see how you spoil the present by concern over the future? Keep strong in your faith that at the proper moment your true path will clearly be opened before you. Patiently wait for signs from the heavenly realm and follow their bidding.

Think in terms of a perfect progression from physical to spiritual, each flowing to the light of God. Every obstacle appears to teach a lesson to be used at the right moment. One does not change when death appears for only the cumbersome body is laid to rest. Therefore, let us remind you to think in terms of the spirit and eternity, rather than to trap your vision in only the physical life. To progress, one must explore his own spiritual body, and find those important messages which ring true in the form of wisdom. Create each day, as if it might be your last on the physical plane, yet it could be the first in the spiritual plane. You see, dear child, they are one and the same, with only a slight change in the dimension. As you live today, so will you live tomorrow.

Fear, unfortunately, appears with the unknown. Human nature finds it easier to think negative thoughts, and this causes untold sorrow. Think of life as the experiment, the testing ground, and the hypotheses of what truly is. The beauty of passing over is to prove one's theories. Those not locked into rigid opinions, prejudices and fear, shall find the spiritual dimension a trip to paradise. Keep open all of your physical senses, for within each dwells the kingdom, the power and the glory of God. Peace be with you always, and remember the words, "in God's own time."

Friday, May 11, 1990
Spirit:

"Love makes the world go round" is a song of truth. Feel and see love in everything. Feel and see positive action in all things, for it is in this belief that changes can take place. Know in your heart this is true, no matter what others may argue or preach. Stand firm in your belief that all things are possible. Learn to be less influenced by others; instead, listen to that silent voice of truth within your spiritual being. Love and joy are at the core of this being, in spite of the outward appearances which seem as a negative force.

Physical life is the testing ground, my child. Continue to find love and joy in every moment for the light around you is contagious and serves to heal others. You cannot see this, but it is there. Leave a mark of love on everything you touch whether it is another human, an animal or a plant. Each can feel the touch of love, and it does matter. Positive vibrations can be used to counter negative forces. Continue to preach your knowledge in daily life to others, even if you feel it has minimal effect. We can see the importance from the spiritual side, while perhaps it is more difficult to view the results from the physical side.

This message is to help you further pursue the talents that lie hidden in your imagination, or so it seems. Talents appear for those who seek. We encourage you with love and energy to strive for your vision of a perfect world, living together in harmony, and sending forth into eternity the rainbow of God's love and joy. Peace be with you!

Wednesday, May 16, 1990

Diane:

How does one learn better concentration, which in turn will help one's recall ability? I also want to work on imagery as they are all connected.

Spirit:

Universal mind can be reached only when one practices and learns the ability to detach oneself totally from activities and thoughts of the physical world. It is that space between consciousness and the sleep state, also known as a semi-trance. One must learn complete self-control where fear is non-existent and the mind is open to explore all phases and realms of one's being. If the heart and motives of one's life are pure with love at its base, then what is there to fear? Ponder more deeply this feeling, for love can and will conquer all things. It is the fear which stands in the way of success.

Know with love that you can do all things, and it will be so. It is the half-hearted attitude which saps the strength to achieve at one's highest level. Help from other sources must work through a clear channel, and this is established through heartfelt prayer and a sincere desire to do God's will. Wisdom appears naturally with little stress, so continue to enjoy all the blessings of your life and be thankful for the small joys which you take for granted. Try to become part of all things and you will understand more about universal law. Stay steady on your course, and let nothing stand in your way to pursue your own special mission. At the perfect moment, it will surface. Walk in peace.

Friday, May 18, 1990

Diane:

Happy birthday, Sue! I know in my heart this is the year good things will happen in Sue's life!

Spirit:

Trust in God, be patient with love in your heart, and all things will work out. Go about life with peace and tranquility, doing one thing at a time quietly. Rushing only causes confusion, and doubt brings uncertainty and fear, so always look to God and see the light of truth flowing into your own heart. By the way that you are and by the way that you live, send out a light which attracts loving thoughts into your life. Mortal life sees such a small section of the overall masterpiece. Broaden your vision to imagine what might be, and God will reveal more of his truth into your life. Enjoy everything which enters into your life for there is always a lesson to be learned. Know that the more difficult life is, the greater the lesson it teaches, and be thankful you are chosen for some special reason. Release your free will to the divine will of God, and your calling will be fully revealed at that right moment.

Weakness and lack of energy are self-imposed, dear child. You must see love, health and happiness always before you—in your inner vision. This is where the mind creates its own blueprint, where God can help make all things perfect. The inner vision knows what must be done, but in the confusion of the material world, the truth gets distorted or ignored. Work to see deeper into your own being, and face what must be done to submit to God's will. We come close to help you always.

Thursday, May 24, 1990
Spirit:

Dear child, great internal strength is needed to do God's will. Grace from God is earned by the continual awareness of suffering and one's desire to act upon this suffering. There is much preparation needed to cast away the selfish ego which lives inside as well. Each experience is of value, but one must look deeply within to find its worth. Again we remind you, dear child, to look through the eyes of eternity when seeking the wisdom of God. If tears appear, welcome them, for this is a sign that progress is being made. Do you not see that one must suffer and feel the weight of others' sadness before being ready to do God's will? It is the caring heart, the selfless love that is given without any desire for a return which God seeks.

Feel joy, for in your heart you know you climb closer to God each day. Discouragement is a negative force and must be dealt with. How, you ask? Let it go and send its heaviness up to the light of God's realms. Know in your heart that each positive thought, prayer and action does make a difference. Faith keeps one on the path, so let its light brighten the darkest moments of your journey. Find ways to live love, and the light from within will glow with unending brilliance. The key, my dear child, is patience. Watch and wait for every opportunity which beckons to you. Trust your intuition for it guides you well. Whenever you feel there is a sign to point the way, then follow.

Remember the questioning mind that tends to doubt and hides the real truth. What can be lost by being so careful and logical? There are many opportunities to follow the call of the inner you, and the chance to broaden your God-given talents and open doors to finding the path you so desire. Build more confidence in your talents. Know you can do what your heart desires and go after it. Do you not know that your Heavenly Father cheers the loudest and laughs with great happiness as you feel his energy and love filling your heart? His heart is a mirror from which you can see your own progress, so take time to view your image and see God smiling through to you. He is always there, and with him comes all his helpers of love. Peace be with you always.

Thursday, June 7, 1990
Spirit:

See the beauty, my child, find the heart of your creator by giving love to all that you meet, and "praise God from whom all blessings flow." With this special formula, great and unexpected talents are born. Remember, with God all things are possible.

Do not question, believe. Direct your thoughts in alignment with your desires, and new roads will open to you. Carry the past deep in your heart for it taught you well, and use it as strength for a new era of accomplishment, for without this love you would not be ready for today. We help you have abundance, but you must take time to feel the presence of those who come to guide. Soon it will be time for the bud to open and each petal will bring you closer to doing God's will. You feel this in your heart; listen to your inner self for it guides you well. May peace be your truest friend. God bless you.

Saturday, June 16, 1990

Diane:

The river is not there this early morning. I'm up at 5:30, and except for the chirping of the birds, there is silence. Not a ripple of water can be heard, and all appears to be a vast emptiness. But I know differently. This too, can be the illusion of life itself, a vast emptiness.

Spirit:

And yet, beyond this mistiness one can find abundant opportunity. It is the ability to wait for the clearing of one's mind, and the ability to find one's hidden talents that God seeks. What do you see beyond the clouds of mist, my child?

Diane:

I see love and beauty and laughter, dear Father in Heaven. Please let me love those who need to be healed of life's wounds. I have much to give, yet I patiently wait for direction. To sit in such peace and tranquility is indeed food for my soul. We each must heal ourselves of the emptiness that life and its problems can so easily cause. It is in the quiet core of one's inner being where peace dwells. I pray that I might go deeper and deeper into this vast emptiness to find the beauty of God within me, and to find that purpose for which I am created. To love, to forgive, to serve are easy words to write, but not so easy to live each day of one's life.

Spirit:

What is the purpose, you ask, of looking out upon the early morning mist of nothingness? So you may see with inner vision, the dreams and desires of your own heart. God speaks to those who seek, those who see what can be, and wait to serve. Smile, laugh and see the beauty in nothing, my child, for beyond this, one finds the treasures which lay dormant in the imagination. Joy is the answer to sorrow, and your loved ones in spirit beg you to see and feel their joy as well. The truth is, beyond that apparent stillness and nothingness, there *is* something. Are you willing to find it? As the mist clears, so shall your life unfold, my child. Wait patiently with only love in your heart. Peace be with you.

Ang:

Nothing is ever over which one chooses to remember. That, dear, is the energy upon which we meet. The thought of the memory itself combines with the present and the future. They unite as one and therein lies eternity. Is it not true that you choose to remember, with love, only the happiness? Loving thoughts pull in good energy—energy we can use together and individually as well. There is so much for you to learn and understand. I marvel at your ability to perceive all of these new ideas, for nothing is impossible in God's world. Work to bring about "Thy will be done on earth as it is in heaven." Seek, dear, seek!

Monday, July 2, 1990
Ang:

Be calm, patient and project only positive thoughts. Many of us are working to clear the way for approval of the Hosmer House Bed and Breakfast you are trying to purchase. If you speak from your heart, others will sense your truth and sincerity. You know, darling, you, yourself are the best seller, for your intent is pure and filled with love. Do you not know how brightly you shine? I do, and it makes me shine with pride as well. We are as one, so the light of love and good deeds brighten both of our auras.

Let God and his realms help you, and wait until your path is clearly shown. Live your life quietly knowing you can do whatever is placed before you. Always live with love as your constant companion for it is the truest friend that exists. Glad you are home, for here in my chair we can hear one another clearly. You look great, dearie, and I love you forever. Walk in peace!

Wednesday, July 4, 1990
Diane:

The birds are bustling about—so busy, perky and cheerful. Guess that's why I love them so. I'm thinking about what Ang would be saying to me.

Ang:

Be as free as those birds that you love. Set no limits and the doors of life will open wide with many opportunities. You are never truly alone; I am always with you in thought and spirit. We work as a team, just as before. When you smile, dearest one, see me smiling back. Hold out your hand and I'm there to grasp it. There is great strength between us. Your tears are the physical proof of love, for true love is bittersweet, and it is felt throughout your whole being.

You are very wise, dear. Let no one tell you differently. Stick to your dreams for they will come to pass if you continue to climb the path of spiritual growth. The article in the newspaper about the bed and breakfast was a good one. A sixty-year-old retired school teacher, huh? Be sure and tell her how much I love her. Be at peace!

Sunday, July 8, 1990

Diane:

How will I learn the necessary techniques to be a healer, and who in particular will help me?

Spirit:

You do not need to work hard to learn; it will just happen. By this we mean, new avenues of knowledge and enlightenment will be easily perceived as you read and study. As you are ready to progress, and we see the need of further enlightenment, it will be so. Continue to trust your own channeling for it is very accurate. We talk to you internally through your own mind. Words are placed within your own mind almost as if you were writing it yourself; yet you know you are not, because no actual effort is going into the writings. You will find this to become true for your other senses—seeing, feeling and even smelling.

We impress upon you again, to have faith in yourself. It matters not what others can do, or how far along you perceive them to be. Healing is not a contest nor should one compare to another. Healing is the enfoldment of one who prepares himself with careful and meticulous preparation, prayer, devotion, sacrifice and self-analysis to find the real core of his being.

Love, unconditional love, begins to emerge, and that, dear child, is the source of the energies of healing. Every healer starts as a novice, for proof of intent and dedication must be proven to those of us who come close to support your efforts. You have begun to take the initiative to learn, and this is an important step.

As you learn new exercises to open your higher sense perception, we will come through on those channels which will be of greatest help. Do not be surprised if we use our ingenuity and find ways of our own. You are right about visiting another realm while you sleep. This is a very important method to prepare you to learn more quickly as new information comes to you. When it is time to reveal more, it will be done. Strive hard in your chosen mission for help can only come as you, yourself, release energy from your own desire and hard work. Is there not always a price to pay for further enlightenment? You, my child, are learning this lesson well. Peace be with you.

Wednesday, July 18, 1990
Diane:

Any discussion or hints about the energy level? What is energy?

Spirit:

Energy is the fuel behind what makes something work. In the human being the main source of energy comes from the spirit—that part of you which is connected to God's original source of universal prime energy. Think for one moment, for without thought and spirit, man would not move at all. Many times too much emphasis is put upon the abilities of only the physical body, but is it not the spirit or will of one's being that truly instigates activity? Listen, my child, to the call of the spirit. It can do all things because of its connection to the creator of all things, God. Without pep talks from the spirit, the physical body would be perfectly happy to do nothing. Energy comes from within and activates the cells of the physical body. Think tired, and you will be tired. Many outside forces affect the energy level, but it is primarily an overload on either the mental or emotional level, or both, which shuts down the energy level to whatever degree it chooses.

Therefore, it is most important to have domain over your thoughts which come directly from your conscious and unconscious will; both belong to God—"Thy will be done." Free will is the extra booster given to each as a gift to find his own potential. The more mastery one achieves in control of his will, the more energy he will find in his physical body. This is an exacting law, but few realize its power. We are not saying to disregard the limits of the physical body, but rather to make each aware of his true self. Seek the truth about yourself, and hide not behind excuses, for herein lies the weakness of mortal men. You are what you think, and this includes your level of energy. Keep striving for the higher level, my child. May peace follow you.

Friday, July 20, 1990
Diane:

I know that what I need will appear at the proper time. My problem is to accept the shortcomings within me are indeed my lack of faith, for all things are possible. I am truly well prepared to be a healer, and if I let go of my insecurities in myself, sending them up to God and his realm, then many doors may open to higher understanding. Progress is happening. I feel this and see it in myself. "I give myself to Thee, Dear Father, do with me as Thou wilt," is my ultimate goal and prayer.[1]

Who am I? A child of God able to do his will, for he can help me know I have the talents for healing. Not to do it for ego sake, but rather to help my fellow man find more love and peace. I do not have to prove anything to another, only to myself; but this must be done with true humility. Any talent is God given—man himself has only the desire to develop this talent. Many talents lay dormant because of the lack of self-control within man himself. Oftentimes I try to figure out what is the most important ingredient in developing oneself, and it must be love.

It is so written in the Bible and also by many famous philosophers and authors. Jesus said "Love thy neighbor as thyself." Shakespeare wrote, "To thine own self be true." The message is that love of oneself expands and fans out to others.

Emmanuel from *Hands of Light* by Barbara Ann Brennan says "It is not a matter of destroying fear, but of knowing its nature and seeing it as a less powerful force than the power of love. It is illusion. Fear is only looking in the mirror and making faces at oneself."[2]

Sunday, July 29, 1990
Spirit:

Interests evolve from a love of life. Do you not see that joy is the result of doing? It is the purpose behind what you do that is worthy of judgment, not so much all that is accomplished. Let us look further into that statement.

Many spend so much time bemoaning their fate and lack of time to do what they desire. They feel there is little energy left in which to perform their duties. The human being puts so much pressure on himself, unknowingly crossing the wires to happiness. Thought comes as a savior or a curse. The interpretation of the message is the key to success or failure. Belief in one's ability to accomplish a desire in the form of thought is of utmost importance. Belief in yourself is the key to success.

We tell you this as reinforcement in your climb to become a healer. What you are ready to absorb will come very easily, but deal patiently with yourself in areas which do not come easily. It is in the *knowing* that answers will come; this allows you the opportunity to climb life's hurdles with patience. Take care to control the concentration of your mind. Let it not go randomly off in many directions. This is detrimental to satisfactory results. One must center himself on the activity at hand. You are better at being aware, but continually practice the ability to center and focus on one thing at a time. More will be accomplished if you master this skill. Help is always close at hand, so call on us anytime. Feel the presence of those who come close. Peace be with you.

Monday, July 30, 1990
Spirit:

Be not dismayed, my child, for you shall see the glory of God as you climb the spiritual path. As we so often repeat to you, continue to have confidence in your own abilities. Pray and meditate for herein lies the vehicle used by those who walk along your chosen path. Prayers *are* heard, my child, especially those desires which lay hidden in the heart. Purity of heart and soul releases the energy through which progress can be made. Ponder all words that you read; search your own soul for those feelings which hamper your progress to finding God's will. Life is beautiful for those who see and feel God's love.

Live a balanced life, my child, but you must leave time to pray, meditate and study. All things come through thought, so one must always leave time to hear one's thoughts, whether from himself, from the world of spirit or from universal thought. Work harder to feel connected to all things. Energy beyond imagination is waiting for those who can use it to do God's will. The human mind cannot comprehend the vastness of God's creation—so simple, yet filled with intricacy most difficult to understand.

Faith in God and yourself is a total commitment you must make. Doubt is negative, and hampers the flow of progress. Send it away as quickly as it appears. Know you will be ready to perform the next task which God places before you—know it even before it happens. When doubt creeps in, pray, pray, pray. Listen not to others, but instead go into thy own self, and right answers and the proper pathway will be placed before you. We come to prepare you for your new adventure. We will be close to help you, so feel our presence. We also thank you for reading to us; so few do with true knowledge of what they do. May peace and love follow you everywhere.

Thursday, August 2, 1990
Spirit:

Faith is built by positive thinking and prayer, until intelligence or innate knowledge releases such awareness. Faith is trusting and knowing that the right path is being prepared for you, hand-crafted with great and careful planning. Know that when you are ready, my child, all things will fall into place. Stay on the sometimes tedious pathway of prayer, meditation and the fulfilling of all conditions that you raise up to God. Obedience is very important for it shows one's willingness to walk the spiritual path. We, in spirit, need true commitment, for this releases the necessary energy through which we can work. Action through your thought process sends signals on a special wave length to those of us who help you. Each on earth is capable of much help, but alas, so few are aware of the magnitude of the world of spirit. We are diligently working to change this and progress is being made. Peace be with you, child.

Tuesday, August 7, 1990
Spirit:

"Surrender your self will to the divine will!" Release that pressure upon yourself. Worry not that you can or cannot do a certain task, but place more faith in yourself and in those who are sent to help you, my child. Just be open, trusting and loyal to God and those experiences which seem to threaten or confront you will dissipate. Let them lighten with unconditional love and gently float away. What is it you are seeking? How deep is the love you follow? Do you not see that there is more sensitivity in your feeling this morning, for we have worked during the night as you rested?

Dear child, feel with your heart and with your desire to help. Try to remove your ego and become one with what you wish to experience. See and feel the energies—those molecular fields which reach out to you. Pass through the valley of self-doubt; only you can do this, for free will is God's gift to you. It is your responsibility. Remember, with God all things are possible. Know that today you will feel more and see more than yesterday because you desire it to be so. Bring the love to the surface for the closer you come to God and the more you desire to do his will, the gifts of healing and helping others will shine forth.

Desire–desire–desire that is filled with love is a winning formula. You must pull all of these forces together within yourself and pray to Heavenly Father, and his love and energy will be there for you. Internalize what you've worked so hard to discover and learn about your true self, my child. We are here to guide—be open in your quest to heal. All pieces of the puzzle will fall into place. Be patient, relax and have faith in yourself. You are God's child.

Wednesday, August 8, 1990
Written while attending a course by healer Barbara Brennan

Spirit:

The fountain of youth *is* eternity. Dwell more upon what you feel you can do well, and less upon those tasks which are more difficult. Do not all things come to pass with patience? Relax and be yourself. Each has something special and unique to offer others; it is in the eyes of the beholder. One who seeks the truth will find it. Trust yourself; give of yourself knowing that help is always present. Blockage is caused by fear, and fear takes on so many different faces. You, my child, are what you are—a child of God. Talents must be nurtured with love, patience and practice. How much you desire the end result, gives you the energy to press onward. Courage is the ability to continue, to pass through the doubts to the rainbow on the other side. You already know all this, but we come to encourage you to keep on keeping on.

Ang:

The colors will come, so put less emphasis on this, dear. Your subconscious knows the colors and will help to clear the chakras; just be intent and concentrate as hard as you can. That is all you need to expect of yourself. Remember, you are the sole judge of yourself; if you have given your best, then be at peace. God and those who help you see your honest intent. If it rings true to you, then be satisfied and at peace. Love—the white light—contains *all* the colors. Remember this as you work.

Friday, August 10, 1990
Diane:

How can healing be done from the positive side? Cannot the suppressed feelings also be released without frenzy? Would you please comment on this?

Spirit:

Work on the opening of your own High Sense Perception (HSP), dear child, and more knowing will unfold before you. As you so often do, you will answer, with guidance, your own questions. You see, dear child, many on the earth plane fail to take the necessary steps to sense their own being, but rather want the easier solution of being enlightened through another. This is the cause of so many problems on earth itself. No one else can account for you, but yourself. Each must live with the truth, and to split this truth splits the well-being of that individual. Divine will, divine love and divine mind are the guides to this truth, but many fail to connect with this higher self for they instead become bogged down in the quests and fears of physical life. They fail to realign themselves with their own divinity. What you seek is a way to open this bridge of transition in a positive mode.

Keep seeking, my child, and the way will be open to you. Keep seeking the missing link, and in the process you will heal yourself of pain and longing. Continue to sort through all the information which you gather, for what rings true will become a part of your own being. Your beloved husband will always be with you, and you know this. There is no realm too high or task more important than being connected to a bond of love. Does love *ever* interfere with the soul? We know it does not, but rather enhances one's being to even higher levels. Ponder this truth, my child. Be confident, always praying for divine guidance, and it will be there. May peace and love follow you everywhere.

Monday, August 13, 1990
Spirit:

The key to purity, dear child, is through the mind. As the mind sees, so shall the physical body follow. Your intuition guides you well so listen and follow its bidding. Keep your conscience clear by revealing those feelings in your heart to each of your family members. Life is not meant to be a game of deceit or dishonest dealing with yourself or with others. Life is a journey to find the purest path to God's heart for therein lies the truth of all eternity.

Can you not see the plan unfolding? That is not to say that you will understand the total picture, but be satisfied, my dear one, with those tiny glimpses of the true meaning and value of physical life. You are indeed blessed, so give great thanks for the privilege of an awareness of God's truth. Each step brings you closer to this truth. How you treat your body is first born in thought; the action of this thought will manifest itself at a much later time. The more you understand your value as a spiritual being in God's eyes, the easier you can resist what is placed before you as temptation.

Growth comes by practicing those thoughts which present themselves. Your value comes, not by setting yourself up as being indispensable, but rather as a link in the outworking of God's will. See with love those who surround you, and watch your actions. No one can follow the light which another sees, but others can follow the light that radiates around one who loves God with his total being. This light shines forth unconditionally for all to see. Continue to seek this light, dear child. "Ask and it will be given to you; seek and you will find; knock and the door will be opened to you." *(Matthew 7:7)*

Purify your life; love without a desire for a return, and peace will fill your heart. We come close to help you. Can you not feel our love and energy? Peace be with you.

Monday, August 20, 1990
Spirit:

Prayer is the important link between the two worlds, my child. When one calls through the love of God, all things can happen. Does the Bible not say this? Believe there is nothing that can interfere with the force and power of prayer from a loving and unconditional heart. This is the law, dear one. Listen within your own heart and do as it bids. The light of love shines for all to see when it is connected to God with prayer.

Always stay steadfast to those conditions which you make, for merit is solely gained by the accomplishment of such conditions. This strengthens the pillars of your own being. To see truth, one must live truth; there is no other path. Charge your battery of life by linking yourself to the lifeline of God's being. The line is always open to those who seek divinity within themselves. Your prayers are of great value, so take the time to express them. We come close always. Peace be with you.

Tuesday, August 21, 1990
Spirit:

As with all things, my child, one's ability to achieve starts from within. Words, thoughts, and ideas are all internal before they erupt into action. One must sense, and does sense with the spiritual senses, but physical life stifles the awareness of spiritual activity. You must spend time letting your inner senses have the opportunity to manifest themselves. Sitting in silence is an important exercise; sense things by feeling what is around you. Take time to do this, my child.

What does nothingness feel like? Sense the message of your own being, both physical and spiritual. Use adjectives to describe your observations. Delve deeper into that realm of silence and much will be revealed unto you. Listen to the power and strength within, hear its message and wallow in its energy. No one else can teach you to find this space of divinity, for it is a solo journey, my dear one. Seek and you will find. Peace be with you.

Sunday, August 26, 1990
Spirit:

You see, dear child, happy are those who learn to give of themselves, for then the blessings of the Lord can flow freely into their life. This lesson you are learning and it will manifest itself in your faith. As this faith grows deeper, many new experiences and talents will appear.

Remember *thought*, the concentrated energy of thought, is the pathway to fulfilling your dreams and desires. Become more *aware* of all that surrounds you, for so many messages and encouragement are given through subtle signs. Focus your mind to observe more closely.

An important key to doing God's will is your ability to hear his message. Be firm on making time in your daily life to pray, meditate and find that inner peace. We know how easy it is to neglect this important part of your daily schedule. Reinforce your commitments each day with concentrated energy and then listen with care. Is it not a sign that the two words you picked were *concentrate* and *listen?* You heard us then before you were even aware that we came so close to help and guide you. It brings us joy to know that you know too! There is comfort between the two worlds—special friends that connect through thought. Peace be with you, child.

Tuesday, August 28, 1990
Ang:

Dear, if you can come up with the feel of a hug through thought and words, we've got it made. Work to recall mentally the feeling of closeness we shared: loving, warm, comforting, soft pressure, tingling sensation, protection, well-being, happiness. Use the special examples you remember, such as the July 4th fireworks or our reunion after summer school in 1955, to name a few. Search for the same comfort mentally through the thought process. In order to physically hug someone, you must first think of it in your mind. Work to perfect this ability, dear, and many avenues of communication will open between us. We must seek to tune into and fine-tune our wave lengths—that is all. What seems to be so difficult while in the physical body is, in reality, very close at hand.

Practice is the key factor. You must not give up on your desire to learn the higher spiritual dimensions. The ability will be found with diligent practice. The love is there; you need only to seek the proper vibration. It will be helpful in all of your endeavors. I'll love you forever. Be at peace as we continue to share our lives together.

Monday, September 3, 1990

Diane:

I miss Ang so very much, but I try not to let anyone see the hurt. It is so very difficult to make myself aware of the finer vibration of spirit. It is my lack of perception, not Ang's, but I know God will help me to open spiritually when the perfect moment arrives. How fickle and changing we humans are with so little consistent faith. I know many beautiful and wonderful truths about spirit and eternity, yet I have to strive so hard to sustain the joy of daily life. Why is this? What do I fail to do correctly?

Spirit:

Dear child, what you fail to remember is the process of healing itself. One cannot expect to be whole after losing a large part of oneself. Do you not think that tears sting the eyes of your beloved husband as well? Perhaps it hurts the most when both of you spend time remembering at the same moment. Could this not be so? It is in the closeness of these moments and the love released in those tears of sorrow which will open the channel of awareness. The beauty of love is there for the taking, but many fail to see the price which must be paid to find eternal love. Tears release the pain, my child, so welcome them. Be grateful you anguish without resentment or guilt for time will continue to heal the pain of separation. One day you will know there is no true separation at all. Keep on keeping on, dear child, for you indeed tread the true pathway. Peace be with you always.

Ang:

Dearie, do what rings true in your own heart. You must follow what aligns itself to the inner truth of your being. Think a positive solution to your concerns and it will be so. This has been proven to you in many ways, so you know it is true. Think us together and it is so. I help you ponder the solutions, and I send answers in many ways; some you recognize and others not. Peace is in the heart, and love releases what stands in the way of peace and tranquility. Remember, to truly know the joy of love, you must feel the pangs of sorrow. To be balanced you must experience both, so dwell on the positive side of life, dearie. We have had so many blessings together, and it will continue to be so if you will keep your faith in God strong, remembering all things are possible. Enjoy the beautiful day. We are together building the bridge of transition between the two worlds.

Tuesday, September 4, 1990

"The way of the disciple…Say little; love much; give all; judge no man; aspire to all that is pure and good; and keep on keeping on."[3]

Spirit:

Have faith in the outworking of God's plan. He can fill the hearts of men, and you must have the trust and patience to let him do so. Be not in a hurry to take the outworking of problems into your hands, my child; leave it to your Heavenly Father. He will not desert his plan to guide those whom he chooses. Have you not learned through poor judgment? This will be true for all whom you love. Regret and harm have indeed been done by those who rush ahead, unsure and centered upon their own ego. Wait, my child, and instead meditate and pray to God for his help and guidance. Is it not possible that the answer is already being sent to those concerned? Ponder well your heart and guard carefully what comes out of your own mouth! Words of ego can hurt; words of the heart do not. Peace be with you.

Saturday, September 8, 1990

Spirit:

To live is to grow; to grow is to live. You cannot separate one from the other, they are interdependent. Many times, my child, you are growing in spirit without even knowing yourself. You are not aware of your loving nature. It shines forth to all. It is your greatest strength and is used knowingly and unknowingly to help and change others for the better. Those who have the ability to love the most must help and be an example to those who are lesser in their ability to love or don't know how to love. The great people in history are those who seek God in everything they do. They seek with their whole heart to hear God's counsel and accomplish accordingly. We are all included in contributing to God's will and plan.

Diane:

I'm trying to clear my mind of my own thoughts, and write only what floats in like a cloud. I seemed to be forcing the words instead of letting them flow, so I stopped.

Saturday, September 15, 1990
Spirit:

Surrending to and allowing God's will to be done in his own time are the key ingredients to a life of faith. To truly understand God's plan while in the physical body, we have to put aside our ego. My child, it is not an easy task, but the end result is worth the effort. It is much like growing a splendid flower; the seed is planted and nurtured by many elements. Then if the conditions are in the right order, is not the beauty well worth the effort? So it is with spiritual growth. There are no shortcuts, so to speak, but rather the sometimes tedious and repetitious effort on the part of one who seeks. Prayer is uplifting and gives one the strength with which to pursue those desires that dwell in the heart. Touch base and tread carefully over each step of the way, for even if you stumble, every obstacle is there for a purpose. When the lesson one needs to learn is accomplished, the pathway is again bright for each to follow.

Be thankful each day for the blessings in your life. The clearer you see and feel them, the brighter will be your guiding light. Praise in the form of appreciation is innate to all of us for we are made in the image of God, so he hears you, my child. Simple prayer, filled with love, concern and joyful purpose are indeed of great value. In the process of asking, thought clears the mind to find the answers. Does this not ring true? A peaceful mind can allow solutions because emotions which confuse are left outside. Truth dwells in the peace of one's being, never in the turmoil. We remind you of this, dear child, so continue to strive for what you most desire: the gift of healing through the energy of God's love.

Have you not come a long way? We urge you to try very hard to forget about time as you now know it in physical life. Instead, imagine time as it might be between the two worlds; this is where you will find more understanding. Continue to reach up with *very* concentrated effort. Feel the energy of the timeless sphere as you meditate, and continue to send out vibrations of love in all that you do, in all that you think, and in all that you aspire to do. Remember always that we come close to help. Peace be with you.

Ang:

I hear you always and what joy it is to be together in our thoughts and our loving energies. I continue to marvel with appreciation at your ability to perceive what many cannot understand. Just remember—eternity is *now*, yet it lasts forever. From God's perspective there are no divisions, only the appearance of such. Mankind is one through God's loving presence and he loves each of us personally. It is quite a mystery, but you, my love, are growing rapidly in understanding and solving it. I love you forever.

Tuesday, September 18, 1990
Spirit:

The secret of life is the acceptance of all things. Acceptance of what is difficult teaches one the greatest lessons. For you see, my child, life will be as difficult as one chooses to make it. Joy can infiltrate the worst of situations if the mind will allow such penetration. Joyful thoughts originate with God as he gave each the ability to find happiness his own way, but mankind fails to realize his own potential to do this. Instead of shouldering their own responsibility, many choose to blame others for their misfortune. Hence, all the negative forces come forth and produce havoc instead. The only weapon one has to counteract negativity is love—the acceptance that love can and will change such forces. It is much more difficult to love and forgive than it is to hate and resent, but it is the only route to happiness and ultimate salvation. One finds God through this door of love, for if one loves deeply enough and has faith in God's love, all things will work out with ultimate joy.

Strive for your own desires, always seeing through the eyes of love, guided by positive thoughts. We, in spirit, cannot emphasize this law too often or too much for it is in reality, the most important of God's laws.

Ponder it well, my child, as you climb the spiritual path of physical life. As you forgive yourself and others, the door upon which you knock will open wider and wider, and your pathway will be seen more clearly. You understand well that to pray and to meditate are top priority and the stronger you become in following this call, the greater will be your effect on others. Always remember that you are the instrument of God's will. Peace be with you, my child.

Wednesday, September 26, 1990

Diane:

What is most important for me to do in my meetings with Roseanne (a healer)?

Spirit:

Find the confidence to do what your heart knows you can do. Dear child, the talent and ability to heal is already there. You must continue to seek until you connect with the missing link. You must have faith that God and those who help will provide all the necessary abilities at the perfect moment. It is in your desire to accomplish that energy be increased. Each step you take can then be transformed into the energy you will need to succeed.

Yes, you know all this, but constant reminders are needed to keep you on the most important of paths—the spiritual pathway to do God's will. Sacrifice is non-existent in the eyes of one who sees the purpose of God's creation. Each is of great importance in the chain of eternity. Always remember this, for God works with splendor and grace to accomplish divine will. Each is chosen, but few realize the magnitude of his own ability to contribute to the whole of creation. Look beyond earth's shadows and see the magnificent rainbow and music of God's world; it is there for all to share as is the beauty of nature. Appreciation and love *are* in the eyes of the beholder, dear child. Open your eyes wide with belief and you will see the inner world of spirit. We come close to encourage you to keep on keeping on. Peace be with you.

Tuesday, October 2, 1990
Spirit:

"Do unto others as you would have them do unto you," but dear one, do unto yourself, as you would have them do unto you. You must learn to care for yourself, and take time to do what you want to do. If it is to read for an entire day or to do nothing, then do it. Do you not see how most of your life is planned around doing for others? How rare it is that you do for yourself. Fault this not, yet you as an individual must allow yourself to ride with the wind in freedom as well. Continue to seek that balance of give and take, for herein lies the secret of ultimate happiness and the readiness to do God's will.

To be all-giving, my child, one must learn the importance of taking, for one can burn out without this balance. Leave room for growth and expansion in your life. Take time to enjoy the beauty for it is in the appreciation of God's gifts that one grows the most. Let all concerns and pressures float within the enjoyment of life as it is. Then and only then does one release the energy to expand and return tenfold.

The human being in physical form desires a timetable, but for the joys of life, there truly is no timetable, my child. Live in the joy of the moment for eternity is the sum total of all of those precious moments. We tell you this so that you can better understand the remainder of your own life in the physical plane. We urge you to relax more, and spend time seeking the world of spirit but without pressure of any kind. We, too, desire closer contact, but have faith and know it will happen, for indeed it will. It will appear in between the joys of life as you live it, my child. Pure heart brings great joy to all, and yours, dear one, sparkles in the sometimes dreariness of earth. Lessen not your desire to serve God, but strive to remove the pressure that you bring to bear on your own being. Your loved ones, your guides, teachers, doctors, sprites and angels, plus those you read to, bring love and support always. May peace follow you everywhere.

Wednesday, October 10, 1990

Diane:

I met with Roseanne, a healer, this noon. Her advice is to find more balance and to give more love to myself. Perhaps she's right. I seek too hard, just as my children, Sue and John, tell me. If I never help another, it would be okay, I guess, but my heart still tells me differently. I will continue to soul search, and perhaps the love which dwells within will find an outlet in time. I'll practice relaxing and doing as I want, yet it seems to me there is much that can be done to help others. Perhaps it is just too soon yet. I shall have faith, be patient and wait for God's own time. There truly is very little guilt, but rather an inner drive to give and to love. Does not the Bible say it is better to give than receive? Where am I missing the lesson to learn? Perhaps, I'm too intense. I will listen and hear some ideas.

Spirit:

Think about the give and take of love. All each of us is trying to tell you is let others do for you; this is true of those in spirit as well. Do you perhaps shoulder too much responsibility yourself? We know what you are thinking: there is no end to the ability to love, so one can always give more. This, dear child, is true, however, you must allow others to give to you. Is it not true that you build an invisible wall about yourself for protection, or is God's love enough to save you from stumbling? Seek the answer deep inside.

Diane:

"My dreams of perfection are the bridges that carry me into the realm of pure ideas. I will purify my mind with the thought that God is guiding every activity."[4]

Spirit:

So shine, my child, that others may see God's light in you. One need say little to influence the life of another, but rather live the life of one who sees God in everything. Every thought then becomes prayer-like, and this bright energy may be used for goodness. It is like a tonic which can be used to heal the planet. Too many on earth fail to realize the powerful energy that positive thinking releases. Those choices which bring one happiness are those which bring goodness into another's life. Is this not true? Goodness comes from God; it is the core of every human being for each is made in the image of God. Perfection is the desire of all of God's children, but few understand its true meaning.

Strive, my child, in your daily life to live a life of purpose, drawing as close to God as possible through prayer, meditation and love. Be always mindful of the power of negativity—that desire to pull one away from God, love and perfection. This is a real force, so master your own being to hear only the call to do God's will. Life can many times seem like a struggle if one allows, in his own mind, the negativity to enter. Everything that happens in life must be seen through the eyes of the beholder. Keep thine eyes upon the good, the loving, the brightest light which can be found, and one's discouragement and sorrow will be surmountable.

Remember, child, physical life *is* the testing ground, the blueprint and framework upon which we, in spirit, can use to better all of mankind. A pure heart is most precious and we encourage all to look within to see the conditions of one's own heart. We know each can change with proper guidance, especially if role models are clearly in sight. Not by preaching, but rather by the manner in which one lives—always with love, never by condemning. Lip service in the form of criticism does little to solve a problem; for instead, it stirs the very emotions which need to be quieted. This lesson is sent to remind the inhabitants of earth to "do unto others as you would have them do unto you." *(Luke 6:31)* This is the way of peace. We come close, my daughter, with great love.

Ang:

Didn't we experience great joy in our life together? How blessed we truly are. Thank you for making the trip north; I rode much of the way with you. Saint Germain's words should be heard by all. He is an inspiration to know. I shall be your unseen escort this afternoon. You can't know the joy *I feel* because you feel and know my presence, but you *do* know the joy. Rest more—you were too tired Friday night. We need you to light the way, so take care. I love you forever, and the bed and breakfast will come to be. How proud I am!

Monday, October 29, 1990
Spirit:

Thought is the common thread which weaves all of one's existence into being. You are and will be what you think. All senses of one's body can be seen, heard and felt through thought, if each would become dedicated to God and strive to find this lost connection between the physical and spiritual aspect of man. Spiritual eyes see more clearly and farther than physical eyes, but one must open himself to universal love which connects all aspects of life together. Fear not that it will elude you, dear child, but rather continue to pray, meditate, fulfill your conditions and wait with untold patience.

The soul is eternal, and all of its capabilities can be mastered, but not on the timetable upon which mankind establishes. Always remember "in God's own time," for he is the master craftsman of each soul. He knows the longings, desires and needs of each of his children. Some would say that this is either impossible or too simple, but you, my child, know differently. Those who love deeply and unconditionally are admired. Why? Not because they boast and strut their own importance, but rather because the light of love makes them sparkle from within for all to see.

Concentrate and listen to those thoughts from within and follow that all-knowing call to be your best. Compromise not, for in doing so one declares doubt in himself, and God needs those with true dedication. We, who come close, know the difficulties which accompany true spiritual growth. Continual self-evaluation is monotonous at times, especially when little progress can be seen from the physical side. However, see through the eyes of thought into that realm of what can be.

Love, my child, is the pathway to all things; let no one influence you otherwise. Love has no end and no beginning—it just *is*, as is God. The more one becomes lost in its infinity, the greater will be its effect on others. All knowing is the gift of a job well done. Spiritual growth is earned. Many times the price is very high, but the reward is so great that one continues to strive ever upward. Listen to this guidance within and follow its message. Peace be with you, my dear child.

Ang:

Dearie, look from the positive side. Have you not come a long, long way from November 28, 1986? It is the effort by which you mount an obstacle which is of value. If you continue to do what is difficult for you to do, each time will become easier. Even though you can no longer see me physically, you know I *am* there by your side. Remember there is nothing that can bring only joy and love, for everything must fall into the laws of balance. You cannot grow spiritually, dear, if the pangs of sorrow are not felt as well. Pray for confidence in yourself and it will be there. The feeling of loneliness is nothing more than lack of confidence in your own ability to cope and to have faith in those who come close to help.

One must also remember the element of fatigue, both of body and spirit. Perhaps it would be good to program in a day of complete rest here and there. Your responsibilities have increased and the distance between has grown in many miles. Know that you can do it, and you can. Decisions have always been difficult for you, but how many wrong ones have you made in your almost sixty years?

Buy the Tappan stove for your birthday from me; I always meant to get you a new one. Dig deeper for that joy we've always had, for it's there. Repeat the words in the card you gave me when I was in the hospital. You bought it without knowing it would become our motto: "I see your smile when I'm alone. I hear you call my name. Remember, love, though we're apart, I'm with you just the same." And this is forever. I'll come shopping with you to Sears, so feel my presence.

Sunday, November 4, 1990

Spirit:

Healing is the art of helping another heal himself, yet it appears under the guise of many methods. It is as diversified as there are talented and worthy people called by its bidding. Look to find your own method to heal, my child, for there is no one book or no one teacher that will be just right for you. Accumulate ideas, send them into your thoughts, and with continued patience, prayer and practice, they shall emerge as an all-knowing and intuitive plan to follow. Believe in yourself and in your desires, for herein lies the pathway to success.

As one visualizes, so it becomes. This is a difficult concept to perceive, for it takes great faith and courage to persist long enough and hard enough to see steady progress. Many give up too soon, oftentimes just before an important breakthrough. Let love be the brightest guiding light for its energy draws to it the most potential help that is available. Pray harder when discouragement hovers near.

Life lived with love is imperative for those who choose to serve God. Love draws to it the light which can be used to heal. Feel internally the connection between love and light energy. It is the eternal quality of love which one must seek and it dwells deep inside the physical body waiting for release through spiritual growth. There is a price to pay for all that is good—an investment of time and energy for which there is no reward, yet energy is returned tenfold. This energy, once felt, becomes the basis for seeking further. To return love given freely is desirable, but to give love where there is little, is divine. "God so loved the world that he gave his only begotten son so all who believe in him shall have everlasting life." *(John 3:16)*

Believe, my child, and follow your desire to do God's will through the gift of healing. We hear, we help, and it shall be if you continue to seek the answers. Peace be with you.

Monday, November 5, 1990
Spirit:

It is true, child, you will do God's work, and yes, you must work to dispel lack of confidence in your own being. This does indeed hamper the progress to the next level of accomplishment. We come close for we see great potential in your ability to love, for you do love all things, and this is a true gift from God. Each on earth has this great potential, but too few have allowed time in their life to seek enlightenment. Those who seek the light can, and indeed will, help others to elevate themselves as well.

Do you not admire certain people for what they were able to accomplish in their lives? Why do you so admire them? Is it not for their love and dedication to helping others? Is this not God's will for each of his children?

Hear the call, my child, shun not the hard work that must be accomplished, but rather take small, consistent steps toward your goal, relying on prayer, meditation and help from those who stand close to walk with you in love. Motivation is present; continue to seek confidence in the God force of your own being. Walk in peace and love.

Tuesday, November 6, 1990
Diane:

Life is busy, life is full, and that which lies ahead will bring joy as well, so I am indeed blessed. It is the pressure of things which must be done, should be done, and want to be done versus that freedom of doing what I want to do. Sometimes, in every life, one must step back and evaluate exactly *what* is important and categorize the priorities. I know this, but like most I fail to do it, but rather feel a bit frantic and wonder how I can do it all. Yet, in hindsight, it always seems to turn out all right. Poor God must shake his blessed head in amazement at times because of what we do to ourselves. At least I see the humor, so I know I am getting better able to come to grips with this situation. I'll see how the day goes.

Saturday, November 10, 1990
Ang:

It is in the altered state of mind that one sees auras. Practice this ability more consistently. What do I say to you on your birthday? Love grows in the heart by sharing with all of mankind—with each whom you meet. The state of grace is that special ability to know in your heart what is true in spite of the traditional values learned during childhood and adolescence. Live life as you know it should be lived, and all good things will happen. Happy birthday, dearie, and enjoy your day. My love follows you everywhere.

Thursday, November 15, 1990
Diane:

Trying to calm those thoughts of worry about my big undertaking of making 48 Elm Street into a bed and breakfast called Hosmer House.

Spirit:

Dispel all doubt, my child. Do you not see that good ideas with good intent draw many to work with you? Knowing this, believing in your own intentions brings that much more force to this conviction. We continue to reinforce this belief in yourself, for success follows positive and affirmative action. Strive continually to banish doubt from your being. See the house in beauty and love, and so shall it be. Small steps of progress will snowball into great results. Pray and strength will be there. Love, and God will bless your intentions with success tenfold. Let not others dampen this belief in yourself with their doubts of the obstacles to surmount.

Would we who love you stand by and let others take advantage? Of course the answer is no. Pray for love and humility to do God's will and it shall be so. Walk and rest with peace in your heart, and send blessings to those who might oppose this project. The energy from such prayers is helpful to those who help you. Be ever mindful of the blessings which flow from your children, especially John, for he labors hard, and much thought and energy comes from his dedicated effort. Without Sue and John's interest, would you have come this far? Work together and include all the ideas which come from such a source of love surrounding you, my child. Not all on earth are so blessed in physical life, and you know this. Peace be with you.

Friday, November 23, 1990
Diane:

How does one comfort another in distress?

Spirit:

Pray for guidance from those in spirit who can help. You see, my child, you can only open the door to another's belief, for they, themselves, must do the necessary work to earn wisdom. Knowledge and wisdom are not of the same mold. The clay which is used differs in many ways. Knowledge comes from books through study and learning; wisdom comes through the heart and is earned by love. It is a true caring for all that is right. Divine love comes directly from God and all seek his love. Encouragement through the power of positive thinking is the doorway through which one must pass to find help from spirit. Continue to impart knowledge and cause it to surface as faith. You, my child, must see with the eyes of the one whom you desire to enlighten. Feel the anguish, and words will be there to comfort. It is difficult to clear one's mind of concerns, but it is necessary in order to see and hear more clearly. Pray for help and it will come one step at a time. Peace be with you.

Saturday, December 1, 1990
Spirit:

Relax and judge yourself less harshly, my child. Live your physical life to the fullest, taking every opportunity to spread the light of love—God's love, which is perfect. Perfect love is letting God use you as an instrument of his great love. Being made in his own image gives each of mankind the ability to seek this perfect love in his daily life, yet many do not see the true value of such love. We remind you, my child, that you must give to your *own* being such love. One cannot love his neighbor until he has first learned to love himself.

How, you ask, does one love oneself? Strive for purity of heart and thought in your life, which will then lead to purity of deed. Love heals all things, and to help others heal themselves, one must become a pure channel of God's will. Do you not feel more strength in your own convictions and beliefs? We come close to help. Peace be with you.

Tuesday, December 4, 1990
Spirit:

My dear one, refuse to let the mind dwell on thoughts of fatigue. The body does rest at night and it revitalizes itself in spite of itself. You, yourself, program through thoughts exactly how you will feel at any given moment. Think and program only positive thoughts, for they, in turn, will become positive action. You accomplish by doing, by carrying out the positive energy which accompanies positive thoughts. Much fatigue is self-imposed because one has not mastered self-control over his own being. Negativity truly saps the physical body of its vitality to accomplish great things.

Work to implement this knowledge in your own daily life, my child. Think energy of mind and it shall be so. Much will be accomplished by this attitude. We remind you to keep control of that lower self which always desires the easy way out of all situations. Instead, let the higher self dictate what must be done, and joy will accompany you in whatever task you do whether it be monotonous, repetitious or inspirational. It is upon this foundation that miracles can happen. Keep on keeping on as you seek communion with our Heavenly Father. Peace be with you.

Monday, December 17, 1990
Diane:

Perhaps those helping me in spirit will counsel me. I seem to spend much of my life pondering decisions. But then, who doesn't?

Spirit:

That past sentence is a key one and of much importance, my child. Singling oneself out as unique in any way leaves the door open to invasion through negativity, fatigue, or any of the pitfalls which can attack the spirit. Refuse to succumb to this through prayer, counting one's blessings, as well as accurately assessing the obstacles and putting them in true perspective of their importance.

You, on earth, tend to make each molehill, so to speak, a mountain. If God is able to move mountains, why must you worry about the molehills to begin with? Dear child, live life with faith, hope and love, and know the perfect outcome will spring forth. Worry or despair only causes interference to this outcome, so banish them forever from your life. One can always control thoughts through diligent practice of a life of prayer. God protects his sheep through their prayers, but so few tune in on a regular, daily basis.

Prayer should be first on the list for each person in his physical body. This dedication releases the energy flow which brings the two worlds closer together. The mind must be trained and conditioned to subjugate evil. Good and love are strongly implanted in each at birth. Circumstances and lack of discipline cause them to become dim and difficult to reach. We come through thought to encourage you to persist in your desire to enlighten others. Your path is that of truth, so forge ahead in all that you do. Enthusiasm spurs one on, so keep it strong and bright in your daily life. A sparkling attitude is contagious, and even though you cannot see its effect on others, believe that it is there.

Dear one, remember that one reaps what one sows; can you not see this more clearly? Trust in those who help you, and find joy in all events of your life. Peace be with you.

Sunday, December 30, 1990
Spirit:

We come, dear child, to comfort you and help you on your spiritual pathway. Everyone has his own helpers, but in the busy throng of physical activity, few can hear or feel the help. You must continue to be diligent and remain always faithful to those conditions upon which we build our bridge of communication. As you become stronger, others will see and follow. Do as I do, not as I say, is much more powerful. If one lives his own convictions and proves it to himself without a doubt, then others will begin to see this truth and perhaps follow. Can you not see, child, that merit is gained through continually pouring out beliefs in what can be. It is this vision, this knowing through faith of what will be, that is so important.

Anyone may hope, but too few truly believe. Faith is this believing and knowing without proof. So many would believe with proof, but little merit can be gained for mankind this way. We come close to further encourage you to walk the difficult path of spiritual growth. We call it difficult because one must discipline himself to take the necessary segment of time each day, without fail, to come into attunement with the finer vibration of the world of spirit. Without total commitment, this task of meeting is lost. Bless you, my child, for your dedication. Peace be with you.

1991

Tuesday, January 1, 1991
Spirit:

Self-control and self-discipline are a road one travels throughout eternity. For certain things, dear child, there is no answer for the road is open-ended. It is in the seeking that greater clarity is achieved through new years, new births, new friends, new experiences, and so it goes on and on. Even death, which so many unfortunately look upon as final, is in itself a new beginning. The narrow-mindedness of mankind is created by the visions of an end rather than of a new beginning. Try in your mind's eye to perceive everything as something new, for each experience in itself *is* new, even if it has been repeated many times. The so-called ending can become the greatest experience, for around each bend the best is yet to come.

Thursday, January 3, 1991
Spirit:

Time is man-made. God worries not about physical clocks. Eternity is timeless and forever. Look beyond earth time and the vista is unending. All things can happen if concern for time is eliminated. What restrictions mankind puts upon itself when the ticking of the clock becomes primary. The seasons know when to change and animals instinctively do what is right, yet man in striving for perfection so often misses that which surrounds him. Why? He cannot find the time. You, my child, must not fall into this trap. Fly free as a bird, knowing what you need will be there at the perfect time. This is the beauty of God's creation.

Wednesday, January 9, 1991
Spirit:

Continue to see beyond the moment, but not so far that you cannot find joy in what is happening in the present. Be not one who tarries in memories or wallows in what might be. Instead, find peace, love and joy in what is. To hope and act for change positively, brings about positive change. This is an exacting law. What you think upon regularly is the driving force that takes you in the direction of such thoughts. In that sense, your thoughts become the blue print of your life that you, in turn, fulfill. Listen carefully to your inner self, for it will always guide you in the right direction and to the right ends.

There is first the appearance of thought in the mind and then if we accept it, consciously or unconsciously, we act upon it. Thoughts *in the mind* are the presentation of possibilities. When acted upon they materialize in our reality externally. Observe carefully what you are thinking before acting so that you act upon the right thoughts and not the wrong thoughts. Self-mastery is derived from discerning and acting correctly on what we think and what we chose to act upon among the thoughts that we think. The choosing of right thoughts leads to right action and the right outcome. Conversely, the opposite is also true. If you are wise you will chose the right thought to lead to the right action, thus complimenting one with the other and enabling you to do God's will at all times. Self-confidence is derived from acting upon right thinking that results in the right outcome. We come to guide you in your endeavor to do God's will. It will come, my child, with love, patience and inner strength. Peace be with you.

Wednesday, January 16, 1991
Diane:

It is a rainy day. It sets the mood of the world, I fear. The midnight deadline passed by last night. All looks calm, but it is not. As a cat crouches silently before it attacks, so is the world today. Pray that love and light might awaken into the hearts of mankind, especially those who are filled with anger. Life is too precious to sacrifice for the ego of man. Yet at this moment the plight of the world is resting on this premise. What can I do to be of help, dear Lord?

Spirit:

Live in love, my child, and send out strong vibrations of pure light. It is a difficult task to see the benefits of positive thinking as we see it from the realm of spirit, but we urge you to use your imagination. Set your sights on the beauty of music, nature and the joy of love. The energy of the light of love is overpowering to all it encounters. Miracles can and do happen, but in truth it is the diligent, painstaking path which the soul must travel in order to do God's will. What about life is truly easy?

Yet with proper thought and mind conditioning, how much of it can be joyful? Each is in control of his own answer for one is what he thinks. It is true that negative thoughts and emotions are difficult to overcome, but with love the task is made easier. Follow love as it reads in the Bible:

"Love is patient, love is kind. It does not want;
It does not boast, it is not proud. It is not rude;
It is not self-seeking; it is not easily angered;
It keeps no record of wrongs. Love does not delight in
Evil but rejoices with the truth. It always protects,
Always trusts, always hopes, always perseveres…
In the end there are three things that last: faith, hope
And love. But the greatest of these is love." *(1 Corinthians 13:4–13)*

Keep the vigil of patience alive within your being, dear child. It takes time to grow in love and spirit. Time spent in development is never wasted. The pressures of physical life can easily pull one away from this spiritual path; be diligent in your daily life. Peace be with you.

Friday, January 18, 1991

Spirit:

Life is a lonely road in spite of family, friends, and support of many kinds. The loneliness turns into contentment, and yes, even joy when one truly discovers the love of God. Hardship and trials can be the best of lessons for one who remains open and free to the realm of the world of spirit. Life is difficult, but the beauty of an experience lasts forever. The imagination, the ability to see mental images of what was, of what is, and of what can be is the essence of life. To recall and truly feel an experience is linked to one's spirit which is of God. God is a part of the whole. Each moment or experience in life does affect one to some degree. Awareness is the reward. If awareness is absent, little joy can be found. We come to tell you that awareness is a form of love. Is this not true? One cannot love what he is not aware of. If the world looked more closely at his neighbor, would there be such trouble? We know not. Strive to see with your heart, my child, and unconditional love will grow in your being. Peace be with you.

Sunday, January 20, 1991
Diane:

I pray for more love, patience and strength within my own being. How does one become more loving and kind to others? It is so difficult to totally drown one's ego in acts of love. I admire those who can give up all to help others. How beautiful must be their aura. Perhaps my admiration for saintly people will help me to remodel my objectives in life. "Seek and you shall find" has to be my theme song. I am not lonely being by myself, but lonely for the answer as to what direction my life is to take. I pray for guidance to be fully aware and not miss the opportunities which will come to me.

Spirit:

Remember the word "patience." To live in love is a contribution in itself, and there are times when one must be satisfied with knowing this. One must continue seeking the God force within, but not let emotion hamper one's effort. Is it not true that frustration can interfere with awareness? Keep mastership over your own being, my child, and leave the pathway open to God's divine will. In how many ways have you been presented with this truth: in God's own time? Try, my child, to learn this lesson, for it is of utmost importance in one's spiritual climb. Time is not so important. Find the balance within. There are many who work with you. Feel their energy and presence. This too is important in your development. Work on your ability to go into deep meditation where you will meet these loving helpers. Live in peace for we come close to help you.

Wednesday January 23, 1991
Spirit:

Spirit is the truth behind reality. The world of illusion and imagination is a real world. Many, and we dare say most of mankind, fail to grasp the fine line between illusion and reality. Reality *is*; it exists because of the world of spirit. Spirit is a world of thought pattern; a world of dreams and imagination. Do you not see that before any happening or event, the seed, the idea, has to be in existence first. This is why everything is interconnected and part of a whole. It is true that each new experience appears as separate and spontaneous, but in real truth, it is not. Each needs the experience of the realm of spirit in which to move forward in his physical life. One is not programmed as a robot because there is free will; but ideas come from this so-called world of illusion and imagination. In fact, illusion is from the great realm of truth.

You see, dear child, ideas are the outcropping, the proof of the existence of the world of spirit. Remember, man is spirit first, physical second. Man always seeks to find and desires to return to God, the creator of all. Try to grasp this profound truth.

We bring you this message so that you will better understand your fellow man and his beliefs. It is true that through the original thought of God, we are all connected. As in physical structure, many of the elements are the same, but in different proportions. This is also true in the world of spirit; thought patterns are also from the same source but in different proportions. Think of each human being as a complex transmitter. Although it is possible for him to tune into the ultimate truth of God, he is limited by the tools of his own thought patterns. He programs his own ability to grow spiritually. The more open one is to new ideas, and the more one seeks the answers from within, the closer his transmitter tunes into the channel of God.

Trust! To live in peace and joy one must trust God, himself and those he loves. You ask, how does one learn to trust another? We answer, with prayer, meditation and honest evaluation of one's own being. To trust another, one must first trust in himself. Let us look at a baby just being born. How must one so vulnerable look upon trust? Totally! Wisdom tells us much about this one-word answer.

When one is born, he is closest to God. He is pure, he loves and he trusts. This is how each is meant to be. Circumstances, experience and conditions build upon this foundation of trust we receive at birth. As life progresses, many are innocently hurt by circumstances, and eventually shut down the flow of energy to this part of their being, and they no longer trust in any situation. This is indeed a problem which affects a loving relationship with others, because one places so many conditions upon another trying to seek happiness in his own life. To trust is basic. What does it say even about money which causes so many problems in the physical world? IN GOD WE TRUST.

We hear your thoughts, dear one. How, once lost, does one find trust? We suggest the exercise of counting one's blessings by writing them down on paper, beginning with all the attributes of being healthy, seeing nature and loving others unconditionally. God gave each of us the opportunity to discover gratitude within, but oftentimes, an earthling spends more time pondering physical conditions which he feels he can control. Unfortunately this leads to confusion and unhappiness.

Wednesday, February 6, 1991
Spirit:

Everything about life can be beautiful if one will truly take the time to look and find it; no matter how small. The eyes which can see beauty are indeed blessed by God. Joy is in the eyes of such a beholder. You ask, dear child, what you can do to further his will. Is this not true? Love everything and everyone with a true heart, a heart that desires to help, and great healing can take place! Do not see with physical eyes, but instead see with faith that all things are possible. Earthlings always want to see instant results, but with God, there is no hurry. Live by eternal time whenever possible and know that your mission unfolds with perfect timing. Your beloved flowers do the same. Is this not also true?

Be patient, and take time to observe the beauty in your life, and joy will bubble forth like an endless brook. Life on earth is what each chooses to make it. Others are not responsible for unhappiness and discontent. Thoughts direct one's life. Take care to fill them with love and forgiveness, for only then will those in the higher realms of spirit be able to use you as a pure channel to help mankind. Peace be with you, dear child.

Sunday, February 17, 1991
Spirit:

Eternity is now. Find the joy in each ion of matter. At all times, try to experience the vibration of creation itself. See beauty and love in every experience. Become a part of it by feeling in your being what you are seeing. Respect all of life whether it be animal, vegetable or mineral, for each is part of the whole. If that which passes through your being is loved by you, it moves forward to help all of mankind. The importance of love is its ability to enhance what already is and to send it onward toward something better. It is simple in scope yet so few understand its message. Think only loving thoughts and send them forth unconditionally. This deed is of utmost importance. Action speaks louder than words, my child, so continue to send forth the light of love from your innermost being. It truly does make a difference and others will see. Peace be with you.

Friday, March 1, 1991
Spirit:

Dear one, we watch out for you no matter where your travels take you, and you know this. Spirit is not affected by time and space. Try to implement and understand this in your daily life. Rise above the judgment and criticism of the physical plane and see life as it truly should be. Each is there for a specific purpose, and heaven on earth will be established when man can see the value of all of God's creation in a positive way and act accordingly. See the good, project what can be and this releases the energy for it to be so. Grateful, giving prayer, my child, releases the most energy. Any act or deed which is given with pure love raises the consciousness of others, even if the awareness does not seem evident. There is so much for each to learn. Be at peace, and that which you know, you *know* is true.

Tuesday, March 5, 1991
Diane:

Days go by too quickly, and it amazes me how many pass before I write in this book. I sense a plateau again. I wish I was better at handling the feelings which accompany such times. Will continue to force my thoughts into only positive projection, and when I feel otherwise shall pray or keep myself busy with worthwhile activity. I must learn to have complete confidence in my own aloneness. All answers and knowledge are within. One must *seek* the ability and means to release this truth, and therein find God. Again it returns:

    Ask—Receive
    Seek—Find
    Knock—Enter

Spirit:

Each plateau reinforces the ability to keep on keeping on. This is the test of one's dedication in pursuing the truth. What, dear one, comes easy in life? Is it not true that one appreciates in equal proportion to what he has invested of himself? That which is given freely and tinged with love teaches one the most important of lessons—happiness. Be not discouraged, dear one, but invest more of yourself in this divine search of self. Divine law is exacting. Peace be with you always. We come close to inspire and guide you.

Friday, March 8, 1991
Spirit:

Your intuition speaks to you well. Gaining in self-confidence is a must, and how else will it happen except through practice and experience? The human being wants too much many times, without the trials and work which must be done to reach one's own potential. Dear one, there is no shortcut. That which is difficult and stands as a stumbling block *must* and *will* be overcome with faith, prayer and finding that strength from within. Failure, or not living up to one's potential, is a strong motivator of examining and scrutinizing one's inner self. Once one discovers the weaknesses and truly admits to the fallen ego, the solution will soon surface. This is the beauty of intuition; your inner self spells out the difficulty. A superficial ego hates to admit its faults, but would rather blame others. The true ego connected to God, continually strives for perfection and cheers itself on learning more truth. Continue to reach for what you desire. We who come close hear your cry for guidance and help. Peace be with you, child.

Sunday, March 10, 1991
Spirit:

There is no ego when one learns to do the Father's will, for the soul seeks to become one with God. This is not accomplished by looking outside one's being, but rather by seeking from within. The ego is fed by forces from without, while the soul seeks only the love of God. To love unconditionally is the pathway to truth. The initiate seeking to do God's will must undergo sacrifice and hardship as it is given from the highest realms. One cannot and will not understand the truth of spiritual matters until mastery over self is won through the pathway of selfless love. Faith, hope and love must be strengthened through prayer each day.

Wednesday, March 13, 1991
Spirit:

Dear child, do more than *want* to believe—believe! Positive thoughts and prayers expressed with true devotion are clearly heard and acted upon by those who come close to help you. If you could but see those of us who spend time with you in your lovely room, the experience would be awesome to you. At this time there are few who truly try on a daily basis to do God's will, not because they do not want to, but because they do not choose to spend the necessary time to climb the spiritual path. Listen to that quiet voice within your own being, child. Is it not growing louder and clearer? Remember that spirit is eternal and not of the physical plane, so its progress must not be measured by time as you live it in the physical world.

This is why one must learn the meaning of the word *patience*. Patience is waiting for divine intervention in the outworking of one's spiritual desires to do God's will. This is why one is never truly alone, even in the direst of situations. Believe, believe, believe, dear child, in God, in yourself, and in the guidance which comes from the world of spirit. Happiness and joy will be present always to one who has learned to balance the fruits of the spirit within, and hence, mastered his own being.

Search for the altered state of mind, for this is the bridge between the two worlds—the dreamlike state where nothing physical matters, for in this state the door is opening to the spiritual. It takes desire, real desire, and practice to begin to even understand the magnitude of discovering eternal truth. Keep on keeping on, and marvel at God's wonders. Peace be with you, my child.

Saturday, March 16, 1991
Spirit:

How much can you love and how much can you give, dear child, before you think of yourself? This is truly the bottom line or the truth of your own existence. When you love another as deeply as you love yourself; when you help another as much as you help yourself and do it unconditionally and without a desire for a return; then, my child, you will begin to see the love of God within your own being.

Where do most people look for God? Is it not outwardly? Please God, do this special prayer for me and I'll be more open to you, if only you will help me. Is this not the most common path? How many look inwardly praying: let me be an instrument of thy will? Be thou one who with undying faith will wait until his will is made known.

Give until you are hurting and standing sometimes alone; then you will begin to know God and his great love. At this crossroad you will see your pathway clearly and hear those who come close to guide you. Selflessness comes from true struggle, sacrifice and doubting of oneself. Finding spiritual confidence oftentimes feels as though you are lacking in ability and direction. Look upon these feelings as progress rather than as signs of little growth. You cannot and do not see yourself as we can from the spiritual side. Kindness, no matter how small you think it to be, does inspire the growth of your spirit. Know this and continue on your present course to do God's will. It shall be so, my dear child. May peace walk with you always.

Monday, March 18, 1991
Ang:
Dear, dig deeply for the joy which comes from just living. Do not be critical, but always find the positive lessons of any situation. Be grateful for your ability to intuitively know the spiritual importance of your own being and its relationship and importance to the whole of creation. Seek and ye shall find what you desire. The truth of love is eternal and its beauty becomes more valuable with the passing of time. True love never lessens, but instead continues to grow and reach out to connect all things. This is the inner desire of each human being, even if many do not understand or realize their true purpose as yet. Continue trying to awaken those around you, leading each a little further on his path to spiritual awareness. Love and the fruits of the spirit can be seen through example, and this is the best method in awakening others.

Diane:
This message from Ang somehow inspires the song "Beautiful Dreamer" by Stephen Foster as a theme song for now. The words follow:
"Beautiful dreamer, wake unto me.
Starlight and dewdrops are waiting for thee.
Sounds of the rude world heard in the day
Lulled by the moonlight have all passed away.

Beautiful dreamer, queen of my song
List while I woo thee with sweet melody.
Gone are the cares of life's busy throng
Beautiful dreamer, awake unto me
Beautiful dreamer, awake unto me.

Beautiful dreamer, out on the sea
Mermaids are chanting the wild Lorelei.
Over the streamlets vapors are borne
Waiting to fade at the bright, coming morn
E'en as the morn on the streamlet and sea;
Then will all clouds of sorrow depart.
Beautiful dreamer, awake unto me
Beautiful dreamer, awake unto me!"

You really are good, and you are always understood by me. May peace and love be your constant strength.

Monday, March 25, 1991
Spirit:

As a man thinks, so he is; therefore what is it *you* think, my child?

Diane:

I think that what we are trying to do (establish a bed and breakfast) is of value and that 48 Elm Street will be a place where people will find peace, friendship and love. I think I am gaining in self-confidence and with continued help from above (which really means from within), all dreams and desires will come to pass. To do God's will, one must firmly accept the challenges placed before him, and with faith and trust do his best. Only then, with this proof of one's intent, can those in spirit come very close to influence and help. Merit is earned by hard, hard work, and happiness is found through the gift of love.

Wednesday, March 27, 1991

Diane:

I wonder what the secret formula is to awaken non-believers. But hasn't this been a problem since the beginning of mankind?

Spirit:

Be true to your own being and to those discoveries which you know to be true. Test the validity within to see if it rings true. When it feels right, it is right. Trust your own instincts and intuition; listen to that small voice within that knows all, and your pathway will be made clear. No one else can hear that voice. This is why each stands apart from another, but never alone, for all things are connected to God. Many have much to learn and are unable to understand as yet.

Do not become discouraged by this, but rather strengthen the truth within your own being. Strength, light, patience and most of all love have a way of shining through to the heart of anyone. Work to brighten the intensity of your own love and in so doing you will brighten the light of your fellow man. Continue to search for the spark in each human being, animal and plant. See the beauty in every surrounding and you shall see and feel your band of helpers more clearly. You see, dear child, one must believe and have total faith in order to be an instrument of God's will. Peace be with you, dear one.

Tuesday, April 2, 1991

Spirit:

Prepare yourself in all things through the power of love. Healing is learned through the ability to love: love of God, love of self and love of all mankind. It is a monumental task; hence it takes great concentration and effort through study and meditation. Listen to your own inner voice, and trust in your own ability to know truth. While in the physical body, man is too content to let someone else advise and plan his life for him, but as you read tonight, each is accountable for his own thoughts and deeds. This is an exact law, and one which you must prepare others to understand and accept. Positive thinking is a gift from God, so be ever thankful for this blessing. The more one can calm his own being and fill it with love, the greater good he can do. Be patient with yourself, dear one. Steady progress is of lasting value, so move forward through prayer and meditation. It matters not who comes to help, for at the right moment more enlightenment will come. Peace be with you.

Saturday, April 6, 1991
Diane:

My body is anxious to get busy working with plants outside, but my heart tells me to take time to speak to God and be thankful for my blessings. To spend time doing for others is always of *utmost* importance; such a difficult lesson to learn, and harder yet to fulfill. I feel as if I am headed in the right direction, but there is a long journey ahead before I reach that place of grace. More and more I rely on the strength from within, the guidance and love from spirit, and as the two come closer to uniting, my spirit grows.

A life of happiness is gained by one's ability to love his fellow man through a desire to help each one he meets. This, of course, includes one's own family. Is it not true that every human being is part of the family with the last name of "world" or "earth"? The world once seemed so large because of the inaccessibility in reaching one another, however modern technology and advancements have now made the world much smaller. The mind becomes better able to accept what was once a distant land. It is the heart of man which needs research to keep abreast of technology. This is the purpose for AIM (Adventures in Mastery, founded by Philip Burley) and other groups as well, who try to enlighten mankind. The plan is unfolding. Continue to see and search for the kingdom of God, my child. Peace be with you.

Thursday, April 18, 1991

Diane:

Sometimes I forget to keep it all in proper perspective. Many times I tend to place too much importance on material problems. It is the atmosphere, love and purpose behind the bed and breakfast which are of importance, not what curtains or blinds dress the windows. I'm always grateful to be brought back on track. I sometimes try to do what others feel is right, but in the end I must do what I feel is right. Herein lies peace of mind.

Spirit:

You see, dear child, if one will go within to meet God, the answers to all problems will filter into the conscious mind. This is the beauty of the mind which God gave to each. It is man's ignorance and dogma which clouds the results. Once one learns to clear away the many layers of mist and clouds, keen awareness and all-knowing wisdom begin to filter through. This then becomes the result, almost as a reward for the hours one spends in prayer, thought and meditation. Be not discouraged, but walk forward with diligent patience to find God. Peace be with you, my child.

Thursday, April 25, 1991

Spirit:

Practice is what makes it perfect; is this not so? Be not discouraged, but rather concentrate upon how far you have come, dear one. The energy grows stronger each time you give concentrated effort and the aura grows brighter, does it not? Eliminate all thoughts of time, for this matters not. As soon as one begins to concern himself with a timetable, it becomes almost a step backwards.

Continue your life of solitude, keeping away from a busy, social schedule, yet find time for those activities that are important to you. Live in the present—drawing from your past experiences and knowing that the future will hold nothing but good. Look positively at everything you see and know it *will* one day be so. Live each moment to the fullest for there is much yet to learn as you travel life's highway. Retreat into yourself to find strength and courage and let the light of love always show. You cannot know how brightly one who manifests love can shine to those in darkness. It helps to light their way. Peace be with you. We come close to help.

Thursday, May 2, 1991
Ang:

Slow down long enough to truly put your priorities in order, and do *not* forget to include those things which you, yourself, desire to do—like arranging the flowers on the dining room table. What is the purpose of doing activities without love in your heart, or at least a small fondness? You see, dear, the mind can be either for or against you because it decides exactly how you will perceive a task to be done. The most important truth is you are in full control of what this mind will think. Work always to make your thoughts positive, for through this discipline of the mind you can visualize a life of joy. Difficult times will always be part of life, but if you put the difficulty in proper perspective, it will become a very important lesson in acquiring more knowledge of spiritual growth.

This message comes to tell you of my support, and I do understand how hard it is to stand alone since communication is more difficult between the two worlds. We're getting better even though you might not think this is true. Think carefully and ponder a moment on what you think my answer would be, and it will be there. We are as one and always shall be. Rely on prayer, for help is *always* there. I marvel at your ability to perceive so much of the truth. Wisdom has always been your forte, hasn't it? Somehow you were never interested in the petty or mundane problems of life unless you could be of help. This is one reason you have been chosen to lead others into an understanding of the world of spirit.

There are so many to help you. If you could but see, you would never be discouraged or feel alone. You will have the energy and strength to accomplish many things. Believe in yourself and your abilities, and take one decision at a time and live one day at a time with joy in your heart. You, too, have brought joy into *my* life, and remember that physical death just opens the door to greater love. It is not an ending, but rather a beautiful new beginning which is ours to enjoy right now. It just takes the ability to think in a different dimension and this takes *practice*.

Thank you, dearie, for spending the time, for I know it is often not an easy task when life (physical that is) pulls you in many directions. Be happy, wife of mine, and remember to do what you want to do, at least some of the time. I'll come out and garden with you for the yard is beautiful indeed. Peace and love be with you always.

Saturday, May 11, 1991
Diane:

I somehow feel that God and his higher realms watch to see the purity of intent in one's life, and only then help to ease the burden. This is the 100 percent of our 5 percent which we show to those who come so close to help. Is this not true?

Spirit:

Yes, dear child, this is so. We lovingly watch the growth of each on earth. It is the intent of each commitment which shows the direction from where help must be sent. Honesty and analyzing one's own abilities to listen to that inner voice are of such great importance. Intuition speaks loud and clear, and it too can be heard in the spirit world, much as prayer is heard. Many times the two are entwined and work as one. We, your guides and teachers, sense the truth of one's dedication and we cooperate to help with the outcome, but there are physical limitations. All things are possible with God. We come close to keep everything in proper perspective. May peace follow you, dear one.

Tuesday, May 14, 1991
Spirit:

Peace is earned through diligent, heartfelt prayer. Strive to love unconditionally, dear one, and life will always contain joy, even when sprinkled with sorrow. What then, is peace? Peace is knowing all things will work out. To truly love God let him show you his will, his way. Think only positive thoughts and take care not to preconceive the outworking of life as you want it to be. Always have faith that the proper solution to problems will come—not as man wishes, but rather, in God's own time. Patience takes the sting out of life if one will only wait.

Take time to listen within and answers will come. Take time to enjoy all those beautiful little moments in life, grabbing not with the physical body, but instead grasping beauty and inhaling it into your spiritual being where it can live forever. Use your spiritual senses while still in the physical body for God meant this to be so. Remain open to all things, dear child, and find the thread of love which permeates and connects all of God's creation together. Peace be with you always.

Monday, May 27, 1991
Diane:

I was reading this morning and found the following inspirational passages: "Our need is to love completely, universally without reservation; in other words, to become love itself."

"Love all that has been created by God, both the whole and every grain of sand. Love every leaf and every ray of light. Love the beasts and the birds, love the plants, and love every separate fragment. If you love each separate fragment, you will understand the mystery of the whole resting in God."[5]

My day is not the same if I fail to pray and read my books. I know this, but so far, lack the discipline to put first things first. There is always something seemingly more important which supersedes, but of course inwardly, I know there is absolutely *nothing* more important than tuning into God's truth and the understanding of his laws.

Why is it then that I sometimes fail to do what I know to be the most important? How can I grow in love of all things when I lack such discipline within myself? How can I help those who turn me off, so to speak, especially those who I know need the most help, but are the hardest to reach?

Spirit:

Continue to see the world and those who live in it with rainbow-filled eyes, or with rose-colored glasses, as many would say. It is the *vision* of goodness and the prayers for love that must be sent forth, for upon these thought waves much can be accomplished. Continue to seek those vibrations which seem just beyond one's reach. It is in this space of quiet unrest, and we do emphasize the word *quiet*, that spiritual growth is achieved. How often have we come back to the passage in the Bible of Matthew 7:7? "Ask and you will receive; seek and you will find; knock and the door will be opened to you. For he who asks receives; he who seeks finds; and he who knocks, enters."

Thursday, June 6, 1991

Diane:

There's much to be done, but none more important than prayer and reflection upon what should be done. I must start putting a writing pad by my bed again. I had a good idea as I went to sleep and at the moment it has left me; perhaps it will return. Time spent in this most beautiful of rooms is *never* wasted, for it always lifts the quality of my life, especially if fatigue tries to wend its way into my being. Yes, the physical body tires, but with a night's sleep that should be sufficient. If after rest one remains tired still, then look to the mental condition and feed the spirit with thankfulness, beauty and meditation.

Spirit:

Behold, dear one, the glory of life. Take into your heart the wonderment of the body and how it performs. Truly open the senses and feel all that surrounds you from the smallest to the largest for the Lord God created them all! Bask in the potential power of his love, for herein lies the creative seed of great deeds to help all mankind. Follow your heart, my dear one, for it is guiding you into righteousness. One who seeks will find for he will be able to see that path which is placed before him. Never doubt this, for faith is the thread which weaves all things together into a magnificent tapestry called eternity. Feel the help from those who have passed on and trust your imagination and intuition. It fails you not for it comes from God. Peace be with you, my child.

"The Lord bless you and keep you; the Lord make his face shine upon you and be gracious to you; the Lord turn his face toward you and give you peace." *(Numbers 6:24–25)*

Saturday, June 22, 1991

Spirit:

    Distractions from the physical life tend to override the messages we send from spirit. As one seeks more solitude, the connection can be quickly resumed. Know that the line between us is ever so fragile, and it is in the true desire to make contact that energy is released. Continue to study and learn more of the beautiful mysteries which can be unlocked for those who desire to love and serve God. Never feel alone or deserted, my child, for many come close to help, guide and love you. The road of those who seek the truth is indeed a lonely one, for you see, dear one, the truth lies within and solitude makes the search possible. Many feel the answers will be given from an outside source, but this is not the way of enlightenment. You see, all fears, anxieties and disturbing emotions must be calmed and brought under control before one can understand the messages of God's plan for his children.

    What makes parenting a success? Is it not the dedication of unconditional love that feeds the many times weary physical body? Love is the brightest and most powerful energy of the spirit. It shines when all else seems to be lost; it feeds strength into an exhausted physical being. You have learned the truth in this, and anyone who lives experiences such a feeling. Unfortunately, many deplete this energy through selfish intent and fail to learn the meaning of the purpose of God's love.

    Love should not be self-serving, but rather used to help another whether family, friend or stranger. God's love never diminishes but grows stronger as each learns to use it unconditionally. It can heal all things when used with faith and hope. Ask, seek and knock, my child, for it will be opened unto you at the perfect moment. Pray for guidance to help others and it will be given. Falter not as you stumble on the lonely road for we see the sincerity of a loving heart. Peace be with you, my child.

Sunday, July 14, 1991

Diane:

    As I sit here looking out the back door, I enjoy watching the hummingbird. I always think of Ang and how he enjoyed watching as well. I guess this bird will be a strong link between us, even into eternity. How lovely to have a garden filled with hummingbirds, chickadees, cardinals and wrens! Birds are lovely creatures indeed. Can't place my finger exactly upon what is troubling me these past few days. I know one factor is fatigue, and I must accept with more grace the fact that I am sixty, and I cannot physically do what I could at thirty. There is a stubborn streak within which seems to refuse acceptance of this, and the result is I'm very tired. This unfortunately influences the spiritual and emotional self as well. Most times life is beautiful, so I must stop dwelling upon this lack of luster. If I reread my journal, I think fatigue would surface each time as a partial cause of this feeling.

Spirit:

To be totally truthful with oneself, it is necessary to probe very deeply into that inner self where one judges himself against the perfect creation of God. Many times it appears, and I repeat the word *appears,* to be discouraging, but he who strengthens himself through faith and prayer can weather any storm of physical life. We are the sum total of the love we contain, so it behooves each one to grow in his capacity to love unconditionally. Did it not occur to you, dear one, that an apparent setback leaves an opening for greater growth? Look through the eyes of one who can see eternity and all things will fall into that perfect place.

Sunday, July 21, 1991

Spirit:

Look for the light and ye shall find it, dear child. Can you not see that the importance of a dream, yet to come, is one's ability to know that it shall be? This is the energy upon which those who help you can work. The mysteries of God's law can be realized in such energy. See with eternal vision which combines what *was,* what *is,* and what *can be.* Aspirations become reality to those who believe it can be so. Faith continually fans this energy of light to become stronger and more powerful until the vision is able to manifest itself.

Continue to watch as you prepare your inner being by praying and seeking the strength from God. The fruits of the spirit are the tools one needs to be of service. Be thou a grateful apprentice, my child, and greatness shall emerge into your being. Yes, it is in the placement and wonder of God's gifts that enlightenment comes.

The words—great and grate—look at them, my child. Is it not the placement of the letters which brings forth the meaning? One must be *grateful* first, and then the forces of energy may bring forth *great* love to accomplish God's will. One must first be grateful, so remember this important lesson. We are but a thought away. Peace be with you!

Sunday, August 11, 1991
Spirit:

Live life as you see it emerge from the love that dwells from within the center of your own being. If only the world would cease to look outwardly for solutions, but instead seek the answers from within the heart of man. We, your friends from the realm of spirit, seek always to awaken and enlighten the soul of each human being. Life need not seem so difficult if each would seek the spiritual being which lies dormant, as is sleeping in so many of earth's inhabitants. Love will one day humble those who search relentlessly for the answers to their questions.

Tuesday, August 13, 1991

"Happiness and sorrow, good and bad, pleasure and pain are the very texture of life on the superficial level. Self-will thrives on these dualities, responding with infinite likes and dislikes, which are the ego's way of self-expression. The less you are bound by likes and dislikes, the more clearly you will be able to see the core of purity and selflessness that is the real Self in everyone, even in people who cause trouble…"[6]

Spirit:

Love life and life will bring to you an abundance of love. As you see more clearly, dear one, the need to assert your own being becomes less and less important. We see you question your own passive attitude and as the truth continues to unfold within in your own being, you realize that you are following the perfect way up the mountain of spiritual growth. Confidence in yourself will continue to grow as you believe in your own intuition. The truth whispers within each being, yet many fail to hear. Listen ever so carefully, my dear one. Peace be with you.

Thursday, August 15, 1991
Diane:

Our thirty-seventh wedding anniversary is today! I still can recall the excitement and happiness of that very special day and how blessed I truly am to have Ang. Thank you, dear Heavenly Father.

Ang:

There is no change in heart and mind for true love can only grow deeper and more beautiful. What joy for me to know you truly understand this great truth. We intertwine within each other's lives while separated, or so it sometimes seems while still on the physical plane. Yet, in heart, we are as one. Look for me in rainbows, hummingbirds and flowers for I'll be there today, tomorrow and forever. I love you always, dearie. May peace follow you everywhere. Happy anniversary!

Diane:

This morning I opened *The Quiet Mind* to this prayer. It answered the question I was pondering on how we seem to get locked up in ourselves and find it difficult to set ourselves free.

"Happiness Beyond Our Dreams. You can purify your own physical atoms by right thinking, right speech, right action, right living, judging no man; then, imperceptibly, will come a raising of your consciousness, a happiness of which you have not dreamed, and a gracious and gentle power will grow within you which will make all crooked places straight, and which will open your prison doors, even as the angel touched the door of Peter's prison and set him free."[7]

Wednesday, August 21, 1991
Diane:

My last page in this book... I wonder what I have learned since November 23, 1990 when I started almost nine months ago?
1. To take each day that comes in a more relaxed way, and only think ahead as far as I can handle and remain at peace.
2. To be more observant of the needs of others, even if it is only a friendly smile.
3. More confidence within myself that I can and will accomplish things I set out to do.
4. Can see the aura around my hands much more vividly.
5. Know that I have lovely guides, teachers, doctors, friends and relatives helping me from the world of spirit.
6. There is a plan unfolding in which the Macci family can help other people know about the world of spirit, through meditation and different forms of healing.
7. Learning about the family genealogy and who works with us is becoming clearer.
8. Faith in the power of God's direction.
9. Remembering more of my dreams.
10. Seeing more color and movement during meditation.
11. Better able to spend long periods of time alone.
12. More forgiving of other's faults; thus more forgiving of myself.
13. Less judgmental and more aware when I criticize others.
14. More confidence in my own intuition and how it speaks to me.
15. Overall progress in learning to master myself.

Thursday, September 5, 1991
Spirit:

Forgive and pray for those in spiritual trouble, and this energy can and will be used for healing by those who come close to help. So often we have mentioned the need to love unconditionally. This is the proper moment to test those beliefs, and yes, skills which you have touched upon for so long.

Deep-seated wounds which cover the ability to love are all too prevalent in the world today. Be not one who fans the fire of hate, envy and anger. Instead, my child, quench it with understanding and love, for many on the physical side of life cannot see the good which comes from forgiveness. Each soul born has the capacity to love, but many times the pathway to God and love becomes crooked and goes downward.

Live what you believe; preach what you feel and only good results will be forthcoming. In truth, each should be his brother's keeper, but too few have the wisdom to practice this law. We come to encourage you to look beyond the trespasses of others and forgive them. It is never impossible to change, for all things are possible with God. Project positive outcomes, place the problem in God's magnificent hands and pray, dear child. May peace abide within and love follow you wherever you may go. Love heals all things.

Thursday, September 12, 1991
Spirit:

All mental blocks are caused by your own insecurities, and the feeling of anxiety comes because one feels he cannot or will not. One must mentally collapse such thoughts and instead know with total faith that the ability is truly there, for indeed it is. One needs only to believe and work to reprogram his mind. This, dear child, is the purpose of meditation. To become proficient at any endeavor, one must practice over and over. Continue with diligence to meditate and what you desire will be there. Can you not see how waves of calmness wash over your being when you seek that inner self laced with the divine presence of God? Peace be with you.

Wednesday, September 18, 1991
Spirit:

It is the challenges of life which keeps one spiritually young. The testing of the spirit is necessary in order to allow room for growth. If one remains in a stationary place with little movement, how is it possible to learn to be God's servant? Can you not see the necessity of trials, stress and trauma? One cannot be used to help many until one learns the lesson of helping himself.

To walk into new situations which warrant peace, love and patience is not an easy task, but a necessary one.

Look upon each as a special calling, for your Heavenly Father needs an abundance of help to awaken others to truth. We come to talk to you often, dear child, so that you will know and feel this truth of the world of spirit. Many come to listen when you read aloud, so continue to do this service. Joy finds its way into the heart of a giver; strength comes to one who climbs every mountain; and love guides each to eternal peace. Ask, seek, knock, and the door will open to those who keep on keeping on. Make perseverance a true friend for without his help the road is lonely and desolate. God helps all of his children, but those he chooses for special tasks must be tested well. If what you desire has not yet become a part of your life, know you are still being taught the lessons of truth. Peace be with you, my child.

Tuesday, October 8, 1991

Diane:

How I miss Ang. We always talked things through and he thought out problems so well. Must listen in my heart to what he is saying, and pray for strength and perseverance. How easy it is to ignore and turn the other way when problems confront one, but it is in the solutions that one grows spiritually.

Spirit:

We again remind you, dear one, to do that which comforts you. To give totally of oneself is the proper goal, but not at the expense of one's own self. When giving is done without a joyful heart, then it is time to regroup one's own priorities and seek communion with God and his spiritual realm of helpers. It is *right* to spend time revitalizing the energy needed to serve others. There can be burnout on all levels of living. Know this and give love to your own being for it truly shines, even though you cannot see its full beauty.

God wants each of his children to find joy, and as you already know, each must learn to find the fruits of the spirit from within. Love, joy, peace, patience, goodness, gentleness, kindness, faith and self-control *(Galatians 5:22–23)* are one's link to God's heart. Follow these rainbows of spirit and happiness shall always present itself in all things. Know, believe and falter not on the pathway of God's love. It will never fail for this road leads to eternal life. May peace comfort you *always*.

Saturday, October 12, 1991

Diane:

How does one open up one's imagination to work more efficiently?

Spirit:

We would say to you, dear one, to put less pressure upon yourself. Spiritual awakening happens naturally, in its own way and at its own time. One must not perceive *how* it is to happen, but rather dwell on the positive thought that it *will* happen. Eliminate *all* thoughts of doubt, no matter how small because this interferes with both concentration and awareness. *Know* it will happen with hard work and desire. Do you not feel the energy? Now work to fine tune the vibration with a positive expectation of success. It will happen, for there is much for you to yet accomplish. Peace be with you as you keep on keeping on so faithfully.

Wednesday, October 16, 1991

> I am only one,
> But still I am one.
> I cannot do everything,
> But still I can do something;
> And because I cannot do everything
> I will not refuse to do the something that I can do.[8]

Spirit:

Do not worry that you will miss the call from God for his energy is most powerful. You *will* hear, dear child. Continue on your spiritual path of prayer and meditation for your belief grows ever stronger with practice and true commitment. Success comes to those who continually move onward to reach their goal. We caution you to be sure and do what brings you joy for the spirit refreshes itself in this manner. Take heed to listen to that child within for it will guide you well as it reaches for beauty, joy and love of all things. Keep this childlike spontaneity as a way of life, and let go of the dullness learned in repetitive, daily living. There are so many new experiences yet to come and within this framework, God's will, which you so desire, will be made known to you.

Positive thoughts and action comes to those who find joy and appreciation in all of God's blessings—even those lessons which momentarily cause great grief and sorrow, for life is the composite of God's heart. To know joy one must know sorrow, but the secret lies in seeing love throughout all of one's experiences. Unconditional love sees with the eyes of God, for he who judges others will one day judge himself. Is it not better to see good, no matter how small, and leave positive energy for growth, than to cover this small light with the darkness of negativity? Continue to see good in all things, my child, and peace will be your constant companion. We come close—feel our presence.

Thursday, October 17, 1991

"I will instruct thee, and teach thee in the way which thou shalt go; I will guide thee with mine eyes." *(Psalm 32:8)*

"God be merciful unto us, and bless us; and cause his face to shine upon us. Selah." *(Psalm 67:1)*

Diane:

My concern is that I am not grasping the messages. I thereby waste valuable time in helping others learn to heal themselves and not fear death, since death is just a natural and beautiful transition into a truth we should all know.

Spirit:

Look at your tears, child, and ponder the meaning. Tears come for many reasons: beauty, sorrow, joy, gratefulness, frustration and anger, to name a few.

Diane:

I feel it is disappointment within me, at myself. My desire to be a channel for healing is so very strong, yet I know not which way to turn. I would study further, but I know not what area to study. I feel I can help free others of unwanted spirits.

Spirit:

Perhaps, my child, it is not quite time. Work to strengthen your own field of protection until it is bright and very strong. This takes great dedication and perseverance. Can you not see in your life the careful preparation of the virtue, patience? It is a true blessing to know patience. Do not be troubled by not being of help to others for your very patience and ambiance heals those around you every day. Man tends to always look elsewhere for being of service and many times the greatest deeds can start right where one is. It is the sowing of the seed which is so important, so let God and his realms do the rest.

There is nothing more valuable in life on earth or in heaven (spirit) than the sowing of love for it is the basic ingredient of true happiness. What you love brings great joy in return. The more love one can sow, the more one can reap; for you see, unconditional love is the Godhead within your own being. Sacrifice, dedication, unselfishness and prayer are the inroads to this life of unconditional love. Those who choose to find it are closely guided by spirit. You *will* know, so have a joyful heart and may peace be your constant companion. God bless you, my child.

Friday, October 18, 1991

"Speak to us of love … Even as he (love) is for your growth, so is he for your pruning … think not you can direct the course of love, for love, if it finds you worthy, directs your course."[9]

Spirit:

If you can give to others what you so desire in your own life, it shall come unto you tenfold. If one sows love in all things, so shall he reap love in all things. Examine well your life, dear child, and see if you have sent only love to counteract all difficulties in your life. Judge not, for that is in God's domain; and yet in truth, the God within each of us in the end does the judging. Free all who are a part of your life and let them be as they must be. Bless each with love: God's love and your own love. This is the greatest healing power there is, and as you ponder this question, more love will be released to you for healing.

Spend time alone, for what is within oneself is of immeasurable importance. The answers to life emerge from within your own being, but one must make time to procure a tranquil heart and a peaceful setting. It is unfortunate that more of mankind has not learned this healing balm of the spirit. Love, dear child, love, and what you so desire will be yours. Peace be with you.

Tuesday, October 22, 1991
Diane:

Watching the birds from Ang's chair, and as we all are, I am sometimes my own worst enemy. I must let what I am yet to accomplish rise slowly from within my being. I torture myself sometimes with a feeling of lack of effort on my part. When, oh when, will I trust my own intuition with confidence knowing I will be prepared for that task for which I will be chosen? Wish there were words which could better explain the emptiness which I feel within at certain times. Frustration, I guess, for I know I have much yet to give, but—How? When? Where? Patience, patience, patience. Where am I missing the message?

Spirit:

Self-mastery is a task of great magnitude which truly lasts throughout all of eternity. How must God feel as he watches the development of his own creation, and yet his patience and love are unending? Life must unfold as naturally as the sun rises each morn and sets each night; as the waves relentlessly break upon the shoreline; as the buds slowly open into full bloom, and so on and so on. As you grow in awareness, so will your calling unfold without effort; it will just come to be. Walk steadily upon your path of prayer and gratitude, helping each that passes into your life, letting go with love at the perfect moment. Love never possesses another, but rather in turn helps to nurture the potential of that which is loved.

The freedom of the spirit is the very essence of its greatness. Conditions of life constantly attempt to hold the spirit as a prisoner. Realization of the world of spirit yet to come opens the mind to release thoughts which contain the truth of God's law. This is the moment one feels freedom to be what he truly is, for love is the center seed planted within each human being. It is activated at birth and though life experiences can cover the light, it is not extinguished totally. God and his high realm spirits can see through to this light of love in humanity, so with enduring patience they strive to awaken mankind to discover the truth. Be grateful for the opportunity to spread the truth to others by unconditional love which you have been using all of your life. Is this not so?

Accept with thanksgiving that you have been chosen to help in this special project called AIM. There is much work to be done, and as it develops, you will be shown your special pathway to help. Peace be with you, my child.

Thursday, October 24, 1991
Diane:

Life must change. I am trying to come to grips with unsettled parts of myself and put everything in its proper place with God-centered perspective. I miss Ang so much—can't believe it will be five years soon! How blessed I am to have been awakened to such truth about the spirit world. It is *my* lack of faith and inability to control my own temple of thought that causes me to lack the joy which should fill my being. We each are responsible for ourselves, and he who is able to continually rise above the physical side is truly blessed. I strive daily for this great joy and many times it comes. One must learn to be alone and not lonely. One must learn to love without a desire for a return. One must learn to *always* give the best of himself to others, and then and only then will the channel from God become pure and true. It is then that one may hear the small voice within and follow the guidance which is truly blessed.

Spirit:

Dear one, to strive for perfection leaves one vulnerable to forces of one's own physical senses. The testing ground is a relentless battle between what *is* right and what the emotions of the body plead for. Remember that prayer and meditation are one's greatest ally for it is possible to rise above these feelings in thought, and to one's amazement there is peace and joy just for the effort shown. Love is truly eternal and all that you love shall be there for eternity. Separation is the challenge to grow into an eternal union. Life becomes boring, dismal and a drudgery only to those who turn away from the truth. The harder one works for something, the more it means. Is this not true?

Search your own being and join forces with those who stand ready to help you in this quest. Age is never considered, for if chosen to do God's work, one will always be supplied with health and energy. Doubting causes pangs of negativity and this leaves one open for attack. In God, who is the source of your strength, love and patience, you have strength, love and patience for everything. Live in this truth every moment, my child, and joy will be your reward enfolded in peace. Be strong in your faith and overcome all thoughts of doubt. You are what you think, and you shall become what you dream you can be. Peace be with you, dear child. We always stand ready to help.

Monday, November 4, 1991

"It is when everything is uncertain like this, when the whirlpool is going round and round, that we must be able to draw upon enormous patience to stay firm and steadfast. Calling on the Lord in our heart by repeating his Name, we find access to our deeper reserves of devotion, firmness and love."[10]

"Instead of demanding your own way, be prepared to yield in humility and say; 'Dear Lord, show me Thy way; I trust in Thee. Lead me according to Thy will, for Thou alone art wise; Thy love is beyond my worldly understanding.' Then your way will be made plain."[11]

Spirit:

Love God with all thy heart and all thy mind, and your way will be made known. Be prepared to be tested, dear child, over and over again. Life is a thing of beauty only if you perceive it to be so. Can you not see that love, peace, patience, joy, gentleness, goodness, self-control, kindness and faith are the strength that each can call upon when the road of life becomes difficult? These are the blessings which can be cultivated by each, but one *must* travel the route which passes by the fruits of the spirit.

When doubt enters, pray, meditate and listen for divine directions. Many times the answers appear, not under stress or non-stop activity, but rather in the solitude of the questioning mind. Train yourself to believe without question, to know the answers will appear at the perfect moment in the proper way. Listen for God's help for it will come with patience and love. Peace be with you.

Thursday, November 7, 1991
Spirit:

Be patient and the answer will come directly to *you*. Your calling will be one of true faith for you ask, seek and knock with a pure heart, and we come to tell you that your prayers are heard. It is your faithful heart and caring love that will lead you to your own special calling. The positive mind will hear the will of God at the perfect moment. It is wise to wait patiently with joy in your heart. Live each moment with childlike thankfulness and wonder. Children accept life with spontaneity and joy, so live as a child, dear one. We are always near to guide you, and to give you peace.

Friday, November 15, 1991
Approval comes for Hosmer House Bed and Breakfast

Spirit:

We, who work closely with you, dear child, are indeed happy as well. Positive, selfless thought combined with love is a hard goal to reach, but we come to encourage you and to tell you, you are indeed on the right pathway. Positive thoughts are so very powerful, and you can do much to convince those around you to see this as well. Positive thoughts become selfless thoughts and the combination becomes part of God's love. It is on this energy that good things happen. Love permeates to a greater degree into one who prays and meditates to become a pure channel to do God's will. Trust, my child, and believe that all things are possible for indeed this is so.

One must have faith in the unseen and grasp the opportunities which almost float in and about one's mind when it is filled with positive ideas. Worry and concern only cloud this pure channel. Always keep on guard and control those emotions which pull negatively upon the spirit. *Always* remember you are spirit first, a child of God throughout eternity, and life in the physical world born of physical parents, is secondary. God uses the growth of a physical body as the vehicle to teach the spirit the beauty of his love. The vibration and well-being of the world depends upon the timbre of its inhabitants. Positive thoughts and actions, no matter how minute or seemingly small, are of great importance, because they are felt eventually in the heart chakra of another. One may deny what this chakra is telling him, but the physical body and life of that person will undeniably be affected. This, my dear child, is an exacting law and there is no exception.

Everything has its purpose and although many slip on the pathway, the seed of love planted in the spirit will be known, if only as a slight glimmer occasionally. It is those who persistently send forth unconditional love that fans this spark in others. Pray for this purity within thy own being, my child, and continually influence those about you. We come with pride and joy to help, love and serve you, dear one, as you help, love and serve us. May peace follow you everywhere.

Ang:

As we become closer as one in our relationship of spirit, the need for physical examples of remembrance will become less. More of our united energy can then be used by spirit to help others. This is hard to express in language, but I know you understand my thoughts. We are as one in love and shall remain so forever. I love you.

Saturday, November 23, 1991

Diane:

The following few lines appeared in my mind last night and I thought they were lovely:

Joy comes on the wings of thought. It is born of God. Those who live within its presence are truly blessed and should be eternally grateful. What greater gift could be bestowed upon them? I have been thinking about joy and love of late. Would like to help someone I know find more of it, but how to begin? Is there help from those in spirit?

Spirit:

Pray for those you wish to help for all things are possible with God's guidance.

Thursday, December 19, 1991

Diane:

Why is it that I do not seem to open my psychic sight more? I know "in God's own time," but could I do more to help the progress?

Spirit:

Have no doubts, my child. You are where you should be at this time. Spiritual awakening to the five senses is a slow process with gradual progress because one must accept it with his whole being. Only positive experiences are desired, so again, dear one, conjure up that ability to be patient. Patience for all things must be learned before new skills become apparent. Trust your intuition, practice meditation, pray to do our Father's will, and it will be so. Those who are diligent and exacting in daily conditions are many times noticed and nurtured without the one chosen even knowing it.

Everything is possible with God for those who believe it will be so. Healing others takes great strength, so prepare yourself for this challenge. Go within and face all anxieties until you are at peace. Be truthful with each feeling and let it go when necessary. Unconditional love is all encompassing and there is no room for doubt or negative thoughts. One will only accomplish that which he knows he wants to do and therefore, knows he can do. Prepare yourself to try whenever possible, for in trying, you allow those who help you to do God's will to come close and align themselves with your energy. *Know* help will be there, and it *will* be there.

Healing is another expression of love. If each loved enough, my child, there would be no disease, for in many cases each brings on his own illness. There is a reason for all happenings, but how many are able to believe this? Look at the condition of the world today, and the answer is all too clear. What, you ask, can one so seemingly small and inconspicuous do to help this situation?

Come forth and tell of your beliefs and knowledge and start soon to practice the gift of healing through God's love. Be humble and childlike in your faith, and know without proof what can be done. We, in spirit, need more credible people to lead the way, for others follow a person who lives a life of truth. Any new endeavor needs much practice and soon you will find that you have the necessary tools to begin. Believe in your ability to do God's will and you shall be chosen to fulfill the calling. Many come close to help—relax and feel their presence. May love and peace follow you as you help humanity.

1992

Wednesday, January 1, 1992

Diane:

Happy New Year to all and may the world find peace and love.

Spirit:

What you give to the world, my child, shall be given back unto you. Project only love and it will be most helpful in righting the ills which are all too prevalent these days upon earth. See only the good in all situations, even when the good seems infinitesimal, for the tides of God's energy are always present. It is up to people like you who care deeply; then the energy can be directed to help others. The law or rule is simple, but man himself has complicated its outworking. Love, positive thoughts and prayer are so much more powerful and effective than can be imagined.

Strive for perfection, visualize your destiny and stay close to Jesus and your Heavenly Father. All questions will be answered, dear child, but only those who listen closely will hear them. Life is the blueprint for eternity, but truth will build the world in which one enters upon leaving the physical body. God is the truth, the light, the love which dwells within each human being. Truth is examining the alignment of your daily life with the perfection of Christ as taught by Jesus as he lived among the people of his time and passed down in the Bible. Jesus is God's son and he understood the yearning and compassion of God's heart. Try, dear one, to be an instrument of his will in all that you do.

Prayer of Saint Francis

Lord, make me an instrument of thy peace.
Where there is hatred, let me sow love;
Where there is injury, pardon;
Where there is doubt, faith;
Where there is despair, hope;
Where there is darkness, light;

Where there is sadness, joy.
O, divine Master, grant that I may not so much seek
To be consoled, as to console,
To be understood as to understand,
To be loved as to love.
For it is in giving that we receive;
It is in pardoning that we are pardoned;
It is in dying (to self) that we are born to eternal life.

Tuesday, January 7, 1992

"Be Patient, have Faith. We know, beloved child, the sorrows and the difficulties of the material life lived in a physical body at present unawakened to the beauty of God's world. We know how hard it is to pursue the shadowed path. You have to walk in darkness, to accept the conditions in which you find yourselves, trusting in the love of the Great White Spirit. This is not easy, we know, but have *patience* and *faith*. Never doubt the power, the wisdom and the love of God."[12]

Diane:

This is a good message from *The Quiet Mind* for me today. I know I tend to block myself with my own frustration as to what I am going to do with the remainder of my life. What good can be accomplished with my desire to be a healer? I have progressed far enough to know that at the perfect moment the course will be set before me, yet there is still impatience forging within. What important lesson have I to learn in order to become worthy as an instrument of God's healing?

Spirit:

Confidence, dear child, work on your confidence. Nothing in life can be accomplished unless you, yourself, know that it will be so. There is *nothing* one cannot do if there is true confidence and desire. We suggest you set more conditions of seemingly small chores and do it without fail and with purpose and joy. Lose those extra pounds, sort all those boxes, refinish the desk, learn the computer, practice the piano, enjoy life and think positively, for this builds confidence. Dwell more upon confidence and less upon patience, for although one can always strive for more perfection, you have already demonstrated the ability to be patient.

Always take the time to pray and listen within yourself, for dear one, the answers are there. Truth is implanted within every human being. The answers come as thoughts and ideas, feelings (intuition) and guidance. As you, yourself release the truth, it manifests itself as action, not coincidence as so many believe. Live your life in love, purity and kindness; the results will be most benevolent, even if you do not see the results.

To want proof of your value is the ego speaking, and this desire thwarts spiritual progress. Love because to love is a beautiful gift from God. To love unconditionally is to know God more intimately. Walk the path of spiritual growth and always feel those who walk with you from spirit. Peace be with you.

Wednesday, January 22, 1992
Spirit:

There is a great deal of energy released in the process of an altered state. By this we mean the transitional period between the two states enhances and multiplies the energy at hand. Can you not feel the heat as it builds? Many times upon waking at night, and it happens more than once, you feel as if you are on fire and must throw off the covers. Is this not true? We work with you, my child, to help you become more aware of the energy within your own being. This is the energy of healing that comes from the energy of God, free to all who ask, seek and knock. You can practice to surface this magnificent healing heat by meditating with the full knowledge that you are indeed a channel.

Desire is the key to success in all endeavors for to desire means the thought has already transpired. We, who come to teach and help you, must bring our knowledge through the subconscious. Between the subconscious and the conscious is a maze filled with emotions of negativity which trap the truth of which we speak. Have you not this morning set yourself free? Believe, dear one, that you will find the energy, color and heat to heal and do phenomena, for indeed you shall.

Everyone has tenacity, but not so many grab it with true desire. Learn to preface every move you make with love, and the mysteries of life will come to you without fail. Let no one dim the star which shines so brightly within and daily leads you to that final purpose for which you know you were born. Feel the energies of the universe and pull them into your own being to use them to help others. Ask for help, seek the truth, and the door to God's splendor will truly be open. Humble yourself always to love, for love holds the key to many wonders. We come close, dear one, and do feel the ecstasy as you discover each new wonder. All answers lie within your own being and are released at that perfect moment. Peace and love be with you, dear one.

Sunday, February 15, 1992
Diane:

To ask in prayer for others is not difficult, but to ask for myself seems not as necessary. My heart tells me God will guide me to do his will if I wait with patience, faith, hope, and most of all, love. Is this correct, dear friends?

Spirit:

If your heart tells you so, dear one, why do you doubt? Intuition is the clearest barometer of one's soul. Much is taught to each during the hours of sleep which rests the physical body. A spirit needs no rest so it continually seeks truth whether consciously or subconsciously. Time is meaningless to spirit; therefore, continually seek for that which lies beyond the moment. Lessons are learned through your subconscious mind first, and then filter into the conscious mind at the perfect moment, especially to one who seeks the inner light.

Continually work to energize your entire being and feel the subtle messages that are sent through thought and feeling. Prayer for others fine-tunes this energy so it can become a working force. Just because you are unable to see it with your physical eyes, does not prove that it isn't there. This is the fallacy of scientific minds and hinders the progress and efficiency of discovery through thought. The energies are there for those who seek God's help. See with broader vision. Imagine what might be and believe that anything is possible with God. Return to meditation for this is the way to travel within.

Wednesday, February 19, 1992
Spirit:

Let us discuss the topic of aloneness this day. Each is born into an affinity with God. We are each whole, unique and filled with all of the qualities needed to find heaven on earth. Life must be lived first as a thought, except perhaps for those reflexes which are built-in protectors of our physical body. All else, dear one, is first experienced in the mind, awakened through a thought. Many ideas lay dormant until the perfect moment when wisdom calls, and this happens not only through physical life but also throughout eternity. Many thoughts and ideas must be learned and experienced throughout one's physical life from infancy, such as communication, factual knowledge, social skills and cultivated interests. These must be practiced to improve one's proficiency, for between thought and achievement much desire, hard work and faith must be shown.

Where then does the greater impetus come from—within or without? You *are* what dwells within your own being. We suggest that time spent alone is the fruition process wherein seeds of wisdom may grow. It is unfortunate that so many fear this time of aloneness and for so many different reasons. However, in truth, it is the fear of meeting oneself with total honesty as to who you really are versus what you have become. How far exactly have you strayed from God? God showed each of us a life of total love, but how many truly live in this image?

This is why learning the art of meditation is of such importance. Meditation brings one into closer attunement with the goodness within. The healing energy of the body lives within one's own being and must manifest itself as unconditional love of God, love of self, love of others and love of Mother Earth. For you see, dear one, God *is* love and we are each in the image of God. To be truly joyful in aloneness brings one into the presence of our loving Creator, as if looking into a mirror. If something of beauty looks in the mirror, what will reflect back?

As you travel within your own being in meditation, note carefully what image you see on that inner mirror. Work unceasingly to build rays of love upon your own inner mirror that others may see this brilliant light reflect in themselves. May peace follow you everywhere. We come close to help.

Thursday, February 27, 1992
Diane:

Is it possible to heal yourself while trying to be a channel to help God heal others? I feel this way, but have no tangible evidence to prove my feelings.

Spirit:

Dear one, intuition has no need to find evidential proof, for in fact, it will in time prove itself. Energies from spirit are blocked by this questioning and doubting of intuition. Let what you believe surface from within, and trust in that indwelling beauty from God within yourself. Positive thinking will release the truth. Through prayer, meditation, reading and actual hands-on activity, you release your own being to expand until your growth can be seen in your physical life. Enlightenment is the result of this difficult task to find love and its truths. We, your friends in spirit, await the call to answer questions and to draw out what is buried deep within your subconscious.

All is connected, each for its own purpose, so when one helps to be a channel for healing, how could one not be healed himself? Healing lights and energies help all who will open the chakras to receive them. The giving of concern and love to another is also a form of healing, dear child. Try to open your mind to the fact that all things are possible. You begin to realize more that there are many methods and ways to heal. Believe that your method will evolve at the perfect moment in your life, and you will not have to find it, for it will find you.

Love is light is God is healing, and is ultimately perfect. Strive *through love* to be a channel of God's healing. Words, touch, eye contact and laughing are all part of healing as is the ability to find joy and peace. Count those blessings and be filled with gratitude to your Creator. Love is your constant companion. We come close to guide you, dear one. Be at peace.

Tuesday, March 3, 1992

Diane:

I am learning more and more that one must love and respect himself in total truth and honesty before he can help another with unconditional love. Love for self and God are interconnected. This is why so few make it to spiritual greatness while in the physical body. To love unconditionally is to see with the eyes of God, and the sacrifice to do this is sometimes unbearable, not only once in a lifetime, but constantly. My gratitude goes to those who come close to help me open the scope of my understanding, for every glimpse is a great gift.

Help me, dear ones, to learn to pray from a heart of love, not from a heart filled with emotion and judgment. Purity of love belongs to God and each must win his trust through daily life. Even situations which might appear as a failure may be reversed with pure thoughts and prayers of love. The answer when one feels heaviness and despair is to pray for intervention of divine love, and know that the right solution will be forthcoming in God's own time. This lesson—in God's own time—I shall always remember.

Tuesday, March 10, 1992

Diane:

What can be seen on the TV-like screen of my inner being or soul? This thought passed through my mind as I woke up this day. It is a good thought, an action thought, a thought each should take to heart. Would it not be better for all, if each spent a little time each day watching their own internal TV?

Spirit:

See self-confidence, strength and courage, patience, faith, hope and love, for it is all there. One only needs to fine-tune the picture with prayer, meditation and desire. Prayer lines one up with God's almighty power. It affirms one's belief to do his will and to follow his rules of goodness and love. Meditation promises to combine the two wills together into a unified desire, and this desire gives one the impetus into action. This, dear one, is how great progress is accomplished. Tire not on your journey, but dig deeply to find the self-control needed to follow the spiritual path. Travel in peace with God's blessing.

Tuesday, March 17, 1992
Diane:

Mother's birthday today—I pray she is at peace and happy. Somehow the energies about me tell me this is so. Many changes are taking place at this time which is probably true for every human being. The better I keep the perspective of my life in line with others and what they endure, the more peace I find within my own being.

Spirit:

Life on earth is the sum total of all of these experiences. How well did one experience teach and guide you to handle the next? Did you learn more about yourself and your ability to love unconditionally? The wonders and wisdom of God are revealed in direct proportion to what you have earned, my child. Selflessness does not just happen spontaneously, but is instead the result of a slow, painful process of internal self-evaluation. One is never so perfected that there is no need to continue the spiritual conquest of self.

Wednesday, March 18, 1992
Spirit:

Cleanse out the debris of your being through prayer and meditation. Once the debris moves on, the flow of love will teach you to do the Father's will. It is so easy to believe when there is physical proof, but this is not so spiritually, for the senses of the spirit are delicate and of a higher and finer vibration. One must truly seek the realm of spirit with pure faith, knowing and trusting that God and all of his creation is there at every moment. Ingest all the marvels of nature as proof enough that indeed the spiritual world is real, for everything has its counterpart in creation. Thought is the connecting link between these two worlds—the purer thoughts allowing more contact.

Meditation is calming and relaxes the tension of physical life and that is why one must diligently practice its technique. Free will must become a part of God's will and this is learned through meditation and prayer which opens up the pathway to pure thought as well. To pray for others lifts one's self-will aside and allows love and its energies to comfort others. Think of beautiful angels being carried to help another on the energies of your prayer of love. Give the energies from your own bank of love and concern, and it shall be filled to capacity at all times.

Selfish concerns shut off this blessed, flowing reservoir from God's love. Jesus constantly tried to teach this to the people of his time. How disappointing and frustrating this must have been, yet his reservoir of true, unconditional love was so pure, he forgave those who persecuted and killed him. The fruits of the spirit all come from this reservoir of energies that each literally pumps from within his own being to that spiritual fountain connected to eternal life. All things are connected and depend upon each other, for the energies which perpetuate God's creation of earth and its inhabitants. We must be grateful and loving. This is the key to peace. We come close to help. Peace be with you.

Monday, March 23, 1992
Spirit:

You must find the depth of your capacity for compassion, and this, as you know, is a most difficult and all-consuming journey. To go beyond the task of daily living is a most difficult and heart-rending experience, but if one is to learn wisdom, the journey must be experienced with all of its peaks and valleys. Spiritual endeavors are of the heart and one's true self must be laid bare to experience the truth of God's realms. One must earn the ability to be all-loving and there is much pain involved to learn the lessons of unconditional love. To be of service one must know the despair of physical life and overcome its difficulties, breaking through to the side where positive solutions reign. Internal light, which comes from our divine center, is always there for those who can see.

When life is easy, one appears superficially happy, yet the important lessons are learned from what appears as failure. In truth, failure is the illusion. The positive outcome is the constant wisdom which continually comforts those who can see more of the total understanding of creation. Each is as a grain of sand or a droplet of water, yet, without each, would there be a whole? Those who understand must continue to seek and help others to see as well. A small seed of an idea can be a new beginning for one who understands little. Always be prepared to plant this seed in all that you meet. Can you know how inspirational one thought might become? Peace be with you.

Wednesday, March 25, 1992
Spirit:

Think not of yourself, dear one, but always of others, and you will know only peace, joy and true happiness. When one learns to do this, he has also learned to be a messenger of God's will. There is so much written about pleasing oneself and gaining confidence through one's own desire, but in truth, those who learn to tap into God's will by setting aside their own will, are those who help the most. This happens many times without one even knowing the influence they instill in others.

Remember, dear child, it is in the *giving* through which one receives; it is in the *believing* that one is answered; for peace comes from within oneself where all wisdom dwells. Keep on keeping on, and that red heart will become stronger and brighter within your inner sight. Peace be with you.

Wednesday, April 1, 1992
Spirit:

Peace and balance ignite the spirit to seek its highest good. Upon this journey of goodness, one learns the meaning of unconditional love. To always give of oneself is unconditional love, but how many truly learn to *always* give? How can one know when and how to give, you ask? Follow that simple rule so eloquently stated: "Do unto others, as you would have them do unto you." *(Luke 6:31)* Lead with the intuition and love dwelling within your own being through empathy. That suffering and sorrow which encompasses another will reach out to you and touch you spiritually if one will only allow it to happen. How, you ask?

Learn to control those selfish thoughts and banish them into the light of God's love. Light diffuses darkness of any kind, and love swallows selfishness and digests it through the other eight fruits of the spirit. Life is the sum total of all of the deeds of the spirit made manifest through your physical body. The spirit is foremost and controls the actions of the body, not the other way around which so many believe to be true. We are spirit first, and the truth of the universe is hidden in the spiritual existence of one's being. Each returns home to this truth of spirit which dwells in all things of the universe.

If man could but learn to live his physical life in tune with his spiritual values, the sorrow and tribulations of earthly life would diminish greatly. The more one is out of contact with his spirit man, the more painful and unhealthy his life. This proves the importance of prayer and meditation, which balances and brings one back to the powerful meaning of life—to love unconditionally. Continue to search for the answers and for the words to enlighten those who still live in darkness. Peace be with you, my child.

Thursday, April 2, 1992
Spirit:

Joy, joy, joy, dear one. See only the joy of each and every thought and situation, and you will contribute more than you know to the overall good of mankind. Light and motion is the source of universal energy, and you, and each human being, is one with this energy. Those who seek deeply within begin to observe and tap into the magnitude of creation and its eternal quality. As you continue to break the ties of physical life and its worries and concerns, your thoughts become free and can climb to greater heights. Desire to help others and it shall be so. Accept daily life with humility and gratitude—in this way the ultimate sacrifices can be accepted on faith, knowing an important lesson would eventually be forthcoming. Once this acceptance is offered, peace and joy will begin to fill the seeming void.

Always find time to seek the peace within, for this ensures vitality and health. Positive thoughts contain only good. Love is a close friend of positive thinking and together they can accomplish many beautiful things. Always remember, dear one, those deeds done in secret are the most worthy of all for the tally is kept deep within and brightens the light of one's eternal spirit. It matters not that it is seen by visible eyes. Teach this secret whenever possible for it will release the atoms of love which are so desperately needed at this time. Life is beautiful only to those who work hard to make it so. Send prayers and love each day of your life, and be on guard to only judge your own being, not another. Keep on keeping on. We hear your heartfelt prayers. Peace be with you always.

Wednesday, April 15, 1992
Diane:

There are many things for me to do. None are more important, however, than time in the meditation room to tune into thoughts and vibrations that will help me to find the peace of God's world, and perhaps raise my ability to better do his will. ASK, SEEK, KNOCK! Know there are so many people yet to help in my lifetime, but this can only come to pass as I internalize the meaning of unconditional love.

Spirit:

Thoughts direct one's life and each must learn to have self-mastery over one's own thoughts. What one chooses to dwell on is the gift of free will. As one slowly trots the spiritual path, the important lessons of life are understood more clearly, for each difficult situation or suffering tends to clear the mists which surround the truth—the core of living with God as one's center. Fear causes so many problems. It paralyzes the spirit and joy of a human being as if with Novocain. What one desires to do is not allowed to grow into manifestation. Over and over we remind you on earth that you *are* what you think. Think of God and his son and their unconditional love, and each can be raised by this love.

Confidence in your own intuition is of great importance, for then one cannot easily be influenced by another through unwanted advice in the form of criticism. This does not mean to disregard helpful suggestions, but rather reminds one to follow his own star, for in truth, no one else can see another's dream in full color. That special rainbow belongs to the one who creates it. Stay on your path, dear one, and become neither discouraged nor downtrodden. See only joy and the possibilities in what your dream can be. Peace be with you. We come close to help.

April 17, 1992—Good Friday
Diane:

Just finished reading in the Bible about the crucifixion of Jesus—such a moving story of total dedication to doing God's will. I pray for guidance to be aware of what I must do to be worthy to hear his will in my life. I sometimes weep with frustration with myself for not finding my pathway to serving God more quickly, but faith tells me to be patient and learn the true meaning of unconditional love.

Spirit:

To always think with pure thoughts of love is an eternal mission, yet, one must train the mind of spirit to lead the physical mind to answer its call of goodness. If each human being could learn to follow this call of goodness, there would be heaven on earth. Live a simple life, my child. See and hear the anguish of those you encounter in your daily travels. Pray for them and set an example of love and purity in your own life. Words are empty if one fails to live his own beliefs. Keep on the pathway to salvation by always being available to one in need. Take the time to hear the sadness and pain of another, for as one painful thought leaves, another may enter. With guidance this new thought can be one of joy and gladness.

Wisdom fills the void left by negative thinking for it is of God. Each has this beautiful knowledge within his own being, but the desire to know and serve God and one's fellow man is an important factor in the releasing of eternal truth. There are many seeming truths, but only one eternal truth. Continue to tap into the power, energy and goodness of God through loving all things, dear one, and your mission will be known in God's own time.

Remember those lessons you have been taught through trials as well as through joy. Life must be lived through both sets of eyes (physical and spiritual) in order to learn wisdom. Weigh the meaning of what is seen by the "hidden" eyes of physical life for this spiritual vision will teach you the meaning of love, goodness and true beauty. Be true to this inner vision and though you might stumble, you will remain on the path of God. Peace be with you, child. We come close to guide you.

Monday, April 20, 1992
Diane:
How does one small soul help another?

Spirit:
The light of the world is only as bright as the sum total of all of the little lights which shine from each human being. Is it not fitting that those whose lights burn brighter should help the dimmer ones to find greater strength and faith? Action always speaks louder than words, my child. Show love and concern for all that you meet. Walk that extra mile when you are fatigued, for the light of wisdom can ignite the truth in another at any moment. Light has no boundaries and can absorb darkness in its wake. Eternal light is a gift from our creator and he watches and helps as each human being strives to intensify this light throughout his physical life. Too few pay attention to this most important light from within, and the world suffers from the lack of love. Illumination of the soul is love itself. Love of God recharges the battery needed for unconditional love of self and of others. Look to the light from God in all that you do, and your mission will be known at that perfect moment. The small acts of love in daily life are the most precious of all, so continue searching for more light in these deeds, dear child. Go in peace and feel the warmth of our love.

Monday, April 27, 1992

"The Master is tender and loving; he knows your need, he understands your difficulties and disappointments and says, 'Come, brother, come above the mists, come unto me, and I will give you that inner peace for which you long …'"[13]

Diane:

Peace comes from the tranquility of one's own sanctuary where love and the light of God dwell. One must trust the outworking of God's love and believe that all things are possible. I'm trying hard to listen to my inner voice, and I do okay until my confidence sags. Are there any words of encouragement from my many friends?

Spirit:

Why do you doubt what you know can and will be true, my child? Persevere always and work through these doubts with positive thinking, praying and meditating. Refuse to let a negative thought remain in your presence, and then right answers will filter through to your conscious mind and bring peace. Trust in the guidance from spirit to soften those who oppose you, and learn to send out only messages of love and understanding. How can you expect others to understand if the vibrations from you, yourself, are not positive? Empathy is a great gift, my child. Use it to be an instrument of God's will. Those on earth, in the physical body, cannot clearly see the path that they must pursue, so this is why finding the God-force within is of such importance. So much work needs to be done to awaken much of the world to the truth of the spirit world. This will be the most powerful weapon to bring forth peace on earth.

How fortunate you understand this truth, and as your life develops you can do much to help others grasp the meaning as well. Life is beautiful and there is joy to be found for those who have beauty dwelling within their own being. Love is the most beautiful of all, so continue each day, dear one, to give forth unconditional love in all that you do. There is no other way to climb the spiritual path. We know your desire is to be a channel for healing and as you learn the ability to love, to pull in the light energy all around you, your confidence will lead you where you so desire to go. We watch closely for dedication, for perseverance, for patience, for goodness, for love, for faith, for joy—all of these lead one closer to the self-discipline of a master. To do what is right, in all situations is to live in God's love. We come close to guide you, dear one.

Saturday, May 2, 1992
Official opening of Hosmer House Bed and Breakfast!
Diane:

I awoke with a lovely thought and it shall be written in the old ledger where people register at the bed and breakfast. It's a tradition Helen M. Hosmer started many years ago: *"The joys of the past have made this new beginning possible!"*

I want this house to be a place of peace where people will find healing within themselves to send forth unto others. This is the only way the world will eventually find peace as well. I am so grateful and filled with joy as each day I understand a little more of the truth and wisdom of God and his world of spirit.

Spirit:

Compassion and love for all things is the route to follow, for along the way one can build the actual visualization of one's dream until it becomes reality. The pure thoughts of such a dream gives energy to produce what is needed to fulfill the desired results. Continue to carefully speak out on what you understand, dear one. We say carefully, for nothing can be accomplished until another is ready to accept, and you must understand the level each is at as you talk to them. This is a skill you are learning well, my child. It is difficult to hold one's tongue, but know that we help through your own thoughts. Peace be with you, child, and know that tomorrow, as today, will be a success. Faith and love never fail those who truly believe. This is God's promise as he spoke through his son.

Wednesday, May 6, 1992
Spirit:

Love makes the world go round so jump on the carousel and dance to the song of life. Live your life without any fears, knowing the power of

God protects you. Pray for others, that they might know the joys of life as they unfold in the events of each day. Rejoice in newly-acquired knowledge for those who strive for unconditional love see with the eyes of truth. Be diligent in your prayer life; meditate daily, search within to find the light from God, and love all things. Peace be with you.

Tuesday, May 12, 1992
Spirit:

Life is what you, yourself, choose to make of it. If one always thinks with love as his guide, joy will follow sorrow, as dawn follows night. This is not to say that night is not beautiful, for we, in spirit know you like the beauty and quiet that nighttime holds in its keeping. However, light holds the creative energy in its grasp and you, on earth, have little understanding of the power it contains. We know that you believe "with God all things are possible," and this belief opens your mind to seek and question all things without skepticism and little prejudice. Continue to dream and look for what some think to be impossible, for in believing, much unseen energy is released from those of us in spirit who come close to you to help. The more one believes in the so-called unknown, the more one will be able to see into spirit.

You think sometimes that your pathway is not known, dear one, but in truth, it *is* known. We encourage you to continue to seek unconditional love through reading, meditating, and most of all, prayer. Prayer teaches humility, gratitude and patience, and gives one the opportunity to come closer to our Heavenly Father and his high realm dynasty. Ask, seek, knock everyday of your life and his will *will* be known unto you. Peace be with you always, my child.

Tuesday, May 19, 1992
Diane:

I have learned many new ideas and concepts over the last few years. Sometimes I amaze myself.

Spirit:

The important factor is steady progress in all that you do. New ideas evolve from the melting pot of creation as each is ready to release the knowledge from within. We all know many things in the subconscious mind, but concern for physical satisfaction and poor control of our emotions keeps the pathway blocked, and little truth escapes to help with spiritual development. One *must* ponder and pray and have purpose. Consider carefully and well what thoughts one allows into the conscious mind. Each *is* in control of his own thoughts and this fact is most important in finding a joyful life. God created all things, so the most important of thoughts is praise and thankfulness for what was bestowed upon every human being. How one uses these gifts is totally controlled by one's thoughts, for one is what he thinks. Joy manifests itself to us through interpretation and reaction to the thoughts we project.

Those who ponder the question of life will find greater satisfaction than those who live only for the joy of the moment. Physical desire is not satisfied because it concerns itself with selfish desires, many times far removed from the righteousness of God's laws. This helps to explain why excessive behavior of any kind causes great strife in life, and eventually, undesirable results. One cannot live outside the boundary of truth and not eventually pay back the trespasses he has committed.

As one seeks this truth of our loving Father, helpful answers do appear in our thoughts, but one must learn to listen and have faith in himself, and give thanks to God and those in spirit who help. Think more in the realms of eternity, for joy and love go on and on and on. There is no end to the possibilities of what is, what will be and what can be. *Live* what you are learning, and prove it through action, not words. The old saying "action speaks louder than words" is indeed the truth. May peace follow you everywhere.

Saturday, May 23, 1992
Spirit:

Who are the tears for, dear one? You, others, God? Where is your faith and trust in God and those who help to direct you? Why do you constantly point out your lacking, and fail to capitalize upon what you do so well? We will always love you unconditionally and think highly of you, even if you never do an expert reading. Give out your own talents, your own uniqueness, your great love and concern and let us supply the results. "Oh you of such little faith" is what Jesus told people, and comparing oneself to another gains little. You seek so deeply; let tears wash away the blockage which holds you back.

Dear one, you are what you are, and that is beautiful to see. If only you could love and be concerned about yourself as you are for others. Would you not try doing this for today? Make it a learning day for yourself; concentrate on what you *know* you do well and see the growth in yourself. If only you could see this growth from our view. It is you, yourself, who is not accepting of your own talents; others only *try* to help this growth.

The more exposed you are to new situations, the more you can grow. No one judges you, so why do you crucify your own being? You are to yourself like the Pharisees were to Jesus. Your heart is pure, your desire to help and heal is sincere, but your ego tries to kill the talent by judging against another. Your cross is lack of confidence and belief in what you are. Love is of most importance, and that, my dear one, you have in abundance. Love your own being as much as you love others. Nurture your own being as you nurture others. Today is another gift from God, so enjoy it with love. We will be with you and shall help you, dear one. Walk in love and peace.

Monday, May 25, 1992
Spirit:

Humility, dear one, is a great virtue, but if one fails to use this humility to help others, what has he gained? Is this not true of all of the fruits of the spirit? When one becomes aware that indeed he is learning to tap into God's powerful and loving energies, is it not a waste to fail to channel this energy into a helpful mission? This, dear one, is the importance of being present at workshops. Continue to be on guard against undermining your own abilities with a negative attitude. There is *nothing* one cannot do, or learn to do, if the desire is present and one is willing to pray and work hard for its fruition. It is at this level that the spirit world can be of great help to you. Know this and continue to keep on keeping on.

Diane:

(At this point I became aware of who it is talking to me.)

Yes, indeed it is Saint Germain talking to you. For you see, Diane, Philip (Burley) is giving so much of himself in this work that he needs those who love him and see his closeness to God. We need people such as these to pray strongly for him each day. We choose you to send forth your love and your energies to him, for we see the dedication of your heart and the willingness to serve others. Thank you, my child.

Monday, June 1, 1992

Diane:

I miss Ang so much, and as the time approaches that I shall be by myself, I pray for the courage, strength and faith to not be a burden to anyone. Life must change, and I with it. Each has his own star to follow and success story to write, and I must give each the freedom to find his own destiny. Please, dear Heavenly Father, show me the pathway for your will be done, not mine. I continue to seek thy strength in myself. How does one find the heart of God? Where do I fail to heed the call of love itself? The questions are many, but the answers are few, and yet, I have truly learned so much. I am most grateful for the enlightenment to this date.

Spirit:

Spiritual growth takes place over time; it is usually a slow, steady process that takes place throughout eternity. Patience is the key to all knowledge, dear one. Peace and tranquility within one's own being gives one the patience needed to find God's will. Each is carefully guided and trained, and the longer it takes to find the truth, because of the suffering involved, the closer one comes to God's heart. Are you not finding that love dwells in the center of all things? To reach perfection one must see with the eyes of a child, filled with wonder, acceptance and an unshakable faith.

Continue to read and study about *faith*. It is a cornerstone of our relationship with God. He who loves with unquestionable faith can do the impossible.

For example, you have experienced the fragrance of roses around you when none where physically present and wondered if, perhaps, the fragrance was coming from those of us in spirit. We do bring such phenomena to you; have faith that it is so. Do not doubt your experiences especially when one of the reasons you are journaling is to open your spiritual senses. Faith opens the door between you and us, whereas doubt closes it. Please depend on faith and belief to strengthen the link between us. We hear your heart's desires and come close to help you. Peace be with you.

Saturday, June 6, 1992

Diane:

I continue to read and think about and meditate upon healing. I do believe that each of us has the ability to realign our molecules to perform properly and produce health. This is not to say that visits to doctors are not wise or necessary at times. But too many people look to medicine and drugs for help, instead of looking within for guidance and listening intuitively to one's own body. I shall strive for a closer relationship within myself to find God's brilliant energy—a tonic for health. The ability to accept change, to adjust to the reality of what is and carry on; this is truly the strength from God within. Health is a by-product of learning the need of being in oneness with God who is all love. How does one strive to learn more of God's love?

Spirit:

Sacrifice is a necessity in giving unconditional love. One must give up their will for God's will. Jesus was all-loving. He served others before himself, for he understood the heart of the Father. Each time we joyfully perform a tedious task or willingly show kindness to another, we are imitating God and learning the meaning of doing God's will. To do God's will, one does not think of self at all.

Look at the saints and people like Mother Teresa of India. Seek within and find the true desire of your being. Write it down and pray for its fruition everyday at least once, and keep it shining brightly before your eyes as you pray and ponder this dream deep within your heart. Then wait with great patience until the seed grows the necessary roots to produce the stem, leaves, and finally, the glorious bloom. This is the reward for finding God's will.

We grow into our dreams and desires, but one must keep on keeping on. The world is filled with beauty and love for those who can see the inner light which shines from all things. One attracts to himself light of equal intensity, so strive to make your light even brighter, dear one. There is no limit to the light of love, so seek within your own being as you meditate this night. It is there for the asking. Ask, seek, knock. Peace be with you.

Saturday, June 12, 1992
Spirit:

Spiritual truths can be available to each human being, but there is a price one needs to pay in order to understand this truth. What, you ask, is this price? From spirit, we say, it can be paid in many ways. To suffer and still keep love and faith alive is the secret formula. Hardship is unbearable first and foremost in the mind. Once the challenge is conquered in the mind, dealing with hardship becomes easier. The love energy which is released is the energy those in spirit can use to send enlightenment. Merit is another way of saying "to be worthy" and those who prove to be deserving are not forgotten. The law is very exacting and even though it appears unfair at times, it is because you, on earth, cannot see the whole picture. Those with strong faith and belief in God understand this, and wait with patience. Master yourself, dear one, and more understanding will open up to you. Walk in love and peace. We come close to help and guide you.

Tuesday June 16, 1992

"Look Into The Light. Your personal contribution toward the great plan for the evolution of man is to dwell continually upon the love of God; to look always into the light and so train yourself to recognize God's great goodness working through everyone else."[14]

Diane:

Believe I am turning into a night person. I seem to come more alive as night approaches. It's amazing how things change, and I with it. I must learn not to become annoyed with myself when I accomplish less than desired. Reading is a productive activity and I do not spend enough time at it. There are so many things in life I would like to learn or try or see or do. The list is limitless; that's another proof to me, of eternity. With so much yet to do, lifetime in the physical world will run out, but not so with life in the spirit world. The doubting Thomas-type people spend so much time looking for physical proof and answers, they allow little time to seek for spiritual answers. This is why meditation becomes so very important. Quieting of the mind and withdrawal from physical distractions and problems leaves the spirit within time to project solutions. Prayer enhances one's ability to listen and join in with the power of God, our creator.

Wednesday, June 17, 1992

"We often forget that the action we are contemplating contains the seed of its result."[15]

Diane:

This statement says so much. Would I be wise enough to write an essay on this thought? How careful are most of us when we contemplate an action?

Spirit:

Again we remind you that the unconditional love one holds in his heart is the guiding light. He who truly loves will not contemplate to hurt another. He instead will see the possible results of the seed and plan his moves wisely. This is not to say that one will never hurt another, for there are times when the truth is hurtful. However, love can ease the pain of the truth for heartfelt sincerity bridges the gap between two people.

Life is made manifest by a continual flow of decisions; many affecting the lives of others. The wise one who seeks to walk the spiritual path will ponder carefully his every move and test his inner being to seek the answer. The subconscious self knows what the conscious self should do, but many fail to listen and heed that place where the truth dwells. Thoughts continually are sent to each, but many fail to listen.

Keep on talking about thought, prayer and meditation whenever possible, dear one. It does make a difference, even if you cannot see results immediately. Wisdom and healing take time. Plant these seeds and let God make them grow. We come close to help you. Walk in peace.

Friday, June 19, 1992

"If you want to judge your spiritual progress (meditation), ask yourself these questions: Am I more loving? Is my judgment sounder? Do I have more energy? Can my mind remain calm under any provocation? Am I free from the conditioning of anger, fear, and greed? Spiritual awareness reveals itself as eloquently in character development and selfless action as in mystical states. Authentic mystical experience changes the way you see the world and the way you live."[16]

Diane:

True joy is found when the mind is still, not when it is excited.

Sunday, June 28, 1992

Diane:

I want to record a few things about Edgar Cayce from the book *The Sleeping Prophet* by Jess Stearns.[17]

"He was aware that most bodily illness was born of the mind, of emotional frustrations, resentments, anger."

"How to bring about lasting peace? The thing is to start with yourself. Unless you can bring about within yourself that which you would have in the nation or in any particular land, don't offer it to others."

"Keep the mental in the attitude of constructive forces. See in every individual that which is hopeful, helpful. Do not look for others' faults but rather for their virtues, and the virtue in self will become magnified. For what we think about, that we become."

"He synchronized long life with selflessness, pointing out that in time the age span of a population would increase most in those nations practicing the greatest altruism."

And from *An Angel in My House* by Tobias Palmer: "Angels enter our lives at the invitation of our spirit."[18]

Diane:

I ponder exactly what I will do with all of these tidbits of meaningful information. If it's only for my own spiritual growth and awareness, it will be time well spent. I am a *very special* person and I try to bombard my head with these thoughts. Everyone should, for if each became capable of truly loving himself and enjoying time spent alone with oneself, the quality of life for all would be raised considerably. Heaven on earth must be the sum total of all of the parts, and each human being is of great importance. Family life will be the savior of mankind for all important forms of love are contained within a happy family.

Monday, July 13, 1992

Spirit:

Fear is the manifestation of negative thoughts and patterns one develops from childhood and beyond. To break through these fears, one must concentrate on his love of God so that faith may teach there is no fear after all, but only lack of trust in God.

Is this an easy task to conquer one's fears? Indeed not, and this is why we come to remind you to pray, meditate and open yourself to universal knowledge which gives one wisdom to cope with the troubles and vicissitudes of daily life. The more one is filled with gratitude and remembers to thank his Heavenly Father for his many gifts, the greater will be one's communication with God.

Pray not only when hard times come, but rather as an ongoing dialogue with your Maker and his Son. Fear is from the dark side and prayer brings light. To pray reinforces one's ability to tightly grasp unto faith and the truth of God's laws. Continue your upward climb, dear one, and remember we are always nearby to help. May peace be your constant companion. God bless you.

Saturday, July 25, 1992

Diane:

So many things to think about—I trust that my mind is up to it, for I have been preparing myself for what is to come.

Spirit:

Watch closely, dear child, for those small signs and signals which are sent to you in many different ways. Your pathway is guided through feelings, intuition, knowledge from books, and awareness of little, subtle signs which point the way. Too many people in the world today are only aware of material gratification and fail to notice the beauty and love close around them. Is not a smile one of God's precious gifts? Analyze its special beauty—so simple, so loving and so easy to give. It cheers, uplifts and sends out signals of peace. Is this not so, my child? And how do you notice the response of others? Do you pay attention to this reaction of others? Yes, we see that you do. Teach this simple gesture to all you meet!

Diane:

My poem:
A smile, so simple, but where does it end?
Its effect is far-reaching to stranger or friend.
The love in one's heart can easily show
To bring comfort and gladness to even a foe.
So each time you meet face to face with another
Smile brightly and treat him as though he's a brother.
For God gave to each one a piece of his heart.
Share it, send it, a smile from the start.

Tuesday, August 4, 1992

"Enthusiasm is no Pollyannish, sweetness and light, unborn and fortuitous concept. It is a strong, rugged mental attitude that is perhaps hard to achieve, difficult to maintain, but powerful, so powerful."[19]

Diane:

Have been annoyed with myself of late, for somehow I am lacking in something, and this small writing hit the nail on the head—enthusiasm. How does one find or rebuild one's enthusiasm for prayer—to become spiritually closer to God and ultimately do his will? To hear that special calling and train oneself to perform those tasks one's heart so deeply desires? Please, dear friends, help me to understand and find my way to help others.

Spirit:

Seek to enjoy and find pleasure and satisfaction in the little experiences of each day in smiles and friendly words spoken. All of those little deeds of selflessness perhaps seem small in your eyes, but vision from the earth plane is very limited, dear child. Many small droplets of water in time will be able to overflow a large container, so it is true that many small kindnesses will fill the heart to overflowing with love as well. As this heart grows with love, the hidden desire will manifest itself at the perfect moment in the perfect way. Plateaus are testing points as well as resting points. To pass the test, one must push forward even if enthusiasm is lacking, knowing with faith that the incentive will again appear. Do you not see how the spirit never tires? It is one's physical body that thwarts the desire, and once this important knowledge is unconditionally accepted, the spirit may always be triumphant.

See these last few nights as a big stepping stone, for you come to pray and meditate in spite of fatigue. We can work with the energy of such decisions. This is the meaning of sacrifice. To walk the extra distance in spite of the difficulties, gains one the wisdom of seeing beyond the hardship of the moment. One grows in strength of spirit. You see, dear child, your intuition guides you so well. Listen closely to its lessons. Seek always for peace in all that you do and walk in love. We come close to help. God bless you.

Thursday, August 6, 1992

Diane:

My faith is growing stronger and there is much less doubt and fear within my being. The classes taken have indeed been a help, and I am looking forward to taking more as each one in my family becomes settled and needs me less. How interesting life is as it unfolds each day! Wonder if I shall one day conquer fatigue, and know that I can call upon those who help me in such situations.

I am thinking about daily life—not energy in a crisis. God has already blessed me with learning his merciful and loving kindness in such situations. To find joy in everything is my goal. To love unconditionally is my goal. To help others to heal themselves is my goal. The ultimate goal is to be a channel pure enough to be worthy to do Heavenly Father's will. So be it. Amen.

Spirit:

Believe, dear child, believe! The brightness of your desire to love unconditionally can be seen, and others will follow this example. Seek the silence within so that you will hear his will. Desire and enthusiasm will carry you where you wish to go, even when the pathway makes you weary and discouraged. Rise above this and see only success. Positive thoughts and ambition are a driving force; yet so much of this power, which molds a person's life, cannot be seen with one's physical eyes. Faith helps one to see into this invisible world of spirit, so believe, dear one, believe. Peace be with you always.

Saturday, August 15, 1992
Diane:

Happy anniversary! Since it is our thirty-eighth anniversary today, I am mindful and grateful for all of the lovely times Ang and I had together for many years. As I sit here thinking about us, the thought of working on my book appears. And here I sit in Ang's chair with energy filling my ears, so I know he is near.

Ang:

Spiritual hugs are a different sensation, but can you feel the energy moving around you? Words are not necessary when true love flows from heart to heart. Instead, within the solitude of the mind, thoughts become as one. Happy anniversary, dearie.

"I see your smile when I'm alone;
I hear you call my name;
Remember, love, though we're apart;
I'm with you just the same."

Life is bittersweet, but concentrate your thoughts upon the sweet. This shows reverence to God who blessed us with the knowledge of eternal love while we are still able to help others to understand this light of love. How brightly your light shines, dear wife of mine. I meet your lonely heart, for I, too, miss the sound of physical life, but continue to seek the solace of the spirit. It takes great fortitude to seek what cannot easily be seen. Strive to turn what you feel so deeply into a vision. Return to the meditative state with relentless effort, for the deeper you let yourself plunge, the freer you will become, and we can meet as you release earthly thoughts. Concentrate on nothingness and open the door to a finer vibration. I'm working to line myself up and tune into this frequency: lower vibration for one from spirit and a higher frequency for one from the physical plane.

Are you not wondering if perhaps I have changed in these years since I passed on? What about you, dearie, are you the same? Take away the physical sensations and what remains? The fruits of the spirit (which remember, each one experiences in life) record those feelings in the form of light which shows up distinctly in the aura. Of course, in each there are flaws and mistakes, and one must work to right all of the unkind and hurtful deeds one commits. Unconditional love forgives, and I thank you for all of the prayers and love you send to me and many others. The priorities of my purpose for being have changed, as have yours, but together as one, we have a great power to help many others.

Continue to see God and good and love in all things, and use this energy to heal, uplift and comfort those in need. I am always there to protect and help you. There's no change in those vows we took thirty-eight years ago. Think of me, and I'm there. Reach out to touch and know I'm there. Outwardly many things change, and one has little control over them. However, inwardly each has the ability to command his thoughts to do those deeds which promote the fruits of one's spirit. See if you can name them. ... "the fruit of the spirit is love, joy, peace, patience, kindness, goodness, faithfulness, gentleness and self-control." (*Galatians 5:22–23*)

We've both changed, for God's laws demand this; but love changes not, for it follows one into eternity. I'll love you forever. Peace be with you.

Sunday, August 16, 1992

Spirit:

Vision is the word for today. It was mentioned in last night's writing, and just before coming to the meditation room, you read an article about it in *Unity* magazine. Vision is the inner sight of one's deepest desire or goal. This vision, dear one, will vitalize your interests and again focus the direction unto prayer, meditation and study. It is true that the spirit does not in itself ever tire, but there are times when the body and lack of self-will trick one into thinking the spirit has weakened. How difficult it is to reverse this feeling into one of enthusiasm and zeal. Analyze less and pray more. Ask for fortitude and guidance. Return to the discipline of your daily routine. Search for the help which surrounds you and find joy in every task. Joy follows right thinking and living; prayer teaches one the right pathway.

Thursday, September 3, 1992

"By moving closer to the Lord in meditation, by calling on him with his holy name, by striving to carry out all the disciplines that wise spiritual counselors have recommended through their own lives, we can gradually ally ourselves with the Lord so completely that we have access to everything that is his. We learn love without limit, courage without fail, wisdom that can penetrate the toughest problems life offers."[20]

"There is always something beautiful to be found if you will look for it. Concentrate on beauty rather than on the reverse. This positive, loving attitude toward life and people is all part of the divine magic which we are endeavoring to reveal to you. It is helping you to perceive the divine Presence, helping you to put into operation the divine magic which heals."[21]

Diane:

The above is most helpful at this moment of my life. Sometimes I think perhaps I look at life too simply, and this leads me astray into more negative thoughts about myself.

Spirit:

Plateaus are okay. Rest is part of God's plan for each, and one must be careful always to stay within the guidelines of positive thinking. You know without a doubt within your own being that God and his spirit world places in front of each the best pathway to be followed. If one fails to notice the first time, and the message is of importance, one must have faith that it will be presented again. Have you not seen this to be true many times, my little one?

You will hear and you will follow, for self-discipline teaches one to listen to the voice from within, which is the voice of God. Affirm many times what you desire, and it shall become so. Never falter, never fear, and love shall take you where you want to be.

As you release your loved ones to find their own way, as indeed you must, many new avenues will cross in front of you—busy avenues in which you will wish to travel. There is much yet to be done, my child, and we see the bright light of service emerging from within. It will not be overlooked or wasted, so continue to strive for perfect discipline and self-control. We shall send signs, experiences and people to help you do the work of our Heavenly Father. You are a special person with talent, so continue to grow inwardly by following those interests which truly appeal to you. If it feels right, act upon it and do it. It is the effort from which energy is released and not always upon the end result. The end result and its meaning from spirit appears quite differently from what you perceive on earth.

This is a difficult task for us, because so few realize the importance of the spirit world and its effect on those still in their physical bodies. This is especially true of one in your age bracket. Skeptical human beings are much more difficult to teach and reach from spirit. When one does not believe without physical proof, our influence passes by almost unnoticed and so much unnecessary suffering is the end result.

We talk to you this way because you understand and it is possible for you to influence many others. The ripples of truth keep moving outward, much more perhaps, than you realize. One does not have to stand up and loudly declare his beliefs, but those who quietly live the truth are seen and believed by others. The truth rings a bell even if it appears to be inaudible within most human beings; yet all who believe must do their part to encourage another to follow this intuition. Peace be with you. We come close to guide you.

Tuesday, September 15, 1992
Diane:

It is very late, but I couldn't let another day go by without coming to ponder and be grateful. I know God and my many friends understand how easy it is to break the habit of meditating because one is too tired, but rationalization must never become an excuse. I shall gain more energy by coming here. I do not understand exactly how it works, but know it is true. How does it work?

Spirit:

Energy of the spirit comes directly from the source of God, so it is an unending supply. To tap into such energy, one must learn its secrets. Life is the doorway, and love is the key with which to open God's eternal source of energy of the spirit. Each time one gives that extra effort to help another through selfless love, he earns the right to find more energy within his own spirit. You must remember, dear one, that the laws of truth are very exacting. They do not change or vary for as the spirit grows in understanding, the body must follow. Too often those on earth let the body dictate to the spirit and unhappiness and poor health are the result. This is not to say that one should fail to heed the fatigue of the body for it must rest, but instead one must be careful to always give dedicated time to the spirit so that it may grow.

Physical life is limited; spiritual life is eternal. Walk steadily on your pathway, dear one. We hear your prayers and know the desires of your heart. Grow in love; we come close to help you. God bless you and walk in peace.

Thursday, September 24, 1992
"Get thy tools ready, God will find the work."²²

Diane:

I'm learning to tap into more energy, but the body does overpower my thinking, sometimes too often. I shall continue to strive for self-mastery and awareness, and give thanks for all of the loving help I receive. Frustration is my enemy for it leads me to less patience with my own being. Life is certainly interesting for I have great patience with others, but not always with myself. Why is this so?

Spirit:

Patience is a God-given virtue and as one spiritually aligns himself with God and becomes closer to his perfection, the individual will become more patient with himself. You see, dear one, the God image within senses this chasm and as it becomes less deep the spirit wants to speed up its union with God. Hence, the impatience factor becomes more acute. Look upon this as real progress, my child. It is the awareness and learning to control one's being, plus the striving to love and bring all things into perfect unity which teaches one the mysteries of eternal wisdom. Be consistent and hard on yourself, yes; but the strength of love comes from first loving and accepting yourself.

How can one love another, if he fails to love himself? One need not accept those traits which turn one away from God. Rejection of self is nothing more than the inner knowing of one's distance from the pure love of God's being. The tools of rejection are many: procrastination, rationalization, pity, selfishness, greed, jealousy, envy and so on. Once one develops total honesty within himself and learns to forgive his own transgressions, he becomes able to forgive others, and in the process he finds peace, joy and truth in the power of love. Continue to seek and you shall find, my child. Let not one day go by without gratitude for all of your many blessings. Thank God personally so his love may manifest through you to help others. We hear your prayers loud and clear. Peace follows you everywhere. God bless you.

Sunday, October 19, 1992

"We must not wish anything other than what happens from moment to moment, all the while, however, exercising ourselves, in goodness. A tremendous amount of our vital energy is squandered in the vacillations of the mind. If things go our way, we get elated; if things do not go our way, we get depressed. Yet elation and depression are made from the same cloth. It is when the mind is getting elated that we need to be very vigilant, because what goes up will inevitably come down. If, through the practice of meditation and repetition of the mantra, we can keep the mind calm when good things are coming our way, then when bad things come, we won't be depressed. Our mind will stay calm. Only then will we be free to be truly spontaneous in our response to life."[23]

Spirit:

The deeper one travels into his own being and finds added strength from God, the greater will become his energy level and ability to control his own thoughts and emotions. This, my child, is a law of truth from God. It is the expanding of one's connection with God, the releasing of one's self will which brings peace and freedom and the ability to love more fully. God's heart encompasses all things; it is up to each human being to search for the pathway into the energy of such love. We who help you from spirit are always making you aware of these great truths, and you feel that progress being made. We salute your tenacity and faithfulness and encourage your battle to remain always on the side of light, of love, of God. It is not an easy battle, but well worth the struggle.

Physical life is difficult but so important for the development of one's spirit. The so-called obstacles that loom in the pathway teach one the tools of the spirit. Each time one becomes more skilled in his own ability to overcome these problems, he grows in truth and spiritual energy. Over physical time, one grows in wisdom and others begin to notice; then, they too begin to search deeper within their own being. Those truly dedicated to God shine forth like a beacon in the dark. They travel the road of life with God's love in their hearts, and their energy level and accomplishments prove, without a doubt, their devotion to God.

The key word is devotion—to give over wholly or purposefully as a cause, use, or end. Give yourself wholly to your Heavenly Father, dear one, and as a master potter, God will mold and use you as a channel of love.

Wednesday, October 28, 1992
Spirit:

Can you not feel the growth of love and understanding within your own heart, dear one? We see your thoughts continually active in ways to help and do for others. This is true progress. Understanding is the ability to pull those bits and pieces from experience which ring true, and focus them into what is known as wisdom.

Wisdom lives within all human beings, but false beliefs and lack of love keep it hidden. Teach all that you meet the secret of reaching God's truth through what you have learned. Many come to listen to you read. Very few in physical life take the time to do this, and your efforts are indeed appreciated. Those in spirit can influence their loved ones on earth, so your reading of the Bible is twofold.

We see your humility, dear one, although you would not say this is so. We come to support your efforts highly and to give you more self-confidence to pursue the task of enlightenment to others. We push you to try new experiences in order to prepare you for even greater tasks. You know unquestioningly that at the perfect moment you will know God's will—the purpose for your remaining years. What joy it brings to know you hear us! Peace be with you, my child. We come close to help you.

Saturday, October 31, 1992

"Oh God, to reach the point of death only to find that you have never lived at all."[24]

Spirit:

The core of one's being belongs to God. The wider the opening to God's source becomes, the brighter and more beautiful one can be spiritually.

The light of your countenance will burn with ever greater intensity. The fuel of love, faith, hope, patience, goodness, kindness, joy, peace and moral strength determines its brightness. Can you not see that the energy of the physical body is fed by the fuel of the spirit?

When this truth is more widely understood, the world will find more love and patience among its inhabitants. Many false truths have clouded the vision; mainly, the misuse of money and the selfish desire for instant self-gratification. So called "death" is feared, and too few understand the beauty of returning to God. Prepare yourself well, my child, to influence all that you come into contact with, for you see, the vision of a few *must* influence the thoughts of many. Continue to open the connection for we know your every desire, and that of your loved ones. Peace be with you.

(Later)
Spirit:

We lead you ever so gently on the pathway of spiritual growth—a tiny glimmer of that which is yet to come. What joy in knowing you hear us as we communicate between the two worlds on wings of thought! The purity and openness of mind widens the channel through which we communicate. Work fervently to hear our message, dear one. Few on earth are aware of the great love and divine help which filters into the physical plane from the spirit world. The answers to all things are within each human being once one opens the channel to God's law of truth. Love, prayer, study and meditation give one the tools with which to practice, but the physical body must listen to the spirit and take the *time* to find this truth.

It is indeed strange, the word, *time*. In physical life, time is so important in one's life, for do not most people live by time? Yet, in the world of spirit time has little meaning. This is a paradox, and it takes much thought and soul-searching to find the answer. Minutes can seem like hours, and yet hours can fly by like minutes. What decides this difference? Is it not love and positive thinking which influences one's attitude toward life the most?

True love dissipates all fear and anxieties in one's life, while positive thinking makes it possible to face all experiences of life with at least a tinge of joy, no matter how small. Always strive for that positive motive which lies behind all moments, and thank your Heavenly Father for the blessings that emerge from these moments. Love, positive thinking and gratitude will take you far along the spiritual pathway, dear one, for this formula leads one to God's laws of truth. Peace within is truly a treasure. We come close to you always.

Tuesday, November 10, 1992
Diane:
Now to see if Ang has a special message for me—must try and calm myself.

Ang:
Happy birthday, dearest one! I joined you for lunch even though you were not aware, except you did notice the rainbow in the water glass. Also, why not give Jo the Wonder Book on rocks since she was interested? I appreciated that compliment about being very knowledgeable. The knowledge available on this side is overwhelming. You'll love it.

I, too, miss talking as we once did in physical life, but what a blessing for us to be able to communicate through our thoughts. Your love and the ability to think and understand who you are within is truly a gift from the high realms. Be as proud of yourself as I am proud of you for you are indeed a beacon of love and light to all those who gaze upon you. You think with such pure thoughts and you give without asking for a return. Do you know how precious this gift is and how far-reaching the results are? Of course you do not, for you are much too busy doing the next good deed.

Kindness is the key to God's unconditional love, so continue on this spiritual pathway. Around each bend in the road you will discover new truths and more wisdom. Your love continues to support and uplift my life in spirit, and I hear your every word. I know my love continues to flourish in your life and gives you courage to carry on, for we are truly blessed by God in eternal marriage. Your faith is so powerful; you turn all you touch into an awareness of love. There is always joy when I come into your realm, for you live life in the heart of a rainbow, always finding a color in even a gloomy atmosphere. I have nothing but pride and love to present to you this day, but, in time, we shall communicate even better. Happy birthday, dearie!

Wednesday, November 11, 1992
Diane:

Striving for more patience to accept each day as it comes, and let go and let God show me the next mission in my life. Sorry to say I have been a bit slack in my prayer life, but vitality will return with diligent effort. I have spent more time writing and reading, so all is not lost. Upon awakening, I received a meaningful message and some thoughts about the symbolism in interpreting dreams.

For example, if I dream someone is dead or has died, it could mean a new beginning. We are so locked into certain thought patterns it behooves each to spend time digging deeper for the true meaning. Death is not the end, but rather the start of a new beginning. So often I am amazed at the wonderful, positive thoughts that are sent to me from spirit whether from angels, master teachers or someone who has passed on. Perhaps one day I shall be able to know, yet that is not really necessary, for love is universal even into the cosmos. One day I shall understand so much more.

Sunday, November 15, 1992
Diane:

I still pray for guidance and help in the specific way in which I am to help this troubled world. I feel in a bit of a lull, but not in a questioning way, and I'm beginning to understand the laws of truth a little more. Yet I have not found the piece of puzzle where I fit in.

Perhaps the problem stems from within my own being. The lack of confidence to *know* I am heard, and make and will continue to make a difference, is such an anguish for me. Why is this so? I can't put my finger on it, but this feeling affects my prayer and meditation life.

Spirit:

If, dear one, we say it is the negative forces working to discourage you, would you believe us? There is never a time when one may stop striving for positive thoughts. One *never* arrives at that plateau of perfection until he is one with God, so can you not see that the struggle to grow must be perceived as a joyful one? As soon as one begins to wonder or doubt what he *knows* to be the truth, apathy begins to show its unwelcome presence.

Continue on as if this feeling was not present, and it shall disappear. What one refuses to think about and dwell upon will dissipate—much as mist or fog dissipates and it is again clear. This is true of thoughts as well. Concentrate instead upon your desire to be of service, and you shall be heard, my child. We need many such as you to help us awaken this world. Peace be with you.

Saturday, November 28, 1992
Diane:

How are you, darling? It's six years since your passing.

Ang:

I couldn't be better except that I miss you too. There is always so much to do and the spirit world constantly revitalizes one's being, so there is no fatigue. This is such a delight. Family members and friends visit you often so there is no need to ever be lonely. How sad that man cut himself off from the glorious world of spirit while he is still in the physical body. God allows those who earn the right a small glimpse of what will be.

Teach others as much as you can for it is of such importance that man becomes aware of the truth. Continue to lead others in this pathway of light. The love between us shall remain throughout eternity. You make me so proud as you continue to grow and find the true meaning of love. As you grow, so do I, for we are as one. Peace be with you.

Sunday, November 29, 1992

"Whatever I am offered in devotion with a pure heart—a leaf, a flower, fruit, or water—I accept with joy."[25]

"We can look upon everything we do, no matter how seemingly insignificant, as a gift to the Lord. If we hoe the garden carefully so that our family, or a neighbor's family, or someone in need can have fresh vegetables for dinner, that is an offering to the Lord. If we work a little more than is expected of us at something that benefits others, that too is an offering to the Lord. Everywhere, in every detail of daily living, it is not a question of quantity or expense that makes our offering acceptable; it is cheerfulness, enthusiasm, and the capacity to forget ourselves in helping others."[26]

"If you want to learn my teachings, you do not have to come with me (to India). Take the money you would spend on the airfare and give it to the poor. There! You have *all* my teachings."[27]

Diane:

Someone I care about deeply does not seem very well at the moment. How can I best help him to find himself and what dwells within his own being? For what is the purpose of concern if one cannot do something to help?

Spirit:

Concern and caring are helpful because these send loving thoughts out into the atmosphere where those who can build a brighter aura are able to utilize the good and positive energy. When one becomes enlightened, his faith will make this energy transfer possible. Pray for him and hold him dear to your own heart and watch the improvement. See it in *your imagination* and let those who work with him help him to do the rest. Many times one must reach "rock bottom" before he can see any light of truth. Strong light from one who cares can help to ignite the desire of another who is struggling. The milk of his life has been spilled so there is no use in lamenting it, yet, there is still time to gather more milk for another try. *This*, my child, is the important fact: there's still time to try again. Send forth your guardian angel to gather those who can influence him and place him upon your healing list.

Tuesday, December 1, 1992

Diane:

A bit late, but there seems little time to spend here, so I must take advantage when I can. Always on the back burner of my mind is "what am

I to do with my remaining years to help others?" I try hard to be patient and yet not miss the helpful hints sent my way. Perhaps one day peace shall reign within and I will just *know*. I am learning everyday to control my thoughts and to make them pure, as if in prayer all the time. I am far from being able to do this, but the desire is there and that is so very important.

Are there any comments from spirit on this topic?

Spirit:

We marvel at your insight, so please give yourself more credit. More help can come through when one keeps positive and uplifting thoughts in mind. It is necessary to give oneself constant pep talks, for one continues searching best when progress is reviewed frequently. Energy comes in many forms so be aware always of warmth, tingling, ringing in ears, and of course, with light. Keep all of these avenues close at hand for awareness makes them stronger and more powerful. Give yourself more credit for your accomplishments.

We cheer and applaud you from here. Remember always to live each day, each moment in gratitude to your Heavenly Father for the bounty of his gifts. What is more precious than the smile of a baby or devotion from your children, or the beauty just outside your window as nature sends its charms in so many ways, or the faithful Smokey who cuddles on the bed?

Be a teacher each day of your life and show others the way by your example. Stray not from the truth as it continues to unfold before you, for others are influenced by your perseverance, patience and love. Keep on keeping on, dear one. We come close to help you. Peace be with you.

Wednesday, December 9, 1992

"To have courage, think courage. We become what we think. As you think courage, courage will fill your thoughts and displace fear. The more courageous your thinking, the greater the courage you will have. Act courageously. Practice that 'as if' principle. Act as if you are courageous and you will become as you think and act. A person should pray for courage as he prays for his daily bread. And your prayer for courage will enable you to think and act with courage."[28]

"Your shoulders are strong and your heart shows compassion, so take that which comes your way with wisdom and grace. Each can grow in love, and there are many different avenues to finding love. Be thou neither critical nor judgmental, but rather use your energies to heal the wounds of life."[29]

"And how, you ask, are we to walk the spiritual path? We answer: Say little; love much; give all; judge no man; aspire to all that is pure and good, and keep on keeping on."[30]

Spirit:

Be faithful to your dream of doing God's will, for at the perfect moment you will know your next mission of physical life. We come to help you in this difficult time. Often others cannot see the pain you must endure. In their misunderstanding it is easy to seemingly attack another and many times, part of it is true, for no one is faultless. However, he who can hold his tongue and respond with kindness does much to heal the world.

Pray for this strength, dear child. It is far easier to blame than it is to forgive. Study your strengths and weaknesses closely, and ask for help from those who know the true meaning of love. If you can stay calm and at peace in all situations, the outcome will not be wasted with emotional outbursts which drain the energies of the spirit. Look beyond and place relationships in their rightful place, for you see, dear one, your children are only loaned to you for a short span of years.

Unconditional love is given freely, so they owe you nothing.

This prayer is most important in times of change: "Let nothing disturb you, let nothing frighten you. Everything passes away except God. God alone is sufficient." Your duties in this instance are indeed over. Mourn them not; for you are becoming stronger each day. If the shoe fits, wear it; if not, seek that which does fit. It is in the seeking that you will find the answers.

Friday, December 11, 1992
Spirit:

The "poor me" syndrome only closes the door to becoming a channel of God's will. Unconditional love is the result of many brief moments in giving of oneself, and taking the time to care and notice when asked, or more importantly, when it is needed. What merit is there in giving only when one feels like it? Very little. The important lesson to learn in one's spiritual growth is to give above and beyond the emotional self.

To forgive before or during a problem is the way of a disciple. See the love which can grow out of understanding before its roots have grown. Is this not what one does when planting a seed? One sees the end result through faith. It is no different in planting seeds of love, dear one. See the joyful outcome for as one lives God's forgiving love, the result can be as a miracle, or as so many would say, a coincidence. Yet, another saying goes, "Coincidence is when God works a miracle and decides to remain anonymous."

Is it not sometimes hard to understand and be patient even when one is older and should have wisdom? How then can the young learn unless they can see such love in action? We come often to help you to understand your mission in life, so set the example for others to see. Does it so matter if you can see the results? Faith teaches one to *know* that the result will one day surface. If you need to see the result, then the love given was not unconditional. The greatest gift is a gift of yourself from that place of love which always shines as a beacon in the dark. How can you truly know how many see it, and again, if you could, does it really matter? Feel the love surrounding you and live in peace. Merry Christmas!

Diane:

As I read in *Words to Live By*, this statement fits so well into today's writing: "Everyone sees the Unseen in proportion to the clarity of his heart, and that depends upon how much he polished it. Whoever has polished it more, sees more; more unseen forms become manifest to him."[31]

And these words by Rumi are so helpful also:

"As your meditation deepens, there will still be occasions when you get upset, but you will be able to watch what goes on in the lab of your mind. It is like getting into a glass-bottomed boat, where you venture out onto the ocean and watch all the deep-sea creatures lurking beneath the surface: resentment sharks, stingrays of greed, scurrying schools of fear. You slowly gain a certain amount of detachment from your mind, by which you can observe what is going on, collect data, and then set things right."[32]

Some of the chronic problems that millions of people suffer from today might be solved by gaining a little detachment from their minds and emotions, so they can stand back a little when the mind is agitated and see the ways in which it makes mountains out of molehills. Many problems simply are not real; they start to seem real only when we dwell on them. The thorniest problems to solve are those that are not real; yet most of us go on giving them our best effort.

Wednesday, December 23, 1992
Diane:

I often wonder if I hear the directions clearly from those who guide me. How does one verify this within oneself?

Spirit:

Follow your heart and listen to your thoughts. If in doubt, wait patiently until the all-knowing answer arrives with that extra impetus. Is it difficult to not answer the call of doing the right thing, or that which you should do? Regret, guilt, annoyance always follows when you fail to listen. Is this not true?

Joy, energy, peace and a pleasant contentment are the signs of following the correct pathway. It is wise to always seek, but you are trying too hard if it causes anxiety of any kind. Rather, dear one, wait with patience and heartfelt prayer for further guidance. Have you not seen the perfect solution or answer appear before you at the right time? Enjoy each moment, be kind to all things and love God with grateful praise, and with this formula great things will come your way. Find peace, my child. We are always close.

Saturday, December 26, 1992
Diane:

As John stated, this is the last Christmas with someone still living in the house with me, and this is true. *Unity* magazine this month has some articles about change. To live life fully, one must be able to face change with hope, faith, joy, love, and oh yes, with patience. I have spent quite a bit of time thinking about it. Will I be fearful, lonely, bored, depressed, and adequately prepared to face challenges alone? How should I best prepare for this great change and challenge, dear friends?

Spirit:

Love is the answer to a life that is full. Love everything that surrounds you, and then there will be no room for unwanted thoughts. Positive, loving and fruitful thoughts will fill your life with an abundance of health, happiness and activity. If you feel truly as you said, that those interests you do not have time for in physical life you will do in eternity, how can you ponder what your life will be in aloneness?

First, God is always with you, for he dwells within your own being as a constant, loving friend and protectorate, always whispering the truth into daily life. He knows your strengths and will always help you find the strength in your weakness; just ask in reverence and humility. Prayer, your personal conversation with him at any hour and in any situation, will always bring forth courage and confidence. Faith is the connecting link to this help. Meditation, dear one, gives you the tools to control your thoughts whenever needed. Remember to practice regularly for it will give you lasting peace.

Perpetual joy is earned; it does not just happen. Joy is seen through magnified tears. It is God's blessing to those who learn to see beyond the toils of life with optimism. The call of love will keep you busy; love of self, love of family, love of friends, the gift of love to those who need it, and most of all, love of God. The richer and more unconditional this love becomes, the more opportunities you will find to serve his will.

It is necessary to *always* be faithful to those conditions of love you offer up to God. Trust is gained through honest self-examination. Be truthful within your own being and make more room for the wisdom and truth from God. We assure you, dear one, if you do this, there will be no space for loneliness. Those who love you dearly, and there are many, come often to spend time with you. Learn to hear and feel our presence. Peace be with you.

1993

Wednesday, January 6, 1993

Diane:

I must think more about change in one's life.

Spirit:

Change is the catalyst in life. It forces one to continually seek the answers as one walks the pathway of life. Would life not be dull and monotonous without the inspiration of change? Each on earth must learn the lessons which accompany the changes in their life. This is the true purpose of change. Those who suffer the most in physical life are the souls who fail to grow in spirit when confronted with change. One must look inward for help, but too few have learned this most important lesson. If one fails to look inward for answers, the external solution looks to attack and blame others for this change, especially if it is unwanted. Every change has a lesson to learn for how else can the spirit grow within the physical body?

You, on earth, tend to listen mainly to the demands and needs of the physical side of life, spending only a small portion of life connecting to the spiritual side of your own being. Many dread change because it causes upheaval in one's life, yet, in hindsight, it is often the change which brings about good, positive progress in one's life. Yes, many times there is a price to pay for positive change, but how else can the spirit within be heard. Too often you on earth miss the daily contact and limitless help from the world of spirit. You must look for the divine Presence within to make more contact with this untapped source of inspiration. Change can always be turned into a positive experience; this is the key to the lesson each must learn.

Saturday, January 9, 1993

At the first sign of a challenge, we affirm: Good will come from this. We hold to this thought as we pray for God's guidance. The spiritual support we receive will sustain us as we wait patiently for our good to unfold.[33]

Diane:

Change is a challenge, and I know at the perfect moment when I have learned the necessary lessons of living alone, the answer for the remaining years of my life will become known to me. I learned a number of years ago to live *this* very day to the fullest and make it a masterpiece, taking time to do unto others as you would have them do unto you.

Spirit:

Yes, my child, it is indeed an upward climb to seek the God within. Seeking good brings goodness into your own aura and being. Compassion is a form of goodness. We know that you feel inadequate in your ability to feel compassion, and yet, we wish to inform you that empathy is a twin sister to compassion. They come from the same seed and form equal roots. Look the meanings up in the dictionary and write them down.

Compassion: The deep feeling of sharing the suffering of another; mercy.

Empathy: Identification with and understanding of another's situation, feelings and motives.

If one has compassion, he shares with another, and with empathy one understands another's needs. Are they so different, my little one? No, they are not, so release your own being to find the glory and joy of unconditional love. It is there for all who seek it with a sincere and humble heart.

As each fear is confronted, one by one and erased, what do you think fills that voided space? Love with a capital L. Simple to write, but oh so difficult to accomplish in physical life. As morals and honesty crumble in this money-hungry world, continue to see the truth and goodness of God gaining strength, for there is great power in collective, positive thinking.

AIM (Adventures in Mastery) is filled with such God-centered people. It is through this group that much can be done to help the world. Think big, bigger and biggest, and your influence shall be so. Continue with your affirmations and believe that they are so, for in truth, they are. Follow the dictate of your heart for it leads you well. We come close, especially Angelo to bring comfort, encouragement and love. Keep on keeping on.

Saturday, February 6, 1993

Diane:

God is spirit—logos—thought—invisible—divine order—universal law.

Spirit:

Spirit world came first, for God is spirit. He thought and thought, and with the thought power of his highest realm, he created the physical world. It is patterned after the spirit world complete with divine order, divine love, universal law and truth. Into each one of his creations he gave a piece of himself, blessing mankind and breathing special life into his beloved man. All the rest of his creation was to serve man, for man was to rule and have dominion over all of creation.

God created the physical world with great love for he is a light and an energy of unfathomable love, and his breath gave to each human being the ability to find perfect love. It was through the fall of man that man lost his ability to understand, and to see and believe the great truth of the eternal spirit world.

The plight of man is written in the books of history. The physical side of life has dominated man ever since the fall. Disobedience in following God's divine order and the pathway to spiritual understanding has become so narrow it is not easily seen; it is hidden by the ignorance and selfishness which prevails life as we know it. The salvation of man will surface more abundantly when each human being takes the time in his daily life to quiet himself, and to learn the ability to detach his thoughts from physical concerns. Then he is better able to search for the thread of spiritual and eternal truth.

To live one's life on earth for only the satisfaction of physical and material desires is seeing life as if blind. Too often the search for physical satisfaction crucifies love and the beauty of the spirit which lies within all human beings. It is difficult to see in many, but the light of love is there; it just needs to be ignited through understanding. The search for understanding and love can be found through the discipline of meditation. It takes commitment, but is not the search for peace, healing and love through greater understanding worth a try?

Sunday, February 7, 1993

Diane:

My mind is going in a thousand different directions tonight; I must reel it in to concentrate on only a few things. I spent a quiet day; not accomplishing much, but sometimes think this is good. Tomorrow I may prove to myself that I am disciplined and not walking aimlessly. I've been alone this week and I'm doing okay. It is a difficult change to look at life, at least with physical sight, that I am alone. I know that my spiritual progress would not be as advanced if Ang were still alive, and I am grateful for the opportunity to grow. I am not sad, yet, in truth I miss him as a part of my life.

The feeling is not one of self-pity for I have accepted the necessity of such a sacrifice, but I must admit to myself, deep within, that the situation is not an easy one. I shall pray and meditate to find the strength to accomplish the will of God. He shall not fail to hear my prayer and I know many are sent to help me personally. It is I who must work harder to reach my calling. The desire to be of service stings my eyes with tears, so I shall look upon this as a good and positive omen. I pray for fortitude to ever move on and out to learn more and become more confident.

Spirit:

Confidence in self is of utmost importance. One must be completely convinced of his own ability to hear the voice of God within, even if the journey seems like a lonely existence, for in truth and reality, it shall be a trip of great joy. To love unconditionally and to live for the purpose of helping others is the greatest feat of all, because then one comes closer to God. Know this in your heart, dear one, when fatigue or loneliness start to cloud your joy of living. Even today, as you felt you relaxed too much, you had the discipline to go to the car, carry up the heavy birdseed and throw it to your friends. Is this not true?

Remember, dear one, it is many times the small, seemingly insignificant tasks which build the discipline for greater tasks. No deed done in love is ever lost. Remind yourself of this very important truth. We love you and come so close to help you. Peace be with you.

Thursday, February 11, 1993
Spirit:

We were happy to hear you say that you would speak out on the truth of the spirit world, for you know it to be so true. These are the jewels you have been collecting these past years, and now it is time to share them with others. Once the fear of being misunderstood disappears, all things are possible. If those who grow in wisdom and understanding stay silent, how can enlightenment grow in others? It can't, so prepare yourself to be a channel of God's will and what you need will be supplied to you. Those who move forward with courage will be victorious. It is time to awaken many more to the reality of the spirit world. This is an important part of your mission. Call upon us who stand close by to help.

Monday, February 22, 1993
Diane:

What is to be learned by this horrible situation that we tried so hard to prevent? I feel like a betrayer and yet I did my part, or so I thought.

Jo called asking to go to the emergency room on Sunday, and due to negligence in not reading my friend's living will, she got put on a respirator—her greatest dread of all. What is the meaning of such an act? I have little problem knowing that God and his realms orchestrate so much more than we on earth realize, but to have the faith to await the outcome, especially when it concerns the passing of a loved one, is very difficult for me. Wishes do not always come to pass due to the legalities in the belief of the medical profession.

When does an individual have the right to simply die? Or does the pain and fear of those last moments cause one to change their mind and desire help? Perhaps this would be a good question to ask Saint Germain at a meeting—shall think on this.

I am truly anguished, why? I have failed the wishes of a dear friend, not with intent, but due to circumstances beyond my control. Is this again to teach me to take more responsibility upon myself, or is it time for me to become more forceful? Yet, this is not the person I desire to be. Love, patience and faith must guide me and I am what I am. The respirator will be removed and then it is God's will and Jo's ability to rally. Could this be so? All things are possible with God. Perhaps Jo's anger is with her loss of control over decisions, but who else does she have to vent this frustration upon?

Spirit:

Many lessons must be learned by each soul, and circumstances differ for each one. Pray for faith to believe what you cannot see, dear one. Fatigue makes situations so much harder to bear. We suggest that you calm the turmoil within with your mantra, and find peace in the knowledge that all will work out according to divine order. Live in the security that you are guided carefully and well, in spite of the outward appearance of chaos. You, on earth, see with such limited vision. Be one who has the courage, stamina and faith to face such challenges knowing God walks beside you always. Seek the inner peace, find the light of love and shine it wherever you walk. We stand close by to help.

Saturday, February 27, 1993

Diane:

Each time I work on my so-called estate it amazes me how little meaning there truly is to material belongings. They matter *so little*, yet, the ego within builds them into such importance. It is the heart, the center, where love bears the truth that is everlasting. This is the priceless gift of living which hides itself from much of mankind, for many seek happiness on the physical side through the annals of material possessions and physical pleasures. Only those who seek the everlasting light touch upon the magnitude of God's heart. One, who upon seeing this glimpse of eternity works to teach others, will find total peace, freedom and love within his being.

Spirit:

It is necessary to teach this lesson over and over again, dear child, until one can love by faith alone when dark shadows play upon life and its predicaments. You now can better read the signs that are sent to guide you and this is indeed progress. There is doubt at times, but as you learn to quickly pass through this darkness, the light which guides you becomes brighter each time. We see the growth on many planes; some of it you are not even aware of for change is subtle and of the spiritual realm. Find these hidden areas so that they may break into the open to help many others. The potential is soon to blossom. What you so desire will happen, but always pray, meditate and most of all, dear one, find God's heart in each you meet through your ability to love. This is God's greatest gift. Peace be with you.

Sunday, February 28, 1993
Spirit:

The beauty and the depth of the human spirit can be compared to the unfathomable depth of the oceans, the summit of the highest mountain, and the beauty of nature's most glorious phenomena. The Lord God made them all for each of his beloved children to know, love and share. It is in difficult times that one seeks the comfort, solace and strength to do what has to be done in spite of surmounting obstacles. It is in this situation that God rushes to fill one's being with the necessary energy to fulfill and complete the difficult task at hand. This is unconditional love and those who learn its lesson well each day shall have a piece of heaven with it.

It is these wisdoms of truth which make up the pot of gold at the end of the rainbow: to see the sun before the storm has passed, and to love from the deepest pangs of sorrow to the heights of great joy and ecstasy. It is the key to God's heart. This, my child is true living and for those who can understand, life is eternal now. Each task completed with love and understanding removes yet another obstacle in the spiritual climb to live within God's heart. Well done, my daughter, well done.

Diane:

This was an answer to my week of anguish.

Wednesday, March 17, 1993

Diane:

On my trip home from Long Island, I was almost in an accident. Someone is watching out for me, and my car has been a good one indeed, coming through in the pinches. I am most grateful for the help. I am not nervous for knowing about the world of spirit and becoming closer to God and his truth has indeed eliminated so many of my fears. Taking events and circumstances in stride is easier, but I've found that I must make time to find quiet and peace within myself. If my schedule gets too rushed, I find I become my own worst enemy, especially if fatigue enters the picture. What can I do about this problem, dear friends? It disturbs my inner peace and I have not yet found a solution.

Spirit:

Balance is the key to inner calmness, my child, and as you know, the focal point or fulcrum must be at that perfect place. Once one disturbs the balance, it is felt in the emotions and erupts as annoyance or depression, to name a few. Balance can only be returned through reevaluating your daily lifestyle and thoughts through meditation, prayer and quiet solitude. You *will not* find the answers anywhere except within your own being by listening to the God-force which dwells there.

Failing to heed the call to inner contemplation will further complicate your daily life. If you are saying to yourself, "I am not spending enough time in prayer, in gratitude, in meditation"—listen, for it is true. Nothing is more important to your spiritual growth than giving time to daily devotions. Helping others is of equal importance, but the energy comes from the spirit. If you fail to fuel the spirit through prayer, gratitude and meditation, the balance becomes unequal and you become less effective in your daily life. It is as simple as that!

Spend this time, my child, and you will reap the rewards in your ability to do God's work. Your channel will become more and more open to be of help to others. Balance is a key to God's truth; learn to use it well. We come very close to help you unlock the wisdom which dwells within your own being. Peace be with you!

Thursday, March 18, 1993

Diane:

I watched the movie "A Trip to Bountiful" on TV and it was very touching. Many experiences in life contain sadness and sorrow, so I am grateful to be learning the lessons of compassion. Only then can one bring the full meaning of love to another. First you must feel the heart of another, and this releases the God-given love within your own being.

Spirit:

This, dear one, is why life is filled with so many trials and difficulties; for it offers one the opportunity to learn compassion. Unconditional love then sends roots deep within the spirit, and if nurtured with prayer and thanksgiving, the bud will open to perfection at the perfect moment. Listen well to your heart, for within its beauty you will hear God speaking to you. One is never alone and as you ask, seek and knock, the answers will gently pour forth.

There is no beauty greater than a spirit filled with God's unconditional love. Make each day, no matter what it brings, a lesson of love. We see your heart growing, dear one, and know that there is no end to love; it grows stronger and deeper through all of eternity. This is the joy of love. There is no end, only wonderful beginnings. Through tears, one washes away the impurities which cloud the true meaning of love. It cleanses the spirit and sends it into higher awareness. Be patient, my child, and peace be with you.

Monday, April 5, 1993

Diane:

I must start making a rough outline about the stages and difficulties of becoming a widow and living alone. There is no one to push one into activity—it is accomplished through one's own mastery of herself. There are times when motivation is difficult, but the key is to get started doing "something" and somehow the rest of the day falls into place. Therefore the key words are *action* and *activity*. Once started, one finds much to do. I found this to be very true today. One activity led to another, and of course, there was much more to do than there was time to do it in.

Spirit:

Life can be and is just as joyful and stimulating as one chooses to make it through his thought power. One's life *is* what one thinks and believes it to be. It is as simple as that in theory, yet, programming the physical body to follow the mind takes courage and hard work. Listening to the body is far easier than listening to the spirit, but so much is gained in wisdom, once one disciplines his behavior. Meditation is so helpful in correctly programming the mind that eventually the body will follow the commands of the spirit in spite of itself. The truth of God hidden deep within slowly awakens and brightens the eternal soul until it begins to overpower the desires of the physical body.

Do you not find this to be true? This is why it is so important to share what you have learned with others. Trust with childlike faith that you and John are being carefully guided in your endeavors. Success will be the outcome; we want you to know this. Peace be with you, and rub more peanut oil on your sore thumb joint—it will help.

Thursday, April 8, 1993

Spirit:

Oh, the beauty of the mind, yet how few listen to its timely messages which come through in so many unique ways: dreams; imagination and intuition; persistent, reoccurring thoughts; and visions and ideas. Teach the importance of listening to oneself, for deep inside there is an answer to guide one through any situation. To reach this wellspring of great knowledge and wisdom, one needs only to train himself to listen.

How can we train ourselves to hear when the clamor of daily life is so great, you ask? Again and again we say to pray and meditate until the secret of quieting down one's nervous system is understood and can be accomplished. Silence is indeed golden and the art of meditation teaches the ability to find peace within, despite the unsettling din of the physical world. Confusion is of the physical world, not a part of one who is spiritually alive. If one overemphasizes the physical side of his life, he becomes distorted and crushed by the negative pressures that appear before him. Those who learn to seek self-mastery find themselves able to control their reaction to difficult situations.

You know this will work without fail, my child, for it has been proven to you over and over, so you now no longer doubt. This is why you work hard to find a way to enlighten others. Life is truly meaningless if wisdom and truth hearken at your doorstep and you fail to share this priceless gift with others. Follow your dreams, dear one, for destiny is the fulfillment of such dreams. Peace be with you always.

Monday, April 12, 1993

Diane:

I am working to focus my thoughts upon planning our meditation circle for tomorrow night. Of late my mind has been going in many directions, and now I must use all of the practice and experience over these years to center myself. John is coming over this evening to finalize our meditations. Perhaps my dear friends in spirit will help me plan this first evening, for we have been working and planning for this event for a very long time. I hope it can be a helpful evening for those who attend, and this way it will grow and more people will come. What do you suggest?

Spirit:

Be yourself, dear one, and all things will work out from deep within your heart. It is the energy behind this desire which brings dreams to fruition. The groundwork has been laid; now enjoy what is to come. Work hard to plan the first evening, but unless you relax and enjoy and send forth your own loving energies, the greatest help for others will not be realized.

Life on the physical plane is a continuous seeking for the truth which lies hidden within each person. Meditation and prayer are the access to this great wisdom. Your goal is to open this pathway through knowledge of the tools of meditation and keep it alive through group meetings. Set the standard and be the example through being who you are—a child of love, faith and hope.

Know you can help and guide those who come, for indeed you can. Anyone can look up facts in a book, but how many try to love *every* moment of their life in love and gratitude to God? Too few, dear one, too few, but AIM's goal is to change this.

Use your intuition and follow your heart; how then can you be led astray? Focus your mind and let it not lose strength by allowing your thoughts to run wildly. Write the healing meditation and know it will be right. We come close to help you and John in this new undertaking. It will be a success. Peace be with you, dear one.

Wednesday, April 14, 1993
Diane:

Last night was our first meditation class, and this lovely room was used for the purpose it was built. It was our maiden voyage. We had five others besides ourselves, so eight in total. I will keep a record of who comes. I know in my heart that more will come in time. The movie "Field of Dreams" reminds me of how I feel. "Build it and they will come."

Our desires are sincere and filled with love, and this is most important. With much help from spirit, I have grown in confidence and depth of spirit. I can now do so many things that used to frighten me, such as speaking out in a group. I am most grateful for the opportunity to grow and meet so many new, loving people. I pray that God will accept my continuous prayer each day as I live life, even though I do not spend as much concentrated time in prayer. There are books to be read and people to be helped, as well as chores to be done, so I ask that my sincere desire be understood.

Spirit:

Prayer for the sake of prayer does not contain the energy and power that living prayer contains. To see God in everything one encounters and does, will lead you to your goal. True prayer comes from the love one shares from deep within his own heart and being, for this shows that one has truly found God within himself. Selfless giving—to always have more love flowing to others—is a true sign of spiritual growth. Keep on keeping on, for the spiritual pathway is filled with wonder.

Sunday, April 18, 1993
Diane:

I'm rather lazy today, which annoys me, but I am trying to be patient with myself as I adjust to my life of "aloneness." Like so many other situations in life, what contains joy in one moment, sometimes shows itself as hard work to overcome in another moment. If I continue to truthfully face myself with my shortcomings, in time I *shall* conquer them and replace weakness with strength. The positive thoughts within the mind *can* and *will* battle any problem, once the problem is truly identified. Finding the problem and understanding the cause is the first step; then the mind can face it head on, and send it away with prayer and positive thoughts.

Tuesday, April 20, 1993
Spirit:

Within love lies the secret of healing energy. To know God is to know love, and this revelation releases the many energies of healing. Each must love himself by aligning his daily actions as close as possible to his God-self, his perfect self. The pressures of living oftentimes separate one from his true self and many health problems are the result. If one can begin to realign his thoughts to find the peace of God, miracles can happen.

See with positive eyes, dear one. Always look to God and his high realm spirits for guidance. God will never fail to hear you. Do you remember your reading with Philip? Jesus was there sending healing energy into your arms. As you touch and pray for others, see this healing energy flowing into their bodies as well. Know that you can be a channel and help your fellow man, and it will be so. Peace be with you, child.

Wednesday, April 28, 1993
Diane:

I have *yet* no ability to see the wondrous workings of the spirit world, and John is right. I must take it on faith with only positive reaction.

Spirit:

How you have grown, dear one. Can you not see the growth within your own being? We see the brightness growing. Never doubt the light of healing which permeates your being through love and compassion. Always take the time to comfort your fellow human being; it is in these brief moments of caring that true healing occurs. So many on earth just need to be accepted for who they are, and the love sent forth will begin the healing process. One heals himself ultimately, but it is so helpful to reach out and touch the wonder of love and caring; to follow the light sent forth by those who follow the truth of universal law.

God lives within each human being, but many fail to grasp this truth. Continue to be a light, never doubting your love, but rather send the healing balm forth to those who need to be loved. Illness is mostly of the mind. It comes as a result of trapped emotions which then cause toxic build-up in the physical body, and eventually erupts in problems too many to list. Knowledge of the spirit will cause many to love, and with love, one takes care of himself and others as well. Is not love the beginning of healing? Give this great message to all that cross your pathway, dear one, and keep on keeping on. Peace be with you always.

Thursday, May 6, 1993

Spirit:

Write down your desires and tackle them one by one. Without a purposeful plan, the pressure of what must be done can become a negative force and then little is accomplished. Look within yourself to find solutions to daily problems such as these. The answers for purposeful living are within you. Take the necessary time to let them surface. Time can be your ally if you chose not to let it control your life. The spirit cries to be heard; listen to the message, even if you must use more self-discipline to find the time. Is it not true that often the most helpful ideas come from these moments of silence and seeking?

To quiet the nervous system, to stop the stress of daily life, to seek the beauty of what surrounds you, can only be accomplished by finding that place of peace where God dwells. Take time to put all things into proper perspective. You, on earth, have a great tendency to place importance upon what in truth is not that important. Sift through the pressing "problems" and decide which is truly important. Your spirit self knows and he will guide you well, if you will but listen. Time spent in attunement is always worthwhile.

Dear one, allow yourself to read without pressure. The spirit is released and uplifted by doing what you so desire to do. So many spirits are locked in a prison by the demands of their physical body. Life passes by so quickly. Teach others the importance of spiritual growth by the example of your own spiritual quest. We come close to help. Peace be with you.

Thursday, May 13, 1993
Spirit:

God finds great joy in one who finds happiness in all of the little moments of life. To see God in everything and know peace on earth is a very special blessing. There are many kinds of prayer and God hears them all, my child. We see you never stray far from your spiritual quest, so it is necessary sometimes to change the usual routine. We, who love you so dearly, understand this, and we desire that you put less pressure on yourself. Prayer comes from the heart and is heard through all the activities of daily life. Know this, relax and rest a bit. Peace be with you.

Monday, May 24, 1993
Spirit:

The most important message for each on earth is to learn that fatigue of the mind causes fatigue of the body. If one becomes discouraged mentally, the body reacts by becoming tired. Is this not true, dear one? Is it also not true that when the mind or spirit prepares itself for a difficult situation, the body's stamina is outstanding? This is not to say that rest and sleep should be discouraged, but rather to help those on the spiritual pathway see the truth fully. As we in spirit often observe, many in physical life allow negative thoughts to program the energy of their physical body. Yet a day of accomplishment, satisfaction and joy can be programmed in one's mind upon rising each day, or just before. Positive and uplifting thoughts *do* give energy to one's physical body. As a man thinks, so he is; as he continues to think, so he remains.

Tuesday, June 1, 1993
Diane:

New month—new beginnings! I woke up this morning remembering a weird dream which I won't even try to interpret. The thought came that each time a lull comes in my life before new events begin, I go through the same emptiness. This causes me annoyance because I have been blessed with wisdom and the desire to understand many things which fall in the realm of seeking spiritual enlightenment. Why, I ask myself, do I experience this same empty feeling of aloneness, but not of loneliness? Why can I not conquer this and climb to the next plateau? It seems apparent to me that in order to help others in a similar situation, I need to more deeply understand life. Then, I can forge ahead and overcome the "plank in my own eye." *(Matthew 7:3)*

Spirit:

The best teacher, the best parent, the best human being is one who shines forth his inner light every moment of his life through example, not with words. Important ideas and thoughts within one's mind have great power, but it is the one who learns to implement these thoughts into his daily life who has the potential to help others. Humbleness is earned, my child, and the lesson it teaches is compassion. To understand another human being, one must experience this pain within his own spirit, and of utmost importance, he must show another the pathway out of his pain and distress.

Are you not aware how often you are touched by events and situations you encounter in daily life? Have you not learned how to move on when pangs of pain or discouragement hit you, dear one? Tears cleanse the soul, so welcome them; then delve a little deeper into your own being, healing what holds you back from achieving what you most desire.

Confrontation of self is the key to changing oneself. This includes an honest appraisal of what you desire, where you are, and most important, how to move continually forward to reach this goal. We come to support your endeavors to seek the truth, to climb ever closer to God through the love which grows stronger within your heart. Serve and love others unconditionally and you will find what you seek. We come close to help you. Peace be with you always.

Thursday, June 10, 1993

Diane:

I am at the campsite near the river, and as I sit in bed listening to the lapping of the waves, I find great comfort and peace. For me there is no place (besides my house) more healing and energizing than this camp that Uncle Sumner built. Happy memories contribute, I know, but the cedars teach me a lesson. They survive harsh, bitter winters and remain strong, always giving out their healing energy. The more I grow spiritually, the more I feel connected to all things. Does this mean I am growing closer to God?

Spirit:

Unconditional love does not just happen. One must go deeply inside and face the truth of what he sees, and change what holds him back from seeking love and truth. Take time everyday, if only for a few minutes, to listen to the God force within. Only then can you be free of all fears and anxieties. Unconditional love brings peace in its wake, as well as waves of energy. Stay on the pathway of gratitude. Find joy and beauty in all things. Find the good in every situation. This is the life of a positive thinker. We come close to guide you, dear one.

Saturday, June 12, 1993

Diane:

What would I do without my flowers? They are an integral part of my personality and I thank God for creating them, and to the sprites that help me implement this interest. I do wish I could see this wonderful kingdom of spirit; perhaps one day I shall. How great would be their company! This sets such an example of unconditional love—to love without any desire for a return.

Spirit:

Keep on keeping on, dear one. You truly see so much more than you are even aware of seeing. Since the fall of man, the human being sees only with the physical senses, and if, perchance, he senses more, it is forgotten if not ignored altogether. Do you not see auras, or notice the changes in color from the physical eyes to the spiritual eyes, or energies dancing as you look skyward? Is this not great progress? How many lament the short life span of a shad fly, as you?

Be encouraged, my daughter, and continue to strive for perfected love with all of its wonders. The value of trips to the river is the peace and tranquility where one can find the time and mood in which to practice getting in touch with the basics, which are the energies of the universe. Many would consider the last statement "far out," but in truth, this distance from the basic energies of life causes mankind many of his woes. Those out of touch with the wholeness of life, of God, have nothing to cling to when difficult times appear in their lives.

To understand the smallness and greatness of one's individual span of a lifetime puts an important perspective into one's being. Never again will one place overemphasis on the mundane necessities of life. To experience the richness, the power, the love that is present in each moment should be the purpose of every human being. Continue to believe that this will one day be so, and God can then see his true ideal—the kingdom of heaven on earth.

It is through people like you, and your loving family in both the spirit and physical worlds, and friends like the Burleys, who give *us* the needed impetus to awaken the unenlightened inhabitants of the world to God's truths. Enjoy each moment of life. Walk in love and each day shall be a masterpiece. Peace be with you, dear one. We thank *you* for hearing our message.

Sunday, June 27, 1993
Spirit:

The best advice we can give you in this endeavor, dear one, is write with simplicity and directly from your heart. Those who need help do not need words which preach at them. Unfortunately, one in sorrow receives too much of this from caring relatives and friends. Rather, help those in bereavement *chart* the course which they must travel for enlightenment. Help them to open their minds to awareness, imagination and mastery of self by writing down your experiences as a widow. You must gently guide them into helping themselves by opening up their pathway to experiencing the touch of the dear one who passed over into spirit. It is that lonely feeling of futility which you must remember, and the empathy to reach the lonely hearts through your own experience with loss.

Search and find what steps helped you to find joy and give this knowledge to others. Wanting to help them is indeed your greatest asset, and as you well know, this opens the energies from spirit to flow freely. We shall help you at every turn, and you know this. Look to us in your mind, as you write, and we shall be there.

Life is a constant adjustment to change, so one must learn to "go with the flow," and enjoy life with some spontaneity and flexibility. This is the secret to finding the hidden joys of life.

Sunday, July 4, 1993
Diane:

God bless America as she celebrates her birthday today. I pray that as a people we become more God-centered and grateful for the blessings that so many of us take for granted. I pray for those that have much (like myself), to share and help others who have much less.

Spirit:

The spiritual climb is a difficult journey. So many times it is hard and painful to bring together the spiritual jewels one learns from within into the physical reality of daily living. The sublime and mundane facets must become as one, and herein lies the secret to happiness in the physical life. For you see, dear one, the spirit already knows of everlasting love and eternal life with God. It is the lag between the two worlds which causes so much friction and despair. Enlightenment is the solution, but too few take the time to travel the road to eternal truth. Do not despair, for there will be, and in fact already is, an awakening of spiritual awareness descending upon America and the world.

Pray for her on her birthday knowing that America's greatest asset has always been, and will continue to be, built on the strength and heart of its people. The greatest leaders in American history have been the ones who called upon the wisdom of God to guide them. Their hearts beat in rhythm with the Almighty One, for these great leaders had learned to ask, seek and knock, which is the humble pathway to greatness.

It is the intent behind the action which leads one to peace, even in times of unrest. Continue to see in your inner sight a world of love and peace; an earth surrounded by an aura of rainbows for it is upon this energy of positive thinking that such a world may be built. Spiritual building is first; the physical follows this foundation. Physical existence is limited, but spiritual existence is forever. How beautiful the earth shall be when many understand this profound truth. Peace be with you, my daughter. Your prayers are indeed heard.

Wednesday, July 14, 1993
Diane:

Thank you, dear Heavenly Father, for giving each one beauty from within which only love can nurture into perfection. Divinity is there for all to grasp; indeed, you live within each of us. Help me to hear your guidance, and as I write these jewels down, let their wisdom reach out to all that read or hear them. I am but a droplet of water or a mere grain of sand, and yet important in your eyes for what I can do to help your cause.

Spirit:

Love is at the very center of all things for its energy creates new life and changes the old into a new beginning. This wellspring of creative energy is within the grasp of each. Spread this great truth, dear one, for so few take the time to love so deeply. Taking is so much easier than giving, but you know differently. Be a guide, a shining light for all to see and you shall do much for the cause of spirit world. So many stand ready from spirit as this door opens in the minds of people upon earth. Prayers and gratitude are necessary to open the channel to God and his high realm spirits.

The practice of meditation is our opportunity to commune with you. No time spent in prayer and meditation is ever wasted, for its energy is transformed into the ability to love unconditionally at all times. This is the beauty of a saint, such as Mother Teresa. The greater this love, the brighter the light shines from within.

Monday, July 19, 1993
Spirit:

Positive thought projects positive results. Any minute which contains joy is *never* wasted, dear one. The intellectual mind has a tendency to overwork, and in doing so, has the ability to cause imbalance in the emotional stability of a person. Is not peace and joy the goal to achieve?

You see, dear one, peace, love and joy bring with them great spiritual energy and light. The power they contain is not so easily seen from the physical side. This is why you, and others, feel they are not accomplishing all that they should be. How can you know the influence you have on others? To know, or the desire to know, negates the good one can do. Follow your heart of love and think not of results, but rather find joy in the gifts from God. Gratitude always sets a pathway of spiritual enlightenment.

Freedom to give for the joy of giving is a great lesson to learn. Let the puzzles of life fall into place as you live each piece naturally. No task done with love behind it is ever lost, for spiritual energy lives forever. We come to remind you to lighten your mental load, and to sing, dance and play with the angels you so enjoy in your imagination. Pray for peace and joy for the entire world. Each has the ability, yet too few take the time to learn the secrets of unconditional love.

Suffering and sorrow is the gateway to spiritual enlightenment. The void left by genuine sorrow is filled with love and a greater awareness of God's truth. This is an exacting law with no exceptions. God's laws of creation always result in justice. It is the weakness of the spirit within which fails to understand and see the glory of his truth.

Diane:

I shall be grateful forever that I see a tiny glimpse of eternity while still in the physical body. My prayer is to help others see this beauty as well. Help me to recognize the signs which are sent to guide me as I travel this pathway.

Spirit:

We are always near, dear one. Live in peace.

Thursday, July 29, 1993

Diane:

I *must* become more disciplined in gathering thoughts for my book. If I do not make a scheduled effort, it will never get written. Isn't this true, dear friends?

Spirit:

Lack of direction is intensified when one fails to daily recharge his energy through prayer and meditation. Even when fatigued, even if one falls asleep in the effort, there is merit in the attempt to be self-disciplined. Look deeper within and find the truth of such a lack in desire to pray and meditate. Those who are spiritually closer to God, are the ones who *always* find time to bask in his will. Then, one can be given great energy to do his will and accomplish one's mission. We are only reinforcing what you already know, dear one. Seek deeper calmness and peace so that you may give courage and strength and love to others without zapping your own source of energy. This is a very important lesson to learn and it takes great fortitude to accomplish. Know we come close to help you.

What one reads in a book and intellectualizes does not become part of one's being without a real effort of prayer and meditation. Life becomes happy and joyful for those who learn to think happy and joyful thoughts by finding positive experiences in everyday life, in all that they do. To do this, one must guard his thoughts at all times, as if each was a jewel unto itself. A perfected spirit is one who thinks with jewels of love, kindness, hope, patience and sees only good. The climb is difficult, but so worth the necessary effort. We come close to give you courage and peace.

Wednesday, August 11, 1993
Spirit:

The more one learns to give love away, the greater the capacity to love. Love grows stronger and more powerful with use. It never tires or wears out, but instead blossoms forth with greater intensity. God's gift to each is his love. "Do I use this love wisely" should be a daily question of each human being. Prayer in the form of gratitude will help to guide one on the proper pathway. Help each you meet, and joy will follow you everywhere. Peace be with you, dear one.

Tuesday, August 24, 1993
Ang:

To always be joyful and full of enthusiasm one needs to be a spiritual giant, and there are *very, very* few who fall into this category. Sorrow teaches great lessons, does it not? Dearie, it is impossible to not be affected by the demise of Frank. How hard it must be to stand by and watch a loved one slowly weaken unto death, but the beauty of it all is the awakening into the world of spirit. I come to remind you how beautiful it is. Words (and you have read much about the spirit world) are inadequate when describing the wonder of it all. Go within and listen and see the joy that your heart tells you to be true. Know that on the other side of sorrow is equal joy, and to have the patience to wait for what you know is true is such a great gift. Be filled with gratitude, dearest one, and thank God for such wisdom. Rewards are given in heaven for those who suffer valiantly through the difficulties of life, and who complain not but seek to love unconditionally.

Many of us watch with pride as you stumble on the rocky road of spiritual growth. Suffer with others, but do learn to conserve your own energy. Fatigue causes molehills to seem like mountains, does it not? Last night sleeping in the meditation room was a wise choice. We can and *do* help you while you sleep, even though you remember not. It is your faith and trust which earns you merit, and we can work with this special energy.

Dearest one, when you feel a lack of sparkle, look to us for renewal and it shall be sent with abounding love. Remember that God promises eternal life for those who share their love with another, and did we not grow together through the years?

Remember my favorite saying? "When everything went wrong, together we were strong." Be at peace and continue to grow in love, for your light shines brightly for many to see. I love you and miss you, but our time will come again.

Friday, September 3, 1993
Spirit:

Courage is the name of the game of life: courage to dare to dream of what can be and the courage to make it happen; courage to seek the truth of unconditional love and its great power to heal; courage to find the heart of God and to become one with it. This is what you seek, dear one, and you shall find it. Peace be with you.

Tuesday, September 14, 1993
Diane:

The more one can love and give of himself unselfishly, the happier one's life will be. One reaps what he sows. I shall pray for more love within my own being so I shall be less judgmental in my life. My heart is far from pure, so I must work harder to become an instrument of God's will. Self-discipline is not an easy task. I read an article about "Flowers: Our Angelic Messengers." Could this be why I have loved them for so long?

Spirit:

The angelic forces are very powerful, and indeed, dear one, they are true friends and worthy of caring thoughts. You, on earth, know and realize very little of what surrounds you. There is help at every turn for those who become aware. Keep an open mind to all things and explore the possibilities. Life is meaningful and exciting for those who ponder the meaning of all things. There is a lesson to be learned in every experience. Take the time to learn the lesson.

Monday, September 20, 1993
Diane:

This has been a good week for me. While waiting to hear from Angelo, I have spent time alone. Time alone causes one to be introspective, and this, in turn, causes one to take a closer look at oneself. What are the true motives of how or why one feels as he does?

Spirit:

Gratitude for each small blessing, which one tends to take for granted, is a move in the right direction, dear one. Seeds are the crux of all living, and he who sees and appreciates the chain of life can live eternity right now. Be humble to this truth and thank God for this ability to see beyond earth's shadows. Many have not learned to be grateful, but with prayers such as yours and many others, the earth and its inhabitants can yet be saved.

Pray about how to best use your writings from spirit and the pathway shall be opened unto you. If only you could see how many pure souls come to help you, but you sense this and that is of equal importance. Is it not true, that just when you become discouraged a wonderful coincidence occurs to lift your energies? Yes, dear one, you know you are indeed traveling the right road.

Continue to hone your ability to sense, hear and feel the touch of spirit. Take the necessary time to practice these special skills; through your thoughts we help you find that unconditional love that you so desire. Profound ideas appear when peace is present, and those who fail to find peace live life on a surface level honoring money, prestige, power and self-ego. Unknown to so many is the beauty of love which comes from God. Pure love is of God and the light which shines from one who deserves such love can be seen by many. This light opens the door for those who are ready to see.

Continue to love, to show kindness to all things, dear one, and the door will continue to open, for you knock with a pure heart. We come close to encourage and support you. Feel our presence and live in peace.

Wednesday, September 29, 1993
Spirit:
Find peace in all that you do for others, dear one. We, from the spirit side, can see the growth you have truly achieved. Spend more time planning and feeling the joy of accomplishment, rather than lamenting what was not done. We see the love in your heart in spite of the fatigue of the physical body. It is very important that each take care of his physical body, for neglect in this area will lead one into some form of illness. You know this, dear one, so accept it and regret not. We come close to bring you love, comfort and peace.

Saturday, October 2, 1993
Diane:
Patience is the name of the game in life, and to become totally under its wisdom and protection is not an easy task. To relinquish one's free will

unto God so that it may serve his will takes great patience, for the ego is strong and fights tenaciously for its survival. I am beginning to understand much more, but to implement this in every moment of one's life is most difficult. It is a constant necessity to check the mental pictures, ideas and thoughts which continue to present themselves, and keep them as pure and truthful as possible.

Spirit:

Positive thinking is truly an art form. Expressing them with love and honesty on the canvas of life takes much dedication and practice. One is sometimes happy and pleased with the result, but many times there is room for great improvement. God stands ready to help, so no one is ever alone. It is our faith that wavers and fails us, *never* because God fails us, for he is omnipresent and filled with light and love. Each must seek the secrets which live within this powerful creation of energy, laws and truth. Each must pray for a glimpse of eternity while still in the physical body for herein lies the secret of love, joy and peace. Seek, dear one, each moment of your life, and you shall find your own special calling. Peace be with you.

Sunday, October 3, 1993

Diane:

Written to a friend who was grieving

Death is a wonderful new beginning for one who leaves a legacy of goodness. His passing has caused such sorrow to many, and in truth, it is sadness which awakens the growing spirit in each to seek the understanding of such a sacrifice. One grows more in sadness and hardship than when all is running smoothly. "There are in the end three things that last; faith, hope and love, and the greatest of these is love." *(1 Corinthians 13:13)*

Your friend supplied great love and now it is up to you to pray for faith to accept his passing and hope to understand its meaning. Weeping cleanses the soul, yet unconditional love goes beyond the self, and in this space of unselfishness one can catch the glimpse of the power of eternal love right now!

Try to look beyond earth's shadows, pray to trust our Father's will. Joy and enthusiasm will return when you least expect it, for you sparkle with a zest for living even in sorrow. To truly care for others is a great gift, but what blessing ever comes without sacrifice? Giving of oneself unselfishly takes a toll, but what returns in love and energy is always tenfold. One truly does reap what one sows. May God bless your friend abundantly and also those who mourn his passing. Please accept my deepest sympathy.

Friday, October 15, 1993
Diane:

Thank you, Heavenly Father, for the opportunity to learn more each day about eternal life. It is such a great gift, yet it's so sad that mankind often abuses your great teaching of LOVE. I pray that the angels, saints, high realm spirits and those good souls from spirit will be heard more clearly, and I shall do my part in awakening those I know. Why do I not feel those loving guides, teachers, family and friends around me, or Ang either? I think I know the answer.

Spirit:

Once one is tuned into the world of spirit, it is not necessary to come close and prove our existence over and over. We know the depth of your faith, dear one, and many of us live within your vibration when necessary. We can slip in and out of your aura easily for indeed we are such close friends. Ang is a part of you and you of him; this is the beauty of eternal love. Once a plateau is reached, one does not slip backwards. Faith continually builds upon itself through service of unconditional love. Enlightenment and understanding are the keys given to open the door to God's truth. Ask, seek, knock. Peace be with you in all things, dear one. We are always by your side guiding you gently upward.

Monday, October 18, 1993
Diane:

There is always help for each of us. No one is barred from this divine love and caring. It is those living in emptiness who fail to know of this magnificent intervention. How I marvel at the awesome wonder of God's great creation. All I can do is shake my head from side to side knowing that all things are possible, learning each day of a new wonder or becoming aware of something I had not noticed in such detail before. My heart sends great gratitude to God for opening my eyes wider to what surrounds me. Thank you, God, and may all praise and glory be yours. Help me, thy servant, become an instrument of thy will.

Spirit:

Love everything with all your being, dear one, and all that you desire shall be yours. Those who wait patiently shall feel the touch of loving spirits who stand close by. Think only good thoughts, productive thoughts, kind and loving thoughts, and this will bring you into the realm of a truly productive and giving life in the physical world. Always place your vision on the spiritual truths that your heart tells you are from God, dear one, and it shall be so. We see within the very core of a heart and know by its light the love contained therein. Ever seek to feel the compassion and love of God, Jesus and his high realm in every task you undertake; this is why one is given the gift of life. We come close to help and guide you. Be at peace.

Wednesday, October 27, 1993
Diane:

Many new changes are coming in the field of health. Each of us can do much to heal ourselves. The immune system is remarkable, and thought is the key in controlling so many important parts of ourselves. Thought is the center of one's being. Its wavelengths control the emotional, physical, mental and spiritual aspects of each life. The reward for balance is peace within. Thoughts that are allowed to run rampant cripple the special talents and purpose which lay hidden, deep inside.

Friday, November 5, 1993
Diane:

Description of a dream and how I interpreted it, in case I need such a narrative in my book: It was very symbolic. At the time I was contemplating whether to attend an art retreat or not.

Then I read the November 5 issue of *Daily Guideposts:* "All things are possible to him who believes." The article continues: "When I noticed that the itinerary for the week-long retreat included chalk drawings, I groaned. You see, I've never been much of an artist; I can't draw a straight line. But the retreat leader explained, 'Defining ourselves in terms of what we think we are NOT can be self-defeating, impeding the life of God in us,' she said."[34]

From now on, I'm making an effort not to say, "I can't" when a new challenge presents itself to me. Instead, I'm going to say, "You know, Diane, there just might be a new adventure awaiting you. Go for it!" God help me to say goodbye to limiting labels and to open myself to the wonderful possibilities in my path. Amen. (The author of this article went on to make a nice drawing.)

The symbolic meaning of the color black in my dream: self-limitation; fears brought about by lack of self-confidence, and doubts about success of a new adventure. Remember—I can do anything with God's help.

Wednesday, November 11, 1993
Diane:

Today is Veteran's Day. May God bless all the men and women who died defending freedom. There are still many mini-wars going on in the world; may those who hate so much find the light of peace and love. There are many things to do. I shall pray for self-mastery so I can zero in and get them done, preferably with enjoyment.

I'm always working to improve myself spiritually, so I shall balance the emotional, physical and mental parts of my being in daily life. I know that the spirit should be in control for it truly knows all and lives forever. The difficult part is listening and following the gems of truth it reveals. I'm thankful always to God for his patient love and for all those wonderful beings and spirits who come to help and support me. Perhaps if I continue to strive for concentration and listen more closely with a heart full of love, my awareness of their presence will be enhanced. There are so many distractions which one must learn to sift through, and how blessed I am, for most of them are joyous ones, and if not that, they are the necessities of physical life which must be done by all.

I am still torn at times between what I feel I should be doing versus what I truly want to do, especially reading. In one way it is selfish, and yet, so much knowledge and understanding seeps into my being through reading. I hear you telling me I am my own worst enemy, and of course this is so true. Procrastination zaps one's spirit and produces such waste of energy by causing fatigue.

Spirit:

Dear one, live as those wonderful examples in nature. Exist like the flowers and birds and children with great love, freedom and trust, for that is how God created you to be. All restrictions are self-imposed for one who does unto others as he would have them do unto him. Relax within your own being, allowing the channel from God to be opened even wider. This is such an important truth, my child. For one who truly loves, all things are indeed possible. Let the joy shine through at all times. Peace be with you.

Monday, November 15, 1993
Diane:

Louise was surprised I called—proud of me, dear?

Ang:

I'm always proud of you. Remember the song this morning "Getting to Know You," and how you wondered why it came to mind? It was my way of saying I marvel at the resourceful way you live your life alone—always showing a new side in development and always with love as well. I can't begin to tell you how helpful and joyous is the eternal love that you send to me in prayer, meditation, and in your every waking moment. This love we use even when you are asleep, for there are countless souls who need to see the light of love.

Your prayers to do God's will are answered in many ways, dearest one, and in ways you are not even aware of. Pure love is so very precious; it is no wonder so many want to come close in spirit. If more could set such an example, the world would not be so dark. Rainbows, even though they are few and far between, are special, as you are. Your gratitude to God has indeed brought you many blessings. Know that I share your joy as if I were standing right there for you to see, for in truth, I am there. I love you more each day as we build together our place in eternity. Peace be with you and know you are never, ever alone.

Friday, November 26, 1993
Spirit:

It is indeed true what you are pondering, dear child. Give and you shall receive; it is an exact law. Self-mastery is gained by the ability to do what is necessary to seek the truth, and to find one's identity with God in spite of circumstances or difficulties at hand. Five minutes spent in prayer above and beyond the normal pace of one's life is responsible for that extra merit which can be used by spirit world to accomplish good and meaningful experiences for many. The more one works to find spiritual perfection, the greater will be his ability to master himself and his thoughts. Each situation can teach an important lesson for those who fine-tune and seek the true meaning. Fatigue is the result of many self-imposed restrictions through one's own thoughts. Find vitality by channeling your energies through the powerful light of God's love.

Sunday, November 28, 1993
Diane:

A date I shall always remember! It has been seven years. Life is full, but I do thank God for letting me know how close you really are, dear husband of mine. I showed the video about Mother Teresa to Flora today; her life is such an inspiration. If only I could begin to love as she does; she accomplishes so much and helps so many without any concern for herself. Her love for God is all-encompassing.

I believe that I will know what it is that I must contribute at the perfect moment. My faith has grown and I deeply believe that all things are possible with God. I feel loved and protected by Heavenly Father and many who come close, especially Ang and relatives. This knowledge has eliminated most fears and I do feel free to explore the oneness of all things. This does bring freedom from the mundane activities of daily life, for this truth of oneness makes me observe the beauty to be found in everything that I do, mundane or not. To take that moment to more fully enjoy is my secret to joy and happiness.

Each must perceive joy through the discipline of his own thoughts; this is self-mastery. Is achieving self-mastery an easy task? No, controlling one's thoughts and actions takes total concentration through prayer, study and meditation each moment of the day. Sometimes I succeed, but more often, it is keep on keeping on.

Sunday, December 5, 1993

Diane:

There is not enough time to accomplish all that I desire, so I must categorize the importance of certain activities. To know what to do is the easy part; to act upon this knowledge is the difficult assignment.

Spirit:

There is much energy released when one does as his inner voice dictates, yet activities of the physical life tend to fatigue one much more readily. Why is this, you ask? God created each in his own image, therefore your spiritual being is subject, and your physical body is object. In this truth, due to the fall, mankind has reversed the importance of his own being. We say to you, dear one, you must repeat to others in your writing, that the reason man is given physical life is to use his body to grow spiritually.

Learn to love unconditionally by always doing "unto others as you would have them do unto you." *(Luke 6:31)*

Think only positive thoughts and see the good in all things. One can only take with him unto death the seeds planted into his own spirit by the doing of good deeds. Love and light travel instantaneously in both worlds, but it is seen most clearly on the spirit side. If it is hard to believe this fact, then one must use his imagination to start his journey into belief. The unconscious mind, the mind of God within knows these truths, but these truths will only be released as the spirit seeks to find the love and goodness of God within.

The journey is not an easy one, for it takes great discipline to love oneself and others at all times. You are all wounded, some more than others, but let us tell you that salvation comes from the ability to love and forgive those who trespass against you. Teach this great truth, my child. We come close to help you and may peace follow you everywhere.

Monday, December 6, 1993
Spirit:

Remember, dear child, to become annoyed at yourself stifles much in the way of productivity. How often do you try very hard to overlook and forgive other's trespasses? Why then, can you not do the same for yourself? Judge yourself, my child, but do not judge so severely. Can you not see this short-circuits the path to receiving added energy?

Sometimes it is much easier to see a fault or shortcoming than it is to *change* it. We understand this, and come to encourage you in your growth through writings, prayer and meditation. Take time to love and forgive yourself. This is most important, for one must be healthy within his own being before he can be helpful to another.

Wednesday, December 15, 1993

Diane:

I am observing a troubled relationship, and I do not know how to deal with my own anxieties.

Spirit:

Firstly, dear one, train your mind to move backward and away from the problem. Too often one tends to observe from too close a position and this distorts your ability to see clearly. This is a problem between two people and there is really no way you can solve it; they must do it themselves. Remember that obstacles are put there for a reason, and each gains as he overcomes the difficulties. You have not been a firsthand observer; you are only seeing the difficulties through another's eyes, and truth is tainted by many emotions. What is faith? Is it not knowing that all will work out as it should with God's help?

Live in that belief and patiently wait for the positive outcome. Negative thoughts feed great energy into any difficulties, so send them scurrying away on contact. See a happy relationship appearing instead, and give those who come to help positive energy to work with. All things are possible with God. This is an all-important lesson that each must learn. Strive to keep an open mind and always be a good listener; so much can be accomplished by letting another talk. Hurts that lay deep inside are allowed to trickle out in such a situation. Breathe in God's love and then send it out to specific people and needs. There is great power in this; far more than you, on earth, are even aware of.

Love heals all things. Immerse yourself in this unconditional love and it will help you to rise above any sadness which you feel. Be there for those who need you with your strength, love and wisdom. Love casts out all fear and animosity, but not always as *you* visualize or as quickly as *you* might wish. Be patient knowing many come to help, and find that place of inner peace.

Tuesday, December 21, 1993

Diane:

The year 1993 is quickly coming to an end. As I reflect upon it, this year has had its great sorrows and difficulties, but also its share of joys. I pray daily that I may keep all things in proper perspective, always seeing a positive solution to my problems, and more importantly, for friends.

Life is the sum total of all of its parts, and there is much to learn from each part as we progress, sometimes trudging but more often skipping through our physical years. Logical thinking helps each to find answers, but dwelling upon the negative catches us as if in a trap, and we become stuck in unwanted feelings.

Help me, dear Heavenly Father to feel the pain of another, but guide me to lead that person into your realm of positive thinking. Your laws of truth are exacting; help me to more fully understand and implement your wisdom into my daily life and into the lives that touch mine. Thank you for the many blessings which surround me. Help me to find joy in everything that needs to be done, and courage for those trials which confront me so that I may indeed be an instrument of your will. Patience continues to be a valuable teacher as it leads me closer to the true meaning of unconditional love. See into my heart, dear Heavenly Father, and teach me to more fully see that which I personally can do to further your cause.

Peace on earth and good will to all men as we approach this holy time of Christmas. Thank you, Heavenly Father, for hearing my prayer.

Tuesday, December 28, 1993

Diane:

Please, dear friends, show me the route to travel to do God's will. How must I work harder?

Spirit:

To grow in unconditional love one must sacrifice and make special conditions. Why do you feel the need to be uncomfortably chilly while in the meditation room for your evening prayer? Why do you seek to be *more* satisfied with what you have accomplished in a given day? Why do you forgive, if only in your private thoughts, those who are unkind? Is it not true that in all of these acts, you are striving to seek a closer understanding of God's heart and his teachings of unconditional love?

Many times an answer shows itself in meaningful questions. Asking is a way of receiving; seeking makes you find. Keep knocking, and the door will open wider and wider to reveal what lies peacefully within your own being, for you are a child of God. Always remember how carefully, how gently, how patiently, how lovingly God prepares you to hear his will.

Love all that surrounds you, and beyond. Count each blessing with great gratitude; pray for those less fortunate than you; and keep on keeping on without fail, even when the mist of uncertainty clouds the pathway. Truth will always lead you in the right direction, and love will brighten the image. Live in peace, dear one, we watch with loving eyes. God bless you.

1994

Friday, January 7, 1994
Spirit:

The bottom line, dear one, is to pray for more love and compassion. How easy it is to philosophize and rationalize oneself into believing you've given your best. Yet, in reality, one can *always* love more for this is the beauty of unconditional love. There is no end to this gift for it travels hand in hand with God throughout eternity. God is love and love is God. His love is the energy, the light, the source of all creativity; thus, accomplishment follows one who taps into this energy of love.

See with renewed vision; pray to find a deeper meaning of unconditional love; and feel a touch of the joy and pain of Heavenly Father's heart. Love is the true essence of eternal life—it is the core of the spirit which guides the physical being. This is the reason why one who seeks to find his spiritual calling is never satisfied. Love is unending until it reaches perfection and joins God in a completed full circle.

Dear one, it is so much easier to criticize another or say you've done the best you can, yet, is there not more one can always give? This is the heart of God calling to those who hear his message of sharing his unconditional love. Futility is not the end, it is only the beginning. This is why it is always the "darkest before dawn." Sometimes one must know total despair before seeing the light of salvation. It is true that each must find his own pathway, but the light of unconditional love can help to guide the way. Be one who is willing to shine forth with such a light by giving more of yourself for the sake of another. Peace be with you.

Saturday, January 8, 1994
Spirit:

Joy and sorrow come from the same wellspring of love. Be proud of your rise to be able to better know and experience the heart of God. One feels his closeness in both sorrow and joy, but one experiences it in a different way. Joy is exhilarating and seems to engulf all things around one—is this not true? Think for a moment of sadness and sorrow; it tends to travel within and releases the vulnerability of a human heart. Empathy and compassion are great treasures. Welcome them into your life with gratitude, dear one, for they are great jewels to behold. In the world of spirit, one who has earned these jewels sees and knows such beauty, and it is indescribable in words. Seeking the meaning of unconditional love opens the pathway to knowing the truth of God's heart.

Is it not true that you have been told this in readings, as well as experiencing this truth in the Bible and other religious books? Continue to pursue your life without fear, for indeed protection is there for those who so love all of mankind. Forgiveness accompanies pure love in spite of the outward appearances of unkind deeds. The evil seed planted by the fall grows too easily in many, yet it is unconditional love in the end which will rout out the evil and transform it into something positive through forgiveness. Money, ego, prestige and the like tend to cloud the issue of forgiveness, and little progress can be made in such an environment.

We beseech you to keep an open heart of pure love and forgiveness. It shows not in the physical world, but the energy and light it sends into the spirit world is great in magnitude. We can work with this energy. Continue to seek and grow, dear one, we come close to help.

Monday, January 10, 1994
Diane:

I'm happy to be back in my meditation room. I missed Saturday totally and only a short visit last evening. I have had a struggle with myself of late—rarely totally satisfied with what I accomplish. But I somehow feel this is necessary to grow more and better prepare myself for whatever mission I am chosen to do. It is not easy to adjust to living all alone when one has been happily married for many years. How blessed I am to have children who truly love and watch out for me! What more could one ask in physical life? And I'm learning so much about the spirit world. I truly have no complaints. Each new experience and hurdle I overcome does teach a lesson in empathy and compassion. I am growing, but there is always some pain in the process. I pray that I can learn more self-control, so that I can walk through the storms in calmness and bring peace to those I encounter along the way. I must write a list of kindnesses which I must do during the month of January.

Monday, January 24, 1994
Spirit:

Keep time in its proper place, dear one, in spite of what others may think about your activities. For you see, it is the so-called rebel or "he who beats to a different drum" who, in the end, moves others into change. To be different because of insecurity is not what this discussion is about, but rather to advance new ideas by focusing the right attention upon them. This is caused through divine intervention and is of God.

True vision opens the door of others' understanding, not through force, but rather through love, compassion and pure example. Words are indeed empty without action to back them up. Is this not true? Continue to be careful in your use of time. Live in the present moment, but pull into it the experiences from the past and vision from what is yet to be—even beyond physical life. Grow unto death with love of all things within your own being, and it shall be contagious unto those whose lives you touch.

Because you are learning the gift of asking, seeking and knocking, this, in itself, does bring more responsibility to rest upon you. How else can we in spirit spread the word of paradise to make known God's great plan for each of his children? Each one is special in his sight, but too few know the deep meaning of this. There is little *time* in their lives to seek the truth of eternity. You, dear one, can bridge this gap because you care deeply for all things, even unto a plant cutting. We see your heart from spirit. No deed done, no matter how small, is *ever* wasted when done in love. Remember this always, for it will bring comfort and healing, and energizes your own being as well. We come close to help you.

Saturday, January 29, 1994

Diane:

Happy birthday, Daddy. Perhaps it was you who tried to arouse me in the night to write that profound statement which I ignored. Maybe one day I shall be in control of my weak physical body. Please try again and I shall be more receptive, no matter what the hour. I must say I have been in a little slump in wholehearted meditation and prayer, focusing more on my reading instead. I shall grow in spite of myself. I have spent many hours alone, but that is okay for I do enjoy my own company. I'm becoming more interesting each day and challenging myself to be of more service. Patience, patience, patience! Perhaps I'll do a writing on the topic of patience one time soon.

Spirit:

Patience is the key-keeper to one's heart. To find that perfect key it is necessary to undergo many trials and tribulations. Is one truly ready to listen to God, to become an instrument of his will and serve mankind? Those who learn patience have also learned to control the emotional outcries of the physical body. Annoyances register, but are quickly put into proper perspective by one who acquires patience. It is God's way of allowing one to listen to the spiritual value of the lesson to be learned. It is in calmness and tranquility where the truth dwells, and patience helps to lead one to these jewels.

To become patient, dear one, is to forever offer one's own will up to God to use for the betterment of all. It is that simple. It is at this moment that one finds the perfect key and opens the door to love, which is the true meaning of one's existence. Live your life with total patience and light the way through example so others may follow. We come close to give you courage with our eternal love. Peace be with you.

Tuesday, February 1, 1994

Diane:

Are there any suggestions you might have about explaining the necessity of patience in one's life—how to wait patiently for the outworking of God's plan? It is easy to say, but so very, very hard to *do* when daily life is difficult to bear.

Spirit:

Patience is the fortress surrounding love and to reach love one must triumphantly climb over the wall, making each stumbling block become a stepping stone. The greater the mission one is chosen to do, the higher and more formidable the fortress can be. As one fights for the patience to find the stepping stones, God watches with his loving eyes, sending his strength and fortitude. Look beyond the moment—both into the past generations as well as into eternity. To save others you must first save yourself by mounting the obstacles placed before you, no matter how great or seemingly impossible they might appear. This takes patient endurance, but *is* possible with one who knows the love which lives in the heart of God.

Changes toward love and understanding, no matter how small, open the door to possible compromise and new beginnings. Patience is one of the nine fruits of the spirit and so very necessary if one is to persuade another into the truth of God's laws. Look at the love and patience Heavenly Father shows toward his wayward children. There are so many lacking in their ability to follow the teachings of his son, Jesus. A teacher's skill is augmented by his ability to set a living example of true values, and what is more important than love, peace and patience! Try to look beyond earth's shadows and pray to find your Father's will.

Friday, February 11, 1994

Diane:

Snow has a peace about it, and I like the way it slows down the fast-paced existence of life today. People are rush-rush-rush, rarely taking the time to appreciate and enjoy life as it presents itself. I pray that I shall organize my mind to present the wisdom that I have received into a practical and meaningful format to help others. My spiritual pursuit is meaningless unless I can use what I have learned to better guide others on their journey.

Spirit:

Like the lesson of a snowstorm, there is great, untold power in the peace which dwells within. The calmness that underlies all other forms of one's external existence is the key to successful living. You, on earth, are rarely or totally satisfied. Instead the better part of one's existence is spent in negativity which appears as criticism, selfishness and unkind deeds, to name a few. It is for those who look to joy, beauty and spiritual uplift, that life becomes a continuous journey toward the realm of peaceful living.

How, you ask, can one enlighten others to this world of peace? We come to remind you that we shall be your constant companion in this endeavor; remember to look for help from those who cross your pathway and are willing to be of service as well. Each human being has a contribution to make, and it is up to each to become aware of those who are sent to help. Use your intuition; listen carefully and quietly to those thoughts which enter your mind. There is great power in thought. Learn how to release and live this guidance as it appears in your daily life.

Too many fear life by dwelling on the negative aspects of living, but we say again and again—there is no room for fear when one becomes completely surrounded by the love of God. Continue to strive for this unconditional love. Each kind deed selflessly performed opens this channel to divine love. A strongly-motivated desire to help mankind is *always* heard, and action will be taken. We come close to help. God bless you, child.

Thursday, February 17, 1994

Diane:

What is the secret to maintaining one's sparkle in life, dear friends?

Spirit:

We answer you, dear one, with the following phrase—keep on keeping on. To live in eternity, to be one with eternal life, one must also learn to understand the meaning of the word *infinite*. Go and look it up in the dictionary: (1) having no bounds or limits; endless; (2) immeasurably great or large; immense.

We come to remind you that the climb to seek God's love is endless as well. You, on earth, are always placing specific goals on yourselves, not satisfied where you are, but instead causing disharmony for not being where you wish to be. Relax, dear one, and *just be*. The greatest joy appears when one allows himself to be gently guided by the rhythm of life, tackling each obstacle with peace and love, and watching it fall into place. With patience, one will change the word "tackling" to "surrounding" challenges with peace and love. The result is one has again found a sparkle and zest for life. Refuse to be overwhelmed, and always look to see the rainbow which shines through the rain. Peace be with you.

Saturday, February 26, 1994

Diane:

I'm so happy about two things: there's a real spurt in my energy level, and I awoke this morning with ideas about the book I must write. I somehow know that great help will be there to support and guide me as I write. I went downstairs until 12:30 a.m., and then came up and typed more writings into the computer. I went to bed quite late, but felt fine. My intuition tells me this is merit for listening to the calling from God in spite of fatigue. Is this indeed true, dear friends?

Spirit:

Desire is a key word in listening to one's intuition. One must know with confidence that he is hearing correctly. Opening the thought channel is not as difficult as many believe, once self-mastery reaches a certain level of attainment. It is necessary to love selflessly and always stand ready to help those in need, and through this desire to help, merit is established. Reward follows one who learns the importance of love. Send forth clear thoughts of what you desire to accomplish, and help will be sent. Work harder to establish rapport with those who come to guide your daily life, and you will receive many new ideas. Uncertainty hinders one's development so always take the time to reevaluate the goals, especially when progress seems too slow. That extra good deed or time spent in quieting one's mind does give us the opportunity to draw closer to your world.

Self-mastery serves all mankind; it weaves greater strength into the tapestry representing all life. Look beyond the physical world and seek to see with your spiritual eyes. We will come as close as you will allow us to come, but remember, dear one, the purity of one's heart allows us to focus, and then we beam in our ideas and support through your thoughts. It is truly remarkable how these energies are used, and you must sense with your imagination our closeness. We see you understanding more and more, and this is because you are willing to go the extra mile to meet us, even when fatigued. Does this not deserve merit? If more on earth could work so diligently, then there would be less hardship and sorrow.

Generation after generation the same mistakes are repeated and oftentimes increased. Many more must step forward and say "Enough! What can I do to reverse this trend?" Then this spiritual desire would grow and love could become the driving force. Continue to shine forth with your quiet determination, and sprinkle the jewels you are learning for others to catch. The most beautiful rainbow appears after God rinses the darkness of the soul with his eternal love.

Wednesday, March 2, 1994
Spirit:

Dear one, you should write yourself a letter of congratulations as well. Your heart of love has grown beyond measure, and the joy it will bring you will be endless, for eternity is indeed the greatest part by far. Vision comes only to those who earn its merit. The more you become part of everything, and love the core value of each, unconditional love will waltz into your life. Can you not begin to hear the magnificent music which accompanies each step?

Remember you waltz with your beloved Ang for he helps you feel the magic and power of such love. Remember, there is nothing that cannot be saved with love and patience. It is from you and the desire which you carry in your heart that gives us the energy to help as well.

We urge you to continue to see the good in each person and situation. This is our answer to the negativity which runs rampant on earth today, but things can and do change. Be that bright light which holds fast to the vision of peace and love. Guide those around you to see with equal vision for it is through families such as yours that new beginnings can come forth. It is the pure heart that others see, even if it appears not to be so. A humble heart radiates love for all to see. Continue on your pathway of seeking unconditional love, dear one.

Thursday, March 3, 1994
Spirit:

In the end of physical life, dear one, it matters not what others say or feel about you, but rather what the God-self within feels about you. This is how each one must truly judge himself—what does the God-self think?

Have you indeed lived up to the rules in the scriptures? How close have you lived to the example that Jesus taught us? Is your life a continuous prayer of gratitude? Do you deeply desire to be an instrument of God's will? How many of the nine fruits of the spirit do you include in your daily life? Do you seek to feel the touch of those from spirit who come close to help? How much can you love and help the unlovable? Is the plank truly out of your own eye so you judge not? Do you take time each day to send out healing energies to others, and to yourself?

Nature teaches us so many lessons; do you listen carefully? How often do you meditate or use the mantra? Are your prayers meaningful or just so many repetitious words? Remember, "Whatever you do to the least of my brothers, that you do unto me." *(Matthew 25:40)*

Ponder well these questions, dear one, and make an honest appraisal of just where you are and where you need to work harder. The climb to spiritual awakening is hard and tedious. Look at the world and see how many have not even started to seek as yet. It is through the energies of the seekers that we can spread the word of God and his spiritual realm. Follow with faith and hope, and love will be the reward. Peace be with you.

Wednesday, March 9, 1994

Diane:

I am all for learning to change, sort out and roll with the punches of life. Only then will I truly be able to live with joy in my heart. It is in giving of oneself that the truth appears, as to just where one *is* spiritually. I examine the progress with scrutiny—sometimes liking what I see, sometimes not, and sometimes realizing that I do not always understand myself at all.

Just when I think I have truly gained in spiritual growth, I surprise myself by not being as self-disciplined as I would wish to be. This is where "keep on keeping on" becomes so important. I fall back on those lovely, pep talks which say one does not necessarily know or see the progress being made. This too shall pass, and I know springtime is just around the corner.

Thursday, March 10, 1994

Diane:

I shall keep trying to accomplish those things that have not come to pass as yet. When it is time, it will happen. With God, all things are possible. I have not done as many writings lately, and I must ponder why. Perhaps it is necessary to assemble those writings which have already been done. This will take great concentration, and I am sure those who come close to help me will be there to give me support with new ideas.

As I write, what I need will be supplied. It is my turn to show the faith that dwells within; to produce the jewels I've been given in an organized way by writing a book. I do not doubt my ability to do this, but I do pray for help to do it well. Life is busy and full with many jobs to do in this physical world I live in, yet I must make time to experience a growth in my spiritual life as well.

Spirit:

Keeping a balance between the two is not always an easy task. The physical life is very demanding for there is much to do to keep the "machine" running properly. The spiritual cries are of a much finer vibration and it is easier to neglect or not hear these needs, but how foolish many are in this respect. The spirit gives great vitality to the physical body. It is the true spark of life and it shines into eternity. Pleasures of the physical body are short-lived, and yet, too many listen intently to these demands sacrificing the opportunity to seek the spiritual side of life. Help others to see more clearly, my child. This is indeed an important mission. We come to help you. Peace be with you always.

Saturday, March 12, 1994

Diane:

As I sometimes do, I find a page at random in *The Quiet Mind*. This is the one tonight:

"Forgive Us Our Trespasses"

"We shall do well to remember how much we ourselves need forgiveness, and to learn to forgive freely, judging no man. We know not any soul; but it is our duty, our surpassing joy, to search ever for the spark of the divine in all men."[35]

I pray that I may see to do this. Please, dear Heavenly Father, let me send blessings to those who are resentful of me. Let me show unconditional love to the seemingly unlovable. Let me judge not, but instead always send out prayers to cover them with love and protection. Keep me ever filled with visions of positive thoughts and outcomes. Your son, Jesus Christ, was indeed a remarkable human being who blessed and forgave those who hated and murdered him. Is it so hard then for us to forgive misunderstanding and resentment toward us from another? Help me to grow in unconditional love, dear Heavenly Father.

Spirit:

Let not another's negativity affect you so deeply. Remember that you cannot live another's life for them or make them happy, but it is possible to visualize a positive outcome. Then put this into words in prayer form and send it forth to be guided to that place where it can be used. There are times when you must seek help from those who come close to you.

Friday, March 18, 1994
Spirit:

Love, dear one, is a simple and beautiful energy which permeates one who seeks God's unconditional love. You must remember that each person comes through a different pathway of life. Some of these roads are filled with stumbling blocks that many fail to turn into stepping stones. As a result, they continue to stumble and feel resentment and anger as they confront each new problem. Open your heart wider, dear one, and all that seems difficult will disappear in time. Remember well, in God's own time, and be patient with yourself and with others too.

Look rather with your spiritual eyes and see that spark of God in every human being. It is true that in many, the spark is harder to find, but love helps one to see more clearly. Try as hard as you can to understand with your empathy just how another is feeling. Judge not whether it is right or just, but rather send prayer and love to straighten out the crooked places. This is the meaning of unconditional love—it matters not what one gets back in return.

Send negative thoughts away without ever speaking them or giving them any attention, and you will travel the spiritual pathway more smoothly. Too many in the world think of self first, and this attitude stunts the spiritual growth of many. One can only live his own life seeking purity; expecting it from another can only be done if you, yourself, shine with selfless love in all that *you* do. This, of course, is a most difficult task, but we implore you to keep on keeping on. We see and hear your prayers, and we come close to help you always. Live in peace, dearest one.

Tuesday, March 22, 1994
Spirit:

Live within the circle of love, dear one. Many fail to join this beautiful circle, and in so doing, shut themselves out of the simple truths which make for a fulfilling life filled with happiness and joy. Life can be a whirlpool of unrest for those inclined to follow the call of the physical senses and heed not the desires of the spiritual senses. The spiritual senses are of a higher quality and far less tangible than those desires which physical life demand. We say "demand" because this is what happens so often: another chance to make more money; being unkind to someone else; taking a pill to make one feel better, and so on, in similar fashion.

You ask what you can do to help this crisis which is affecting mankind, and we answer to continue to love, to pray and to send out vibrations of concern and caring. There is so much that cannot be seen and understood from the physical side of life. Try to use your imagination beyond what science has uncovered. All things are possible for those who believe with faith those unseen forces from the energies of God. Spread your spiritual wings and fly beyond what can be seen with the naked eye. You perhaps think this is not possible, but we tell you to continue to ask, seek and knock. The veil between the two worlds can be lifted for those who seek to know and feel the love and suffering of the true heart of God.

It is beneficial to the spirit to place less emphasis on time where or whenever possible. Concern about time hampers the freedom of the desires of the spirit. How can it be allowed to grow if there is a constant worry about time? This stifles the opportunity to sense and feel the beauty of what is yet to come. The unknown causes so much worry and fear to many. Whenever possible, help these unenlightened people to look beyond the moment, for each moment has the potential to teach an important lesson to those who take the time to notice. Help is within the grasp of each of God's children; guide others to see this truth, dear one. We are always but a thought away. Peace be with you.

Friday, March 25, 1994
Diane:

I'm very proud of myself this morning. I was out of the house a little before 6:00 and took a two-and-a-half mile walk, then meditated, read daily books and wrote in my journal—all by 8:00. I've wanted to change my daily schedule for a long while; perhaps this first move will do it. The answer to so many problems is really quite simple—just do it. The human being oftentimes makes life so complicated with procrastination, stubborn resistance, and most of all, a lack of proper direction. The spirit knows this proper direction, but the physical side of our being more often dictates than not. It is a hard upward climb to overcome the mountains placed before us as a test of our spiritual growth. Why do we not listen more carefully?

Spirit:

If the answer was simple, dear one, the world would not be in such an unhappy state as it is today. Is it easier to love or hate? To one who is spiritually enlightened the answer is easy—to love brings such joy. However, to one who follows the dictates of physical satisfaction, is it not easier to hate in order to achieve the desired goals? Selfishness hovers around most decisions. Another cigarette or drink will calm the nerves, or perhaps a pill or more junk food, or more money will surely make me happy and so what if I cheat a little here and there—who will know? Does a piece of this not ring true for all of us?

It is not an easy decision to change oneself, but the pride of accomplishment will, in the end, be well worth the effort, for indeed the light of one's spirit can be felt and seen. This energy is called happiness. The dust and debris of the mind is often overlooked until one day when the light of the spirit reveals it. This is the day one starts anew.

Diane:

This truth came to me the other day as I was cleaning dust off of a plant. In the shade of the living room the plant looked okay as I quickly cleaned the leaves. What a surprise when the sun, that bright all-revealing sun, shone on the leaves. They were covered with dust and unwanted grime. What can be hidden in darkness will one day be revealed in the light! This is true of our spirit, and what a profound truth. Each of us knows this truth within our own being, but the darkness too often covers this gift from God. It does indeed matter what we do each moment of our lives. It is so important that each decision we make is carefully placed into the bright light of the spirit. Is there unwanted dust or debris clinging to it?

Spirit:

If so, dear one, reevaluate, and guide others to do likewise. You are a beacon of light to us as we send you important messages. Peace follows those who seek the truth. We come close to help.

Saturday, April 2, 1994

Diane:

This is Holy Week, but to me every week should be a special week. We should always think of God and his Son with great reverence. I'm not sure where I come from in my religious beliefs, but somehow think I understand ahead of my time. Is this true?

Spirit:

Mankind finds the truth on many different levels, dear one. This is perhaps the biggest reason for such turmoil over the centuries. Each thinks his own beliefs are the correct ones, and others are indeed on the wrong track. God meant each human being to be a loving and beautiful soul, quick to feel the needs of another. Through loving care of himself, he would treat others as himself. Although many strive to achieve this goal, heaven on earth is far from completed. Perfection, finding the need to see through the eyes of God, is far from being accomplished.

Our advice to you, dear one, is listen to your own heart for it guides you well. Try to understand your own needs, and do not push your own physical and emotional being so hard. If there must be a period of rest, so be it. Ideally, one's spiritual being needs no rest, but the physical body does. Work to find the perfect balance, and spend less time agonizing over what you did not do, but rather see into eternity with what you have done. Any negative thoughts do take their toll. You, in physical life, cannot see what energy is wasted from negativity—even a little literally zaps your being of much vitality. Protect yourself carefully by not allowing any negative idea to enter your thought pattern. This is a difficult assignment, but possible for those with great dedication.

You see, dear child, we can see and feel the truth of a heart, so no apology is ever needed. Perhaps it is our prompting that sends you to bed early for we see the need. Keep peace within, always calming the storms which arise in your own being. This is the key to the door of eternal happiness which can be used while still in the physical body. Think of this profound truth, for do you not always ask, seek and knock? We offer you the key to enter. May peace follow you everywhere.

Friday, April 8, 1994

Diane:

How blessed I am to know so much intuitively about the spirit world. I almost feel as though I have visited it already.

Spirit:

And indeed you have, my child. We come very often when you are sleeping and you travel many places as our guest. If we told you much healing has been done by the love light which shines from your aura, would you believe this to be true? Yes, we know you would. Unconditional love is a most precious gift for it does not shy away from those who need it the most, and it matters not which world receives this light of love. This is why we tell you there is so much that cannot be understood by most people in the physical world at this time.

Continue to send out prayers of love and concern for all of mankind. These vibrations will make a difference, even though progress seems slow, and many times it seems as though mankind moves backwards. Think positive thoughts of a peaceful world being built with love. Constantly encourage others to see and live only positive thoughts. This is possible with prayer and meditation. Mind control comes from within, regardless of the turmoil surrounding one at any given moment. Fear, distrust, selfishness, greed and the like welcome negative thoughts for they feed on such ideas. It is only love, kindness and positive thinking which heals people, countries, and ultimately, the world.

As we have so often told you, the secret is trying to see good in everything, no matter how infinitesimal it may seem at the moment. There is evil, dear one, but its power is greatly reduced by the vibration of love. Love, pure love, does not fear; it has a strong armor of protection for those who earn its refuge. We come to always encourage you to keep on keeping on in your desire to know more of the beauty of unconditional love. Happiness and joy of insurmountable understanding lives within its confines. Peace be with you, my dear one.

Monday, April 11, 1994

"The root of all violence is in the world of thoughts, and that is why training the mind is so important."[36]

Diane:

My gratitude goes to God, his realms and to all those who come and help me on the spiritual ladder. I have come far when I look at myself with detachment from criticism. When one looks at oneself in truth and with love, it is not a negative judgment but rather a very positive experience, or so it should be. Life is always springing unexpected experiences both difficult and easy. It is one's reaction which brings joy or sorrow into one's life. Positivity brings the eventual reward of joy; negativity reacts with more negativity and tends to bring hardship and sorrow. Life is a continuing process unto death.

Those who seek the light of God's love are more able to see beyond physical life. Perhaps a good term would be intuitive vision. The beauty of each human being is his individual difference which is guided by free will. Such a glorious gift from God, yet how often do we thank him for this gift? How easy it is for each of us to be greedy and selfish, thinking of our own desires first, and only giving love when it is convenient.

Ideally, love should be given to others first, then we would be filled automatically. This is God's law stated so beautifully as "do unto others as you would have them do unto you." *(Luke 6:31)* Over and over this truth appears before us, and if one listens, this truth can be proven beyond a doubt.

When do you feel the happiest? Write down ten circumstances and evaluate the situation—were you taking or giving? Do this exercise and ponder within yourself honestly, stripping away all rationalization down to the bare truth. What do you see?

Wednesday, April 13, 1994

Diane:

It is early morning. Why is it so difficult for me to get up and go downstairs to pray and meditate? I'm getting better in my spiritual practice each morning, but I would rather this be the rule and not the exception. As I lie in bed pondering, I have decided that I am thwarting my own ability to help both myself and others by allowing a fine mist of negativity to appear and lie about. This is my own lack of control, and it *will stop* because my thoughts will not allow its intrusion.

Spirit:

When times get difficult, send those concerns through prayer, then trust God and his realms to help you find the perfect solutions. Listen to your heart and to your intuition, dear one, for it will never fail. Solutions are presented, grasp them and move forward. Dwell upon those attributes which you do well, and the door will be opened wider. Faith, hope and love are earned through diligent service to others—remember this *always*. If another is hurting, then you, yourself, should feel the pain. Reach out your hand in love to help all those who cross your path. Know that we guide you to complete your mission in physical life, a mission to inspire and encourage others to climb the spiritual pathway to God.

If one attempt does not work as you wish, seek another. We remind you over and over that you, on earth, cannot truly see the real progress which is being made. Live your life with love, integrity and gratitude to God, and all crooked places shall be made straight. We encourage you to think only *positive*, gentle thoughts, and a rainbow of love shall surround those in your prayers.

World peace begins in the mind of each human being; send vibrations of love which can be used to open all minds. Understanding filters into the mind of those who seek to become a part of the whole. We encourage you to continue on the pathway to seek unconditional love, for herein lies the secret to heaven on earth. We come close to help you find what you seek. Peace be with you always.

Tuesday, April 19, 1994

Diane:

So many people are suffering in this life due to the lack of love. It is sad and somehow I wish I was better prepared to be of service to those who suffer from within, yet one can always pray for them. This energy can be used by those who come close to help.

Spirit:

Prayer has great power and can do much more than you in physical life are aware of, for you see not with spiritual eyes. Have faith, dear one, and do not allow yourself any negative feelings or thoughts. See only good coming from each difficult situation, and with patience, it shall be so. Give negativity an inch and it will take a mile. The spirit will choose joy over sorrow and the quicker one views life's difficulties from afar, the sooner solutions will come forth. The void one feels is the journey to that place where one can visualize clearly. Trust your Heavenly Father to make all crooked places straight. Find peace in quiet contemplation, dear one, and in prayer.

Thursday, April 21, 1994

Diane:

I wonder why so many either run away from hurtful situations, or cause unrest within, trying to protect themselves from the inevitable hurt which is part of living. Can you please comment on this thought, dear friends?

Spirit:

When one's being is filled with spiritual energy, it is far easier to cope with the emotional traumas of life. Once one becomes depleted of this energy, problems mount and unhappiness appears instead. How, you ask, can this be prevented?

It is truly necessary for one to carefully guard this energy by seeking God's help through prayer and meditation. A mind cluttered with too many thoughts is on overload and zaps the spirit very quickly. Control of the mind through quiet moments like meditation, allows concerns to move back so helpful messages and ideas may enter to solve the problems and to quiet the unrest. Slowing down the activity of the mind causes one to become more patient, and this is necessary since many solutions take time to work.

To help another, one must be careful to have compassion and empathy without tapping into the precious energy of one's own being. Those who learn unconditional love rarely have problems with vitality. Why is this? Without desiring any return, their energy and love is returned automatically, if in fact, it leaves at all. To be able to give such love, one must make time to spend alone in prayer and contemplation—*this is a must.* Quality time is needed to seek the God force within.

Diane:

Lately I have done a poor job of this for my mind seems too scattered to receive meaningful writings, and I have done more rambling than usual. However, I shall use this opportunity to learn the ability to focus my mind regardless of outside problems. Is it easy to do? Indeed not! Yet, my faith tells me this too shall pass, and more important knowledge shall appear at the perfect moment.

Spirit:

Life is a continuous fountain of opportunity to help one's fellow man. Those who have true desire to learn the truth and serve will always shine with special light. How else can we in spirit know of such desires? Peace be with you.

Tuesday, April 26, 1994

"Place yourself as an instrument in the hands of God who does his own work in his own way."[37]

Diane:

It seems that I am frequently sending situations, for which I have no real control, into God's loving hands.

Spirit:

Yes, dear one, this is indeed progress. Negativity comes in so many forms and it does much to thwart spiritual progress. It is difficult to solve problems out of one's control without thinking any negative thoughts, so to send it to God is, in truth, a form of prayer. God and his realms can work with this form of positive energy. We have cautioned you many times to control your every thought and only allow attention to what can be of use in helping another. Can you not see real progress in your ability to do this? Training the mind to always listen to the inner you, that God force and true Master within, is a giant step to self-mastery.

We come less often to guide you through writings because you, yourself, can answer questions which arise in your life. Wisdom is growing within *you*, my child. Your thoughts and prayers are of a more universal scope, and this energy can be used to heal the world. Falter not in your daily routine of prayer and meditation. The world of spirit now depends upon your discipline to do this. We come close to bring love and peace. Follow your intuition for it speaks the truth.

Saturday, April 30, 1994
Spirit:

Friendship is, indeed, a most important part of life. We urge you, dear one, to be a good friend to yourself at all times. Through this friendship one can learn many lessons of life, and as each lesson is learned carefully and with great patience and love, it can be passed on to others. How often have you heard, "it is good talking to you"? This is the proof that your wisdom is growing in scope, and it can and will help many people. How one lives his life, every small moment of it, is seen by those who watch. Pray for others that they may find the true meaning of life and thus tap into the sparkle of the spirit. As you continue to prepare yourself and learn to relax and find total peace in God's love, so will all things work out in the perfect way. This is the meaning of faith, knowing good will come out of what one cannot yet see.

If one can do this while living life alone, how much more fulfilling your days will become as more people enter in and share it. Change brings progress, so one should always welcome it into his life. If one loves God with all of his heart, the energy and power which returns is almost a miracle. Feel the love and encouragement from those who stand ready to help you. To know their names is not of such importance, but to tune into their helpful ideas will be of much comfort and help. Pray with gratitude, ask with humility and love, and always love those less fortunate than yourself. We hear such prayers and feel the intensity of caring which one sends from his heart. If more were enlightened to the power of unconditional love, the world would be better able to cure itself of many ills.

A positive thought is that we *have* people like you who are willing to find the truth, and then do something to help others. Your book will fall into place at the perfect moment for many come to aid the cause. Keep on keeping on, dear one, and we do continually collect the energy which accompanies unconditional love. It shines with great radiance. Peace be with you.

Wednesday, May 11, 1994
Diane:

It amazes me how much constant self-discipline it takes to walk the spiritual pathway. Just when one feels progress is being made, a slump appears. Perhaps it would be more positive to say, it is a period to re-energize oneself. It does take energy, even when watching the struggles of others. To always keep on top of one's true feelings and purpose is not an easy task. Sometimes I find prayer more difficult when I become unbalanced in my own thinking. Why should this be?

Spirit:

Soul-searching is not an easy task for one more easily catches only glimpses of the real truth about himself. It is in this close-range scrutiny that the flaws become more painful and difficult to behold. It is far easier to blame another than take responsibility oneself. Is this not but another form of rationalization? We are what we think, and each does have the ability to control what is allowed within his own thought pattern. This thought pattern contains energy and brings to it similar energies. This is such an important truth and few realize the magnitude and potential of their own thought pattern. How can it be explained or proven in a more practical format?

Experiment with:
1. Counting your blessings when negativity enters the mind.
2. What occurs when one does something nice for another? Can it cause a mood change?

3. Does listening to music help?
4. What about a bouquet of flowers or beauty of some kind?
5. Learn a mantra.
6. Take time to pray or read spiritual writings.
7. Laugh, for laughter always distracts negativity.

Tuesday, May 17, 1994
Spirit:

Each must live his own life. Everyday each must take the responsibility for his own thoughts. No one else can move into this sacred territory. In order to be of help to another, one must try to understand with love and support, but there are times when no opportunity is available. Prayer then becomes the only path for one in need. There is little or no help in negative thinking, so look to God for guidance.

It is indeed sad when a relationship ends, but always look to the new beginning. Each new day is a new beginning; joy and happiness can suddenly appear the next minute, hour or day. Live your life in peace, dear one, helping all whom you can and extend prayer for those who stray beyond your reach. Use every experience of your life as you research the true meaning of God's truth, for his laws of justice were born of his creation. Is it not true that the more one learns, the less one truly knows?

Self-will closes the door to so much wisdom. The divinity within, that part which belongs to God, wants to speak its truth but too often it remains hidden, as if a prisoner. When will mankind allow this message of love and all of the fruits of the spirit to emerge as a conquering hero? What will it take to cleanse the world of pain, suffering and unkindness? Perhaps the most important message you can send forth, dear one, is that of the importance of each thought which one allows into his own being. Thoughts *can* and *must* be controlled by every human being. Negative thoughts feed on other negative thoughts until they become very powerful. It takes less energy to find fault with everyday occurrences than to see the positive possibilities instead.

Stand guard with diligence as each thought is born within your mind. To become proficient in any endeavor, it does take practice. Meditation and prayer do teach one to look at his own thoughts, for as the body relaxes and slows down its pace, the clear answers from spirit can be heard. Time so spent is never wasted, for it brings peace.

Thursday, June 2, 1994
Diane:
Trying to put my thoughts together about the meaning of angels and particularly about their importance in my life. I know my deep interest means something special, but I'm not able to comprehend the real reason or message, as yet. Thought I might receive a writing about it, although I haven't been as concentrated on spiritual endeavors of late. This probably interferes with communication.

Spirit:
Your mission, dear one, is to quietly listen to others, and in that perfect moment speak a gem of wisdom. You see accomplishment in others, but rarely do you see it in yourself. Know that you do indeed make a difference. Could it not be that the angels are trying to tell you this very message? Unconditional love given through every moment of the day, or a desire to do this, is a rare accomplishment, and so few even dare to try.

Angels are messengers of love and light, so use them as helpful guides in your daily life. Visualize them standing by as a forever friend, and their aura of light and love will join forces with yours, and you will grow with the ability to help others even more. Talk to them as you talk to Ang and your sprites; they will enhance your life with the sparkle of joy. Look for their sparkles of light in your imagination, in your crystals, in your diamond and in the space surrounding you. Faith that they are there, and teach you in many ways, is the key to finding them.

Monday, June 6, 1994

Diane:

I need more time to study, and yet there is much to do otherwise. How does one find a balance in one's life to pursue God's will? Please help me, all who come to guide me, as I climb the spiritual ladder. My garden is my gift to all who come close for it is a living prayer to God for his gift of such beauty. My sprites flit about daily helping me as I work. Somehow my energy reverberates as I work in the soil of Mother Earth for she gives back so much through the grace of God. My awareness is growing daily, and I thank Heavenly Father for his love and patience. The angel consciousness continually surrounds my life with love, joy and peace. I am less critical of myself and others, so there is more room for love to grow.

Spirit:

Goodness ushers in wisdom. This profound truth keeps one seeking daily to be a being of goodness filled with the light of love. Words are not always necessary, my child, for action speaks louder than words. Giving of yourself to help another is doing God's will. It is the simple acts of service that cause the spirit to grow. The journey to unconditional love is learned by giving beyond the call of duty each time there is a need. This is not an easy task but the rewards are many.

Can you name a few that bless your life?

Diane:

1. To find joy in everything
2. A heart bursting with love
3. Another day full of surprises
4. A loving family
5. Good friends
6. The peace of camp and the river
7. My beautiful house, yard and gardens
8. Devotion of Smokey
9. Books to read
10. Happy memories
11. Ang and the peace of knowing he is near, as we wait for that glorious day to be reunited

12. Meditation room and its ambiance
13. Watching my grandchildren grow
14. Beauty of music
15. Breezy summer nights
16. Blue sky, rain and rainbows, and on, and on, and on, and on.

Spirit:

Teach those who allow negativity to interfere with their lives to find more joy in living. This is a great contribution, my child. Walk in peace.

Saturday, June 11, 1994

"Ask and it will be given to you; seek and you will find; knock and the door will be opened to you." *(Matthew 7:7)*

"Most of us have not tried knocking on the door that Jesus is talking about. We are content to spend all our time exploring the outside of the house. The lawn, the shrubs, the trellis and the porch swing receive all our attention, so that we never even get inside, never seek out the One who is waiting there. We turn our cottage into *House Beautiful*, paint it and repaint it, but never so much as knock on the door.

"Not only are we not looking for anybody inside, we are convinced that no one is there. If there is a God, we think he is surely outside, as is everything else that catches our attention. Vaguely, fondly even, we may sometimes imagine as we go about our business that someone is probably keeping an eye on us. But if we will open our ears, we can hear the murmuring from within, the faint stir and rustle of a presence deep inside of us, and a voice hauntingly beautiful. Once we hear that, we will pound on the door with all of our might, so that we can enter and meet the one who has been waiting so long."[38]

Diane:

Why do these words ring so true to me?

Spirit:

As you no longer doubt the ability to communicate with spirit world, you become very apt at hearing our messages. Ang is indeed right at hand,

and we continually encourage you to walk the pathway to God's heart by asking, seeking and knocking. Has this not been a kind of theme song throughout this period of purification, dear one? You write less for there is less need to bring words of wisdom, for you have listened well, my daughter. Now is the time to gather these gems in concentrated order to help others. We shall inspire you to do this great work. Yes, it will be a great work for you have opened the doors to your many talents. Watch your abilities grow until you will amaze yourself. God releases his magnificent energy into those who open their will to do his will. We watch as you pass each test, and at the perfect moment—voila!—a servant of God is born.

Angels and saints come to help you, dear one. This is the reason you have such a strong desire to learn about them. You are drawn by their love and vibration, and the more you become aware of their aspiration to guide and work with you, the greater will be this heaven-sent connection. We see and feel your excitement as you continue to realize the potential which has been locked inside. Without time alone in perfect silence as you link yourself to nature, the task would be far more burdensome. This is why you seek solitude, my child. You are indeed not a loner, but rather you seek the need to look within; this is what releases your potential and ability to love unconditionally. We are always close by. Peace be with you, dear one.

Friday, July 1, 1994

Diane:

Today I am a bundle of mixed emotions: great sorrow, gratefulness, forgiveness for my own shortcomings and for others, and seeking unconditional love to better serve God. Joy is present as well, for each heartfelt experience teaches me more about the sorrow in God's heart as he watches his misguided and foolish children. Thank you, dear Heavenly Father, for your truth and mercy which is always evident in your love, and the joy which is built within each of us. Help me to find better skills on this good side of myself.

Spirit:

Life's happenings cannot bring defeat to one who seeks for love and joy in all things, my dearest one. Your compassion grows with each experience, and you never stand alone. This is true for each; find solace and peace knowing this is true. Each must bear his own trials, so pray that those in need will wisely reach out and find this God-given right. You can only control the thoughts and the actions of your own being, dear one, so release the futility of thinking you are responsible. This only decreases the light within your own being and for what cause? Better to see only positive results of fairness and justice; let God help those who help themselves. Love and be there for others, but see only positive results, and it shall be so.

Many work for you, your son and your grandson, so fear not. Your empathy for those who are troubled will not go unnoticed, but each life must be healed by their own family. This is where truth must be seen very clearly, so that you may continue to climb the spiritual mountain to accomplish what is written in God's book of destiny. Pray always and pray diligently for others because this energy of prayer will one day save the world, but remember the eternal truth of positive thinking. You are in control of your own thoughts and the more you project love, beauty, peace and joy (plus the remaining nine fruits of the spirit), the easier it is for us in spirit to enter into your aura. Humility keeps you on the correct pathway, and love raises you closer to serving God. Joy and happiness brings success to all. Walk in peace, dear one, you are never alone.

"Rejoice in the Lord always! I say it again. Rejoice ... Dismiss all anxiety from your minds. Present your needs to God in every form of prayer and in petitions full of gratitude. Then God's own peace, which is beyond all understanding, will stand guard over your hearts and minds, in Christ Jesus. Finally, my brothers, your thoughts should be wholly directed to all that is true, all that deserves respect, all that is honest, pure, admirable, decent, virtuous, or worthy of praise. Live according to what you have learned and accepted; what you have heard me say and seen me do. Then will the God of peace be with you." *(Philippians 4:4–10)*

Saturday, July 23, 1994

Diane:

How easy it is to think one is better and more well-adjusted than another, but in truth we all have insecurities and problems to face. As long as one can be disturbed by what another does, self-will has not fully been extinguished, and unconditional love has not manifested itself as God meant it to be. This is why one must work a lifetime to become an instrument of God's will. Just when one thinks true progress is being made, another hurdle is placed before him to test the sincerity of that progress. One must look within on a daily basis, and sometimes more than once, to seek the truth and intent of one's own heart. Is there not always more that one can do?

Spirit:

Heavenly Father always helps those who help themselves in their search for truth. Not only feel empathy with others, dear one, but act upon what you feel with unconditional love. Then, and only then, have you done your very best. Ask, seek and knock, for your prayers are always heard. Peace be with you.

Thursday, July 28, 1994

"The best way to deal with a problem is this: Write it down on a piece of paper. Study its components. Think it through. Then put it aside and think of God. Forget the problem. Think of God. The more you think of him, the more he will put ideas into your mind when you pick up the problem again. You will get your answer. God answers. If you don't get it the first time, you will the second or the third. Shift from the problem to God."[39]

Diane:

How does one feel kindness and compassion toward someone who has hurt and manipulated many people, myself included? How do I accomplish this, dear Heavenly Father? I can pray for them and wish that their life will fall into place, but forgiveness is not that easy. Please help me to accomplish more understanding so I may be released as well.

Spirit:

Keep praying for those involved and wait for the right moment to send a note. We shall help you decide when that is. There will be a sign. Sometimes when one stands accused, there is nothing to do but just wait, and send forgiving energies and love in prayer. Each experience, no matter how difficult, can open the heart to greater acceptance and unconditional love. You can still forgive and send loving energies without getting them in return—at least not immediately. Keep on keeping on with prayer, and with God all things are possible. Find peace with yourself, dear one.

The final answer: send no letter yet. Sometimes when one stands falsely accused it is best to say nothing. Did not Jesus show us this when he was wrongfully attacked? This then is the answer to your concerns. Be silent and patiently wait as you send out prayers.

Wednesday, August 17, 1994

Diane:

I woke up very early this morning with thoughts about how to protect someone from negativity, even from a distance. The following was the first thought that came to me.

Spirit:

There is great power in love and light, especially when it comes from a pure heart. As it is with spirit, the most important part of one's being is indeed invisible, yet its force and power go beyond the comprehension of physical life as one lives it. Faith is the key because it unlocks God's love within; and *all* things are possible with God.

Believe, my child, believe. Continue to pray and send these loving thoughts of protection to counter any negativity which surrounds this one you love. Banish all doubts and concerns. These thoughts only diminish the healing capabilities of God's love which channels through you, your son, and all that pray for him—and there are many. Find comfort knowing this.

The tests of physical life are placed before each to teach mastery over self. Those who see with their physical eyes only are missing the important link which joins all of creation together. This knowledge opens the door to help one learn to tap into its great power. Love is potent, and you and your son awaken many to come to the "rescue" when you project a loving thought. This is true of all, but many are not aware of this potential and so it remains dormant.

We come, this early morning, to comfort you and to remind you to remain positive no matter what the circumstances appear to dictate, for underneath the turmoil there is peace and tranquility. We help greatly in protecting your loved one. His sparkle and joy may appear diminished, but the joy and love within him *will* be rekindled soon. Calm the storm within your own being with faith and "know that you know" all will turn out with justice prevailing. God is love and truth; strengthen your faith with prayer and meditation, dear one. We always stand close by to help and comfort you. Peace be with you always.

Friday, August 19, 1994

"In the silence, I am renewed. I find rest and renewal in the silence of prayer. This is because, in prayer, I am consciously reconnecting with God, the source of all life. Prayer recharges my spiritual battery, and I am revitalized.

"Each time I pray, I am immersed in divine love and peace. Any leftover tension vanishes, for I am in the presence of God. People or situations or circumstances that may have troubled me earlier no longer seem threatening. I give every concern over to God, and I trust God to take care of all in the perfect way. In the silence, I become still and listen. God speaks to me through divinely inspired thoughts. Realizations come to me for the best ways to work through a challenge or to achieve a goal. As I turn within in the silence, God truly does renew me."[40]

"But they who wait for the Lord shall renew their strength." *(Isaiah 40:31)*

Diane:

I'm trying to maintain inner calm and tranquility through the nightmare of John's divorce. I pray that a beautiful and powerful light of protection covers my grandson at all times until justice and love overtake the situation again. This situation shows me what God endures all the time as he watches and tries to save his children. My heart is so heavy as the black cloud hangs about, but just behind the storm is a beautiful rainbow. I shall focus my mind on the brilliant colors of this rainbow, for true love is connected to God and all problems which are placed in his loving hands will be made right. I pray for stronger faith and also to try and send more loving thoughts to those who persecute others. Help me to understand better, dear Heavenly Father, your laws of truth, and to always see life from the positive side. Thank you for listening.

Monday, August 22, 1994

Diane:

Once I offer difficulties into God's loving hands, I know the right and just solution will come at that perfect moment. Trying to control my energy level and enthusiasm is indeed another matter. Why is this so, dear friends?

Spirit:

Have you not been reading about the power of thoughts? Redirect *all* of your thoughts and project them all with only positive outcomes—and so it shall be. Try diligently to prevent and or screen out any unwanted thoughts. You are what you think, and God gave each the power to be in *full* control of what one feels is worthy to be allowed into his thought process. As it is with so many of God's truths, this law is simple in structure yet so hard to implement in one's physical life.

Difficulties placed before one gives each the practice to learn the skills of the spirit like faith, love, joy, patience, goodness, gentleness, kindness, self-control and peace. These fruits of the spirit are developed and perfected during one's lifetime. Banish doubts and fears for justice will ultimately prevail. Pray for those who persecute you and yours, for they know not what they do. Those not awakened to God's world of spirit walk blindly. Much of the world still walks in darkness, and you and those who know must shine the light upon them and bring them out of this darkness. We hear your whispers. Peace be with you.

Wednesday, August 31, 1994

Diane:

Nine days have passed since my last entry, and somehow I can't believe how quickly time passes, and yet sometimes when living through especially difficult situations, time drags. I guess this is why time is connected to eternity; it appears simple in theory, but beyond true comprehension while living the physical life.

This is not the topic of my concerns this new morning, but indeed a fascinating one. Instead, I am struggling with negative thoughts rather than positive, constructive ones. What is it that I am to learn from this most frustrating of situations? It continually chips away at the joy and enthusiasm I usually feel toward life. Perhaps the idea of veneer versus solid wood came in as a thought and this makes sense to me.

Spirit:

Work, dear one, on strengthening your ability to only find the positive in all things as if using pure, solid oak, and doing away with any form of a shallow veneer. You *are* what you think and you are in control of what you think. Being positive is the fulcrum—that point where the two meet. Once one has learned this ability, even in the darkest moments, joy is never far from sight.

Remember, you are only in control of yourself, so be careful to not let despair enter into your being through the lack of control in another. Even help is many times not accepted by another, so learn to accept this fact within yourself. Too often mankind desires to control the outcome not only of himself, but also of others—this is *not* possible. So much sadness and negativity comes from this desire to control others.

Look within your own heart and find the correct answers for God is always listening to all who seek his love and truth. It takes great faith in God and in yourself to wallow through despair and still remain positive. We come close to remind you to keep on keeping on, and always visualize a joyful outcome. Thy will be done, dear Father, not my will.

Tuesday, September 13, 1994

Spirit:

It seems like a constant battle to think positive thoughts when negativity circles around so persistently. Keep on keeping on is what one must do, until all of the negativity is swallowed up through faith, prayer, meditation and love. Joy will appear again—that is the law of God's truth. It is always the intent of the heart which is important, so remember this well, my child. Clouds can cover the beauty for a short time, but they dissipate quickly at the perfect moment.

Diane:

I have had little experience with a heart full of malice, so I guess that is what causes me the most distress. Why would someone allow this to happen to them?

Spirit:

God's pathway and his laws are direct and eternal. However many do not follow his road but instead get lost and take matters into their own hands. The road they follow is crooked and leads to great despair. Give of your kindness, your knowledge and your love, but guard your spiritual energy well, and recharge by tapping into God's eternal energy.

Diane:

There is so *much* I do not understand, but each day lived in the right way brings me closer to the answers.

Spirit:

Pray for those you love in these troubled days for their energy and aura can be strengthened by your light. Think of mercury. As your energy gets close to those you love their aura can "zap" it in—it becomes part of them. This is how prayer works; this is how love works; this is how the energy of auric fields works as well. It is the love behind it, and the intent of the heart, which decides the strength and power of prayer.

Be not discouraged, dear one, all will work out, and though damage may be done, it is repairable as well. Think only good results, and it shall be so. What one thinks about all day *is* what one becomes. If you think about God, goodness, love and joy, so will your life and the life of your family become. Even as you head into the stormy parts of life, always see the joy on the other side. This is faith at its best. Rest, and find peace in your heart. Can you not feel how close we come to comfort you?

Thursday, September 22, 1994
Diane:

John [our son] just went up to try and see his son. It is indeed a nightmare, and the child is the one who suffers the most. I will write down thoughts I am having as I attempt to calm my own being. I've been reading a lot lately—perhaps some of the ideas expressed will be of help.

Spirit:

All energy is of God. He created everything from the one source, hence, all things are connected through this eternal energy. Since love is such an important part of this energy, push your thoughts to dwell *only* upon this love. Do you not see, dear one, that those who tackle problems with love increase the healing channel for God, so that Heavenly Father may intervene on the energy of love. Send positive energy only to the one you love, and let it not be mixed with *anything* but a positive energy.

Forgive those who see with such a warped vision and, if possible, help them to see the positive side as well. At least send positive energy to them. Each is ultimately responsible for his own choices for free will is a gift from God. The tragedy is the misuse of this gift. Pray for your loved one from a quiet, calm, serene center, my child. *This* will help the situation, and even when you cannot see the results, know the result *is there*.

Now you are learning, firsthand, what self-control is. Your energy level is high; share this with the one you love for protection. Talk to John about it as well. We come to teach you to not let any light from God escape your being to be used randomly; instead, dear one, remain calm, and direct this light of God directly to the needed source. A child is his own being, and a parent *never* has control over the energy of his child regardless of how it might appear in a physical sense.

See with your spiritual eyes and know with your intuition that all of the positive forces are working toward a God-centered solution. One reaps what he sows—this is truth. Peace be with you. Know that we come close always to help.

Saturday, September 24, 1994
Spirit:
What profound thought or wisdom have you truly learned during the recent difficulties in your life, especially concerning that feeling of almost utter futility?

Diane:
To trust the solution that Heavenly Father will send forth once you place the difficulty in his loving hands. And to minimize time, as it is known in the physical world, and wait with love and patience for this right solution to be forthcoming. I must use the spiritual energies within my own being as I feel directed to do, as they appear in my own thoughts.

Spirit:
It takes hard work to "live" in the realm of spiritual truths while still in the physical body, but enlightenment comes as one continually tries. Do you not see this, dear one? We remind you that merit is earned by right thinking, right action and right loving every moment of life. To love God and oneself, to love mankind and all of creation, one must be master of his own thoughts. Allow only positive thoughts to permeate the mind which indeed affects the light within and around each person.

Continually program this truth into your own being, even as the battle rages within. Stand firm and the invaders will retreat; not even negativity can remain where it is not wanted or allowed. Love and forgiveness are the heroes of such battles. The light from love has the power to transform all negativity, but only as the mind which harbors these negative thoughts begins to open and accept new ideas. Continue to love with a pure heart, and all that you dream will come to be—in God's own time, dear one.

Sunday, October 9, 1994

Diane:

My notes from *Spiritual Enfoldment 4* by White Eagle:[41]

The major initiations applying to humanity come under four elements: earth, air, fire and water. Air controls and purifies the mental body and mastery of it. The lesson of the air element is that of brotherhood... Not enough to live by themselves, but their humanity must expand to touch all lives.

With the Fire element, its lesson is that of using love. The soul that truly radiates love radiates a certain magnetism. Those under this fiery influence must endeavor to use this magical principle to give light, comfort and joy to their brothers and sisters on earth. They will also have "green fingers" for growing things, and fire will respond to them quickly too.

Water controls the emotional body and its purification. Water teaches the lesson of peace and mainly affects the soul, the astral plane, the psyche and psychic things. You have to learn to control this element *within yourself* before you can advance toward the next step, and control astral forces and astral life.

Earth controls the body and also the crucifixion of the lower nature. Earth element teaches the lesson of service and sacrifice. The soul comes to know that ultimately all that has been learned of spiritual truth, all that has been gained, must be surrendered, given back in loving humble service on earth. The keynote of the element is humility.

Diane:

I spent this day in reading; it is important for me to devote time to reading spiritual books. I *must* spend more time in meditation so that I can line up and match these intellectual truths to the divine truths and laws which dwell within my own being. This brings me to the song:

"It's in every one of us to be wise
Find your heart, open up both your eyes
We can all know everything without ever knowing why,
It's in every one of us, you and I."[42]

I marvel at the simplicity and beauty of God's spiritual and divine laws, yet, oh so difficult to live in daily, physical life. How do I purify and perfect my own being enough to do God's will?

Spirit:

Read, study, pray, meditate and follow the dictates of your heart and intuition. One cannot only study the mystery and magic of love, one must jump in and do it. Unconditional love guides one to do what is needed; one just knows. This is why true love from the heart takes control of the mind and one sacrifices himself without feeling pain or sorrow, but instead experiences true joy. Is this not true, dear one?

Proof can readily be found by looking closely within one's own being. The pathway of God's will is found by waiting, with patient endurance and love and peace in one's heart until the perfect moment. Prayer and meditation keeps one from slipping off the current step in his spiritual climb to find God within. We remind you again to listen to the song in your heart for this is of primary importance. The mind can take you on many detours, whereas the heart knows the proper and best route to travel. This does not mean one must disregard the mind, but rather place its desire on the other end of the scale.

Is there balance between heart and mind? If not, wait patiently until the balance is perfected. Keep on keeping on, dear one, for the light of love grows brighter every day. Peace be with you always.

Thursday, October 13, 1994

Diane:

Each day I learn a little more about myself and the need to have more faith in the goodness of God. *Daily Word* for this day states it perfectly:

"I have absolute, unshakable faith in the goodness of God. I have faith in God and in God's power to pour abundant good into my life.

"I do not think thoughts of lack. Instead, I fill my mind with images of radiant health and abundant prosperity, and I faithfully expect health and prosperity to be my experiences.

"I have faith in God to guide and protect the ones I love. I place my loved ones in God's care and keeping, and know that the indwelling spirit of God is leading them on the paths that are right for them.

"My prayers are prayers of faith. I pray believing, and I give thanks that my prayers are heard and answered in ways that are best for all concerned. I have absolute, unshakable faith in God's wisdom and love. Confident of my relationship with God, I am at peace."[43]

What a helpful writing! Why does every little change, comment or incident concerning the current problem, drain me of energy and positive thinking? Please, dear Heavenly Father, help me to address my own inadequacy so that I may be forever victorious over my own thoughts and emotional reaction.

Spirit:

The word *faith* is of utmost importance, dear one. Feel it throughout your entire spiritual being and beyond. Do you not see that again you become the prisoner of your physical being? You project outcomes on the physical level. Perhaps the reason for this is to precondition yourself for disappointment because you have heard things turn out certain ways in certain situations, or you allow negative energies to steal or suck from your own strong faith. We strongly urge you to become master of your own being, and simply stop allowing this to happen. We understand how simple it is to state, yet most difficult to accomplish. Think of it as just interference and simply turn the channel until the message of faith rings clear as a bell—right from the God center within.

Restore your faith through Heavenly Father that justice shall prevail, and it will. Refrain from preconceiving how it all shall be accomplished, but know truth and love are the most powerful of tools to pray for during the court hearing. We remind you again that you are not responsible for how another reacts; instead examine the motives of your own reaction. If there is forgiveness and a degree of love coming from your heart, what more can you do? You think you do not love enough in so many instances, dear one, but the light of understanding and forgiveness shines forth brightly.

Be more confident in your own abilities to project justice and the proper outcome, and it shall be so. The means through which this is accomplished sometimes must be placed in the hands of others, but know that Heavenly Father and his high realms will help, as will your dear ones in spirit. It is only through faith that one finds peace. See with both sets of eyes, and as you have learned through much prayer, meditation, suffering and study; the spiritual truth is what truly matters, and it shall, in all its glory, show itself to be victorious.

We encourage you to continue the climb to self-mastery. Faith grows stronger under duress and this situation is indeed living proof of the need to master one's thoughts into loving messengers of divine truth. Peace be with you.

Monday, October 17, 1994
Diane:

The most important of Heavenly Father's gifts is unconditional love, and this is the most important, single task before me—to truly have love for those who are difficult to love. I am gaining on this monumental task, for there is so much more forgiveness within my own being, and this is true progress.

I shall continue to see a courtroom filled with love and justice for all present. I try hard *not* to judge or verbally criticize others, but instead send healing energies that they too, may love themselves and others, and find inner peace. It is the unloved who do need the most forgiveness, and since I know the power of prayer and positive thinking, it is up to me to do my part in helping another to find more love and peace.

The most precious truth about unconditional love is its capacity to enfold more and more people within its waves of protection, beauty and peace. Forgiveness is the pathway to unconditional love. I pray that my heart center will continue to open wide so that this beautiful truth can happen within my own being. I know then that I will be better able to serve and do God's will. The marvel that the more one spiritually grows, new wisdom, ideas and avenues awaken almost like magic. Thank you, dear Heavenly Father.

Monday, October 24, 1994

Diane:

I read this article in *Unity Magazine* by Jan DeVries, and I thought it had very good advice.

"Four simple steps to abundance:
1. Working with what is available
2. Giving thanks for it
3. Keeping the mind free from negative thoughts
4. Continually listening for the still, small voice within for directions."[44]

Thursday, November 3, 1994

Spirit:

Healing can be brought about by focusing one's mind, and allowing only thoughts of love, light and energy to draw out only positive reactions. Health and well-being begins within the mind. Again, too many look for health from an outside force, when in reality it comes from within. The mind, connected to God in energy, can control the workings and health of the body far beyond what man is aware of.

This is an exciting time to live, dear one, for new ideas and so-called discoveries are appearing each day. Those who strive to find the beauty of God and continue to experience life with an open mind will be awestruck by the potential available to the ones who ask, seek and knock.

"The sky's the limit," so to speak. We come to remind you that all things *are* possible for those who believe with faith. Protection in so many ways is possible provided one learns, accepts and follows spiritual laws. Questioning as one seeks the truth is indeed acceptable, provided he who seeks understands the true nature of God, and hence, unconditional love.

Love releases self-will, which is the cause of all ills upon earth. Those who can see a spark of good even in the least lovable, begin to find and see the possibilities released by this core energy of love. It is encouraging to us from the spirit world to see how the avenues of spiritual growth are opening on earth at this time. Mankind is thirsting for such exposure, yet, the most important lesson to learn is unconditional love.

Be one who continually sets an example of this type of love. Always find time for the downtrodden, the injured, the suffering—whether animal, vegetable or mineral. All things *are* connected, and this is where the strength of God's core energy lies. To be worthy to tap into this power, all self-will must be released, and only love, which is God's voice, will be heard and followed. We come close always. Peace be with you, dear one.

Thursday, November 17, 1994
Diane:

My problem is priorities. There is much to do to prepare for my sister-in-law Flora's visit and then Thanksgiving. Plus, the many other activities which I must do such as writing in the computer, watering my faithful plants, Smokey and the bird, writing of cards—to name but a few. This is indeed not a complaint for I love doing all things (raking is not high on the list however), yet it is necessary to keep everything in proper perspective.

Spirit:

Do this, dear one, by taking one job at a time and completing it with a joyful heart before moving on to the next item on your list. Trust in that built-in wisdom that dwells within each human being. Take the time to listen for without careful connection to this wellspring of knowledge, do you not tend to run helter-skelter and accomplish little? What made you listen to the advice to come to the meditation room and seek more peace? Was it not the spirit self taking control of the situation? You see, in spite of what *you think* you think, did you not perceive the spiritual pathway? We heard your concerns in prayer last night and know that you are growing in unconditional love as more peace, tranquility and self-control enter your being.

To control one's thoughts is a big hurdle on the spiritual pathway to finding God within. So many people believe that the external qualities control one's life, but in truth, the most important happenings of life are decided from within. How many times have you seen others make mountains out of molehills, or destroy an opportunity to find joy by interference and the failure to listen from within their own being? Many short circuit their own energy through wrong thought which inevitably causes wrong action.

Take the time, dear one, to put things in their proper perspective and this must *always* be done with calmness. The purer your heart becomes, the more unconditional love it can contain and this formula produces a peaceful, God-centered person. Pep talks, so to speak, are released from within to guide you. Listen well, my child. "God did not give us a spirit of timidity but a spirit of power and love and self-control." *(2 Timothy 1:7)*

Thursday, December 1, 1994
Spirit:

Hate only feeds the fire one wishes to extinguish. It is a negative force, and though it appears as a legitimate emotion, it destroys the foundation of God's love. Hate is destructive for it survives only on negative thoughts and this undermines the beauty of love. Frustration is an ally, a channel through which hate can manifest and grow. It would be our suggestion that you use great strength and self-control to minimize this strong, undermining emotion, and instead place that which you hate in the hands of Jesus who can teach love and the fruits of the spirit. Always be pure hearted and loving, then all that is loving will appear in your life. God works through those who understand his heart, his love, and his great sacrifices to save mankind. Stand firm in your desire to be an instrument of his will, and see through your emotions until you find God's divine love. This is not an easy task, but those who are chosen to do an important work involving many souls must learn to withstand great pressure. There are many who stand close by to help you. Peace be with you.

Wednesday, December 14, 1994

Diane:

Today's *Daily Word* is about faith. From the Bible "For we walk by faith, not by sight." *(II Corinthians 5:7)*

I am trying to live always by faith, forgiving myself and others for our trespasses, and knowing that justice will come in time in all situations. This is God's law. I need not harbor unkind thoughts for this does nothing to right any situation.

Spirit:

To stand accused is not an easy thing to accept, but to accuse another of wrongdoing does not solve the problem. Instead, release the negativity from your being so that the good, the positive, the loving may fill the void. One is *always* in control of what he thinks and ultimately what he does. Love and kindness handle any negativity the right way, even if the result hoped for does not show itself immediately.

There are many reasons time is necessary before justice is accomplished. Many times one must learn an important lesson about himself before the answer comes. What is there to gain in one's spiritual growth if lessons are not learned? To read and nod one's head in agreement with a revealing truth is important, but this truth must be lived in daily life without fail. If it is a difficult test and one that is hard to abide by, many times one must wait and learn the lesson with more diligence.

This is why spiritual growth is a slow process. It can never be hurried for one must learn to act correctly in all situations which call upon this truth. Wisdom and more understanding is the reward as one climbs closer to God within himself. We each belong to God for he is our creator, our loving Mother/Father image which all, whether they know it or not, continually seek to find. Do not tire as you turn the stumbling blocks into stepping stones, dear one. We come close to help you. Find peace in all that you do.

1995

Monday, January 9, 1995

Diane:

There is much to do, and some of it doesn't seem to get done. I haven't been very faithful to meditation; and yet, my heart grows bigger to harbor more love and a special feeling of understanding continues to grow in spite of less time downstairs. Perhaps the quality is surpassing the quantity. Is this possible?

Spirit:

How, dear one, does one grow in love? Is it not in doing small deeds of kindness without expecting or asking for something in return? Is it not a secret you keep locked in your heart rather than always forming into words what you did? If one person is affected by your presence each day, where does that special moment go? Could it not continue onward into a good deed performed by the one you encountered, and so on, and so on? The heart grows in compassion ever so slowly, and nothing that God nurtures is done in haste, but rather with great patience and faith.

"And now here is my secret, a very simple secret; it is only with the heart that one can see rightly; what is essential is invisible to the eye."[45]

Peace be with you, dear one, as you grow in love.

Saturday, January 21, 1995

Diane:

The justice system does not serve justice, and freedoms are being taken away due to the crumbling of morality. How painful for Heavenly Father, who gives us *so much*, to watch his truth being badly abused causing injustice to many on the physical plane. I thank God for the great privilege of some understanding about the world of spirit where truth does reign, for those deserving will live in love, beauty and peace.

Spirit:

Write your book, dear one, and continue to love even if at times it seems futile. Love can penetrate and cure all ills; there just is not enough love present to go around. However, let not this scarcity discourage you, for love is *most* powerful and it works in ways not visible to the physical body. The energy of true love can be magnified and its aura is far-reaching.

We beg you to continue to love even into futility for love is *never* wasted. We who come close to you, promise you this. Find healing in all of the gifts Heavenly Father gives freely to you and to everyone through his unconditional love. Continue to learn his great truth. We come to remind you that one discovers the truth more quickly under duress and sorrow. As the heart bleeds, love grows and like magic it blossoms into the realm of all-knowing. This is the reward for treading the spiritual pathway to finding God's heart. Peace be with you.

Sunday, January 29, 1995

Diane:

I'm pondering the following thoughts: to understand, to accept, to see a wider spectrum—but faith is *knowing* "Thy will be done" in God's own time. There *is* a purpose even when the soul cries out in despair, injustice and sorrow. If one cannot feel the heart of God in all of his glory, no matter what the situation seems, how can he do his Father's will?

Spirit:

Have you not been praying to understand the heart of God more fully, dear one? *This* is the pathway. To live on the outside of suffering by accepting it only intellectually is not the same as allowing every pain, anguish, injustice or sorrow to penetrate to one's heart emotionally. It is through prayer and meditation that one is able to cope and turn agony into a positive force to find self-mastery. Each in physical life must experience the wide range of emotions deep inside. In this internal battle, knowledge, facts, emotions and feelings are chewed, churned, digested and spit out accordingly. If the spark of God's love can soften the negativity which often accompanies problems of the physical world, the fruits of the spirit will grow and conquer all problems.

You, dear one, must pray often and with total concentration to dissipate the hate, fear and anxiety which surrounds the planet earth. The peace, love and understanding sent through prayer does much to heal the hearts of many, both on earth and in the spirit world. One small flame can ignite the wicks of many until the light of understanding shines forth brightly for all to see. Keep on keeping on; we hear your every prayer. Peace be with you.

Wednesday, February 8, 1995
Diane:

Last night I watched the movie about Bernadette, the girl who saw the visions at Lourdes. It is an old movie, but very touching. There are so many miracles and happenings that we are not even aware of while in our physical bodies. I am learning to be more satisfied with my own spiritual progress, realizing that enlightenment comes as each is ready. Nothing in God's domain is in a hurry. Is there not all of eternity in which to grow and continue the pathway into God's loving arms? It is we, ourselves that make the journey so tedious and long.

Spirit:

Have faith, dear one, and continue to grow in love, truth and health each moment of each day—truly making it a masterpiece. Unconditional love shines as a great beacon and much good can be accomplished with its power and energy. Just because this energy of love cannot be seen readily, does not make it any less real. This is the fallacy of physical life for those scientifically- and intellectually-oriented.

The true greatness is in the unseen world which God created first. To love is innate; to learn otherwise and recoil from it, is the great sin of man. This condition of recoiling from love is caused by the flaws created by man's ego, and his distance from the love and goodness of God.

Align your prayers and thoughts to coincide with God's love, dear one, and the energy can be used to right the wrongs which man has created in his ignorance and disbelief. Learn to banish all fear, all anxieties, all insecurities and worries in your life, and send them into the light of God's love where they may be dissipated forever. Forgive those who trespass against you and pray for others to forgive your trespasses. We stand ready to help always. Peace be with you.

Friday, February 17, 1995
Diane:

Oh, for peace on this earth, where each takes the time to love all of creation and to learn the energies behind every animal, vegetable and mineral! It takes eternity, for there are so many of these energies to know and experience. The more I study, the less I know because the possibilities of God's creation are endless. This is a wondrous discovery, and it brings unlimited joy into one's being. Love and gratitude are the keys to opening these wonders of creation. Thanks be to God.

I pray for guidance and help so that I can travel the road to finding God's will. I must incorporate the following into my life:
1. One day a week of juice or liquid fasting
2. Exercise—either walking or 30 minutes of floor work
3. Daily prayer and meditation
4. Scheduled time for work on my book
5. One day of sorting items in the house

If I can accomplish the self-discipline to do these things on a regular basis, new avenues will open up for me. My intuition speaks to me, but I do not always listen and heed the message. This is *my* weakness, but one that I can work on.

Friday, February 24, 1995

Diane:

Today I was reading about the medical field, and so many of the preventative tests and treatments are now being looked at as unreliable and perhaps harmful. It amazes me how my inner knowing already told me this; some don't understand me, but that's okay. If we follow good nutrition and a healthy spiritual lifestyle, giving praise and gratitude to our creator and listening carefully to the guidance within, health is truly within our grasp.

I continually seek for my true pathway, and at the perfect moment the light shall guide my way. It is my own lack of self-control which looms in the way. My twitching eye condition is indeed an indication that *all* is not peaceful within, even if I think it is so. It is twitching less, but not totally gone. My writings are less frequent, but this is good for I *must* tabulate all the ones I have already written.

The most profound truths are simple in theory. It is the implementation that causes such stress because many are not aware of the importance these truths play in their lives. It is the realization that everything is part of the whole and deserves love, respect and honor. If one disappears and becomes lost to us, we will all suffer in some way. Selfishness, greed, jealousy, hate, envy and all like emotions must be put in their rightful place which is "out of mind." Negative thoughts are all-consuming, and they leave little room for the truth of love.

Tuesday, February 28, 1995

Spirit:

Let go of the past, dear one, and move into a new freedom of love, heart and mind. It is all too easy to stay entrapped within old mindsets and lack of motivation. Too often one looks to others to give them the necessary incentive to accomplish a desired goal. In truth, the greatest help will come to those who continually strive to find the God-force within their own being. Each human being has the potential to connect with this great force of love, light and energy. One must continually seek this unseen world of spiritual energy. It is far more difficult to align oneself with an invisible spiritual power than to be influenced by the many easier trappings of the physical world.

Keep on keeping on, dear one. Set your deepest desires into motion by mastering total control over your own being. Reset the goals as needed, and spend little time in criticism and regret. These negative thoughts only zap energy from the true source of accomplishment which comes from the spiritual side of your being. Once you make the full commitment to write, help will be sent tenfold. We see the strength of this commitment growing stronger each day. Face physical life with all of its experiences head on. Each must confront himself with eternal truth if progress is to continue.

To reach another plateau, one must continue to seek within. Prayer from a heart filled with honest effort is clearly heard. Empty words will not save the plight of mankind, but rather the energy from those who seek to find God's heart via the fruits of the spirit. Peace be with you, dear one.

Tuesday, March 14, 1995
Diane:

I am getting more proficient in letting dear Heavenly Father help in working out problems. He knows what needs to be done, and if I live by the fruits of the spirit and have gratitude in my heart, all things are possible with God. The reward for learning this lesson is more peace in one's life. Peace is learning to live inside a circle of unconditional love where compassion and forgiveness sweep away unkind thoughts.

Spirit:

Even when you think you are not growing spiritually, dear one, the truth of the matter is, you are. Each day is a new beginning, and if you do your best, God will help to turn it into a masterpiece. Selfless love feeds not only yourself, but those that you help and far beyond. This is why kind deeds bring such joy.

One day you must write about each of the fruits of the spirit and how it affects your life. Jewels shared only increase their brilliance. Remember, dear one, the physical world was created *first* in the realm of spirit, and that is where each shall return when the physical body becomes sick, destroyed or old. Fear is caused by the misunderstanding of this great, eternal truth, and imagination and creativity help to guide in finding one's own thread to weave into the tapestry of eternal life. Those who ask, seek and knock will find the seemingly hidden truths, for they dwell within each who lives. Peace be with you, dear one.

Wednesday, March 15, 1995
Diane:

Watching and becoming aware of the subtle ways God's realm of beauty, nurtured by all of his workers, touch and enhance my life. I'm taking time every day to notice this wondrous love. The crocuses in my garden, with their abundance and beauty, tell me of this love. How do I know? It is as if each bloom sends a kiss filled with great love and joy. This uplifting feeling can be transferred to more mundane tasks through the mastery of my own thought patterns.

It is so easy to become caught in the trap of daily stress, but one who learns the art of meditation and quiet contemplation will become more aware of these "hidden" joys. To perfect any new venture takes great practice, but few truly explore this realm of energy. Each has the ability; few take the time to notice its power. Perhaps in my book I should write a chapter on "Hidden Treasures." Faith is feeling and knowing what can be, even before it is seen.

Tuesday, March 28, 1995
Diane:

I pray that my grandson may soon stay overnight with his father. I'm thinking and projecting these positive thoughts, and growing stronger in them. This is an important universal law which too few truly understand. Thought has great potential power when used with God's blessing. It is the human mind that fails to discipline itself and the results can indeed be disastrous.

Spirit:

Continue to enlighten in your own way, dear one, for it does make a difference. Little ideas planted as seeds will grow, even without proper nourishment. Then when given more attention, these thoughts will flourish. The more consistently one seeks the wonders of God, more of his seeds of truth can germinate. Little deeds and thoughts of kindness travel far beyond what is visible with the physical eyes. The intuitive and spiritual senses are what live into eternity, yet they are fed by the acts of one's physical life on earth. The hidden truth, the secret, is how very important each day becomes to the growth of the spirit. What one does every moment of each day is so vital for it gives the needed nourishment. Continue to love *all* things, dear one, and it will make a difference. Peace be with you.

Thursday, March 30, 1995
Diane:

We, as a country are *so* wasteful—myself included. I shall try to be more careful and do less wasting of Mother Nature's treasures. Again, if *each* human being would place attention upon this carelessness and waste, Mother Earth might begin to breathe more easily.

This journey to begin to love all things is a difficult but rewarding one. It was a pleasure to remember old friends again as I worked through many old Christmas cards. Some are still in physical life, yet others have moved into eternal life, and these dear people especially brought a smile to my heart. It is these little joys which bring such happiness into my life. Oh, to share this great secret with those too busy to find the time.

Spirit:

Be of good cheer, dear one, for more and more people will be forced to discover this secret since a stressed-out person will eventually be shut down by his own being; then there is little else to do but listen from within. Money and all of its purported attributes do not satisfy the spirit, the eternal spirit, and sooner or later this message will make itself known. The irony and tragedy comes when many find that they have discovered the true meaning of life too late, for much precious time has already passed by them. However, it's better late than never.

Live your life with joy as you discover the meaning of unconditional love. The light of faith and knowledge brightens in those who continually ask, seek and knock. See and feel the joy of the end result, even as you labor to complete it. This is the answer to finding happiness—lips with an eternal smile! Peace be with you always, my child.

Saturday, April 8, 1995
Diane:

I pray for fortitude to continue the process of moving my possessions, collected over thirty-six years in this lovely house, to the other side of the house. It is a healing process as well because letting go of the past does cleanse and free one to move on into the next chapter of life.

I continue to learn more important lessons of wisdom within my own life, and I pray that I may pass this feeling of peace onto others. It is so easy to stray from one's ultimate desire of accomplishment and I cry for help to do what I am destined to do in this lifetime. Pitfalls constantly appear, and yet, the glory of faith is knowing that the difficulties will pass, and the result will teach the lesson needed to grow spiritually. Each moment can contain the seed of joy; it is our nurturing that brings this seed into fruition. This is a most *difficult* lesson to learn, but with each new awakening, life becomes more meaningful. Time spent in quiet contemplation is never wasted, but instead brings the peace needed to look at each moment with a clearer vision.

Spirit:

You are learning this lesson well, dear one. Continue to live your life in this manner, and those wise enough to see will find time for meditation as well. Action speaks louder than words. Find peace in all that you do. We come close to help.

Monday, April 10, 1995

Diane:

If I breathe in the light and love of God and send it forth to the world, it must truly touch my being as well. This lovely truth came to me this morning in the meditation room during my prayer time. This is how one replenishes his own being by putting others first—*it just is.*

Friday, April 14, 1995

Diane:

All of us want a loving and compassionate spirit, so that love will be the ruling principle of our lives. And we have it! If people seem unfair in their dealings with us, we bless them and release judgmental thoughts about them. We then direct our energy into being the loving and compassionate people that we are in spirit. "This is my commandment, that you love one another as I have loved you." *(John 15:12)*

I still have problems within myself with the feeling of anger. I can keep it under control to an annoyance now, and I am working hard on blessing and releasing judgment on others, as certain injustices happen frequently in the lives of my loved ones. What gives someone the right to control others?

In my heart I know that it is necessary to stop allowing unrest within my own being, but the road of life is a difficult, spiritual climb. It is far easier to write the words of truth down on paper than it is to live them every moment of every day. But I continue to try to wipe out any negative feelings through forgiveness and blessings of those who trespass against us. I am sure I hurt others in their interpretation of me. Perhaps that is a key word in this writing—interpretation. How does one interpret life through the eyes of goodness and truth, dear friends?

Spirit:

Unconditional love contains all of these: peace, faith, joy, patience, kindness, goodness, gentleness, self-control, plus non-judgment as well. Did you have anything to do with the creation of man? Do you not need to explore within your own being the meaning of life first, before judging another? God knows and understands his creation, so when in doubt, release your anxieties into his great hands and wait with patience for his helpful solutions. The physical eyes see only one side of the coin, and so human interpretation is indeed lacking in many ways.

Love enough, dear one, to allow faith and patience to bring joy through acts of kindness, goodness and gentleness; for peace will then abide within you. This is self-mastery. Follow the example of Jesus every day of your life. He turned persecution into a beacon of light; should you do any less? Work on your own weaknesses and it will strengthen all of mankind. As each droplet of water contributes to making a mighty ocean, so shall a pure heart light the way for others. If one life shines, the life next to it will catch the light. Walk in peace and love, dear one.

Tuesday, April 18, 1995
Diane:

There is much to accomplish today, so I will take one task at a time, calmly and with peace in my heart, so nothing can overwhelm me. Heavenly Father and his light of energy and love walk beside me, so there is no problem so great that it cannot be solved. It is we, ourselves, within our own minds, who fail to keep things in proper perspective and to seek peace through gratitude and love. How am I to convey all this wisdom to others when I still struggle to put a proper perspective on daily living myself?

Spirit:

Again, and again we say to you, trust in God and his high realm spirits to show you the way. The reason it is so hard for those of us in spirit to help mankind is the lack of faith—a true, abiding faith in the laws of truth upon which God built his creation. Many tend to give of themselves halfheartedly, pretending their faith and love is genuine, but little time is ever spent seeking this God force within. How precious life would become for each if he learned how to tap into this all-knowing, all-encompassing energy of God's unconditional love.

The secret lies, dear one, in your ability to totally trust as you place yourself in Heavenly Father's hands, and wait, with great patience, his answer. It is in the rushing forth with scattered faith that problems become unmanageable. Instead, dear one, sit quietly in prayer so you can control the random thoughts which strive to destroy the peace within. Again, self-mastery within one's own mind will decide the outcome. As a man thinks, so he is. Peace be with you.

Tuesday, April 25, 1995
Diane:

I found a good line from a booklet called *After the Rain* by Unity writer, Barrie Jones: "The difference between mourning and morning is U."

What we see through the eyes of our thoughts is the answer to finding joy. Will it be a new beginning like a dawn, or the somber thoughts which accompany mourning? Help me, Heavenly Father, to always see the light of love.

Sunday, April 30, 1995

"For wisdom is better than jewels, and all that you may desire cannot compare with her." *(Proverbs 8:11)*

Diane:

The month of May is here. It is a very special month—the season for rebirth. Mother Earth awakens and sends forth her beauty. For a few days I am truly resting my knee so that it can repair itself. It is amazing how we humans know what *should* be done, but oftentimes fail to heed the warnings. Time marches onward, and the body is not able to do what it did in youth, so the wise *will learn* to pace themselves. I am in the process of learning this.

Monday, May 8, 1995

Diane:

Things come in and things go out. There are lots of changes in my life at this time. However, now I know I can grow old gracefully, for change has indeed become an adventure for me. Life is always changing and so it must. My secret, with God's help, is to change with it.

I have no complaints because I am learning to enjoy whatever must be done by concentrating on the moment. One's attitude comes from controlling the thoughts which are allowed to dwell therein. Positive thoughts beget positive outcomes. One must practice through prayer and meditation to secure the necessary skills to empower oneself with positive thinking at all times.

The link to God's love lies within the stillness of a quiet mind, and clarity of thought dwells within this realm of calmness. Each must continue to ask, seek and knock at this place of beauty, finding daily refuge in the stillness of one's own mind. Thanks be to God.

Wednesday, May 10, 1995

"We cannot change the past, but we can change the thoughts and feelings we hold about the past. And we can change the way past events affect us in the present."[46]

Diane:

I must meditate and pray more to line myself up with God's grace. There's been no important writing for a long while and this comes about because I am lax in my self-discipline. The laws of a spiritual life are not so complex; it is in learning the self-discipline of living such a life which becomes complex and difficult to achieve. This is why there are so few saintly people. Oh, to begin to achieve what lies hidden within my own heart! Progress is indeed *so slow*.

Action speaks louder than words, so I shall work on the computer for awhile this morning. My energies are lower than usual, but that changes very quickly when I refuse to dwell upon it. I have so much to be grateful for, and I thank Heavenly Father for granting so much good in my life.

May I grow in unconditional love each day and in my small way lighten the load of those I encounter along the way.

Thank you, dear Father. When there is so much to do, I miss Ang and his energy to get started. We did have a great team effort, and I try to not draw on his energy now that he has moved on into the world of spirit. I know he talks to me and comforts me in my thoughts and as I sleep. But he has much to do in his world and I do not wish to interfere with that special work. In God's own time we shall join forces again.

Spirit:

To be a good listener one must hear what another is saying, not what *you wish* to hear. It is so easy to force your beliefs upon one who suffers, yet this helps them not. Rare is the person who can listen with total compassion, neither passing judgment nor giving of advice. Is this not unconditional love, dear one? Is this not what you strive to achieve? Happy are we when you take the special time to clear your mind of daily affairs, for your channel is indeed pure, more than you give yourself credit for. Kindness, goodness and gentleness do not go unnoticed, my little one. It is the love within a heart at all times which gives merit. We come to remind you that we hear the quiet cries which come from within you for all of humanity. Positive prayer is needed abundantly to reverse the trend of negativity. Keep on keeping on, dear one.

Monday, May 17, 1995

"During my prayers, I release myself into God's care and keeping. I gladly let go of all tension from my mind and body and immerse myself in God's wellspring of life."[47]

"Those who wait for the Lord shall renew their strength." *(Isaiah 40:31)*

"...nature as a vast community of interacting, intercommunicating, cooperating centers of life. Far from being the exception, collaboration is the rule in which entirely different species find ways to help each other. Biologists call such a relationship *symbiosis*—'to live together.' Are we drawn to nature because there we encounter something quietly working in every species—something that guides species to find in each other a way to connect—unifying us all?"[48]

Diane:

Dear, dear friends, is there not wisdom in all living things? What is it that makes us continually seek such wisdom?

Spirit:

For all to live together in peace—this common thread must touch all things, dear one. Heavenly Father in his magnificence imparted into each of his creations a link of continuity which connects everything together whether out of physical or spiritual need. There is a piece of Heavenly Father in all things. Each grows in wisdom as he discovers and appreciates the divinity in all things!

God's greatest reward must come from watching each of his children discover this oneness as he grows in love and joy. Sorrow and sadness are the storms of life, but without this nourishment the spirit could not grow. The key to finding joy is found in learning the meaning behind these storms of life. Mother Nature helps each to unlock the many hidden doors of the soul where wisdom patiently waits to be released. We must work diligently through prayer, meditation and love to see the wonder of God's love. It is there, freely given to all who learn its secrets.

Be thou one who steadily treads onward through the storms of life, blessing those who trespass against you, asking forgiveness from those whom you hurt, and continually seek to love all things. Survival of mankind will depend upon such love for it is indeed the foundation of Heavenly Father's creation. Peace be with you.

Thursday, May 18, 1995

"... I now know that the Christ spirit is within and I no longer look beyond myself for the strength to step out into new territory, the faith to do what I truly desire to do."[49]

Diane:

I need to center myself again into more consistent prayer and meditation. The pull to always accomplish "outside" things is so very strong. I wish I was able to put spiritual desires above all else but it takes such dedication and concentration to do this. I do not mean half-hearted devotion or the kind of prayer that I consider "lip-service" or rote-type prayer, but rather compassion and true, heartfelt concern for all of Heavenly Father's creation. I so desire to be closer to his heart and to live in the realm of unconditional love, humility and service.

Write a book, write a book, write a book—this always seems to crop up as my answer. Is my wisdom and faith strong enough to walk this bridge of creativity?

Spirit:

Faith in self, dear one, is in direct correlation to your faith in Heavenly Father. Do you truly believe that all things are possible with God? If so, the sky is the limit and only good can come from an all-believing heart and mind. Thoughts want to follow the built-in wisdom from God, but it is the free will of each which must decide to follow his will. This is the true beauty of each soul.

Once the heart and mind become as one, Heavenly Father rejoices for one is then on the right pathway to discover the truth of his spiritual laws. The one, who continually asks, seeks and knocks with diligence and love, finds the door opening. Be strong in your conviction and practice the art of prayer and meditation daily. The deeper the dedication, the greater is the power of its energy. We come close to bless your endeavors. Always walk in peace and love.

Thursday, May 25, 1995

Diane:

As a person thinks, so he *is*. The beauty is one can *always* change the direction of his thought patterns. Faith can use its strength and power to influence the seemingly impossible, for with God, all things are possible. If one can truly see positive outcomes in his mind's eye, so it shall be accomplished. Our thought patterns are connected to the creativity of all things; it is there for each to tap into when one's faith leads the way. Did Jesus not say "your faith has healed you?"

Spirit:

Seek always, dear one, but do so with a heart full of love and compassion. See only positive outcomes and then watch them develop into a reality. What cannot be seen holds the secrets of that which can be seen. Life is a living riddle. Discover the paradox and move one step closer to Heavenly Father's truth. Do not be dismayed by those who have lost their way in the mire of negativity, for change is but a thought away. Heartfelt prayer can and will change the trend of the world today. Despair does nothing to alleviate problems; positive thoughts lead to positive action.

One cannot see his influence using only his physical senses, for the true value of a person finds itself in the spirit. To see life filled with joy, as if a child, is such a great gift. Cherish this, my child, and give its beauty to all who touch your life. We come to bring you peace. All will work out in God's own time for those who practice the gift of loving. "A tranquil mind gives life to the flesh." *(Proverbs 14:30)*

Wednesday, June 7, 1995

Spirit:

Nothing arouses one more emotionally than anger, dear one. Anger itself is not the culprit, for out of anger many good seeds are fertilized by its energy and power. Rather, it is the lack of self-control that anger causes. Persecution and injustice are most difficult to bear, but those who fight back with an assemblage of love create the atmosphere for justice to prevail. Two wrongs never constitute a right; instead, good and justice must overshadow the wrong. Corruption has and can cause havoc in many peoples' lives, but those with patience and steadfast perseverance *can* win the battle.

High realm spirits choose those who have these qualities to lead this cause to change the direction of mankind. Do not compromise your own values in fighting the battle of injustice, but find guidance and solace within your own being through prayer and meditation. The greater the mission, the more one is tested by being put in situations which cause duress and turmoil within. Pray for guidance to control the anger, and though it is necessary to fight back, let it be done with love and justice.

Love lives in one's heart and it cannot be judged by another. Only Heavenly Father and the person himself know the truth of his own being. Superficial judgment runs rampant in these times because too few take the time to judge themselves. It is far easier to judge another, because then a person need not judge oneself.

As you are learning well, my daughter, anger is anger, rage is rage, and those who love enough can transform this energy into a worthwhile cause. Evil must be fought at every crossroad for it is indeed present. Heavenly Father gave each of us the nine fruits of the spirit to use in this never-ending battle for righteousness. Write them down again, dear one: love, joy, peace, patience, faith, goodness, kindness, gentleness and self-control from the Book of Galatians. Pray for those who fight injustice and peace be with you, my child.

Diane:

This message is not written as well as some, but its contents are important for me. It amazes me how much of life is spent in judging how someone else is reacting, rather than how I, myself, am reacting. This is an important key to spiritual development. If we all would spend as much time on self-criticism as we do on criticizing others, the world would be a better place at this time in history.

Thursday, June 15, 1995
Spirit:

Yes, dear one, it is in the doing that one releases the energy to travel farther on the spiritual climb to Heavenly Father. You have asked and are receiving. Now with great desire, you must continue to seek the avenues to serve. We shall never desert you, but rather work harder to help you find your perfect calling. Keep ever alert as you live each day in love and peace. It takes many rocks to make a mountain, many grains of sand to make a beach, many droplets of water to make an ocean. So it goes that many small deeds of selfless love will build a ladder to Heavenly Father's arms. Work diligently, but see the beauty in all things as you walk a path of peace.

Monday, June 19, 1995
Spirit:

We shall always continue to encourage you to share, to enlighten, to introduce the knowledge, and yes, expertise that you have gained through the diligence of your desire to ask, seek and knock over these years. This was done through an avenue of prayer, seeking unconditional love and using your talents in the service of Heavenly Father. Yes, dear one, the time has come to enlighten others; to help them to understand the power of the realms of spirit which lie beyond the physical life. Yours is a life of credibility, so even unbelievers will listen to what you say, even as you recommend books to read. It is time for you to truly share your gift of understanding, and is this not the perfect opportunity to begin?

Silence helps no one. Such information will be accepted by those who are ready to climb the spiritual ladder either through desire or necessity. We are with you constantly as you gain strength and courage to pursue this avenue of work with a grateful heart. *Always* strengthen your own aura through prayer, for this gives protection for you to walk the corridors of unrest with sparkles of love. Love can and will conquer the despair caused by darkness because it shines with Heavenly Father's brilliance. Those who serve without fear can enter the dark places because they are protected by their own faith which shows itself in love. It is time to step out into this unknown space and be of service. May peace walk with you, my child.

Saturday, June 24, 1995

"And nothing will be impossible for you." *(Matthew: 17–20)*

Diane:

I'm taking an early morning retreat into my own thoughts. It is such a vast area to explore. As I become more comfortable within, so shall I become worthy to do my Father's will. There is no lack there, only my own resistance to see the truth as it lives in each second of reality; each moment that passes should be appreciated as a learning experience to become part of the whole of creation. We spend so much time judging life and our piece of it that there is little time left to live it with appreciation, peace and love.

I am reading the book *The Miracle of Mindfulness* by the Buddhist monk Thich Nhat Hanh and it is very helpful to me.[50] How easy it is to let the busyness of life steal away its joy. I pray that God will enlighten me more to the beauty of peace. Freedom to live in peace is the reward for one who masters his own mind through concentration and control. I shall continue to strive for this, and pray that all of God's children will find peace within as well.

Monday, June 26, 1995
Spirit:

Get more rest, little one, and do not push yourself so hard. Can you not see that this overloads the communication line between us? Give all of your energy to finding that place of peace and serenity in spite of the circumstances of daily living. This skill *must* be mastered, for then you can and will place all things into their proper place. Love can only enter into a peaceful environment. Fatigue is an ally of negative thinking, so when weary, think of joyful things and give gratitude, always gratitude, to Heavenly Father for his many blessings.

We have come to encourage you countless times through the years since your beloved Ang passed over into spirit. Have you not progressed far since that time? Press on, but do so in a gentle manner concerning yourself. Let go and let God be your tour guide. Only say the word and you shall be healed. Peace be with you.

Tuesday, July 18, 1995
Diane:

Today I would like to put a few more writings into the computer for I'm finally down to this last book. I have not done any new writings of late, probably because I do not sit quietly often enough. I *must* get back into my old routine of a scheduled quiet time. It will happen because I will make it happen. As I am learning continuously, *I am* in control of my thought patterns and what I do. The hidden secret is using prayer, meditation and quiet contemplation as a means to connect into the will of God.

Sometimes I wonder why some of the supposed unknowns seem so clear to me—as if I have no doubt lingering in my mind. This brings such joy into my life even in difficult situations when I'm usually fatigued. I notice this happens less frequently. Some things which once seemed of importance, no longer seem so. Why is this so, dear friends?

Spirit:

Once one has joined the "eternal circuit," what was once so important takes a place further away from the brightness of what stands in the center of all life—to do the will of God as you outgrow your own will. This causes one to place less emphasis on physical or earthly needs. As one continues to travel with this invisible light, Heavenly Father's wisdom and insight grows into the conscious mind and understanding occurs, as if by magic. All-knowing lies hidden and dormant within all of mankind, and is released only as one seeks the answers through the fruits of the spirit.

Do you not remember your desire to ask, seek and knock, and your attraction for the nine fruits of the spirit? Herein lies the answer to your question, oh dearest of ones. You seek for a pure heart every moment of each day and we can work to enlighten one with such aspirations. Continue to know, that you know with the deepest humility, for all things are possible with God. Peace be with you.

Tuesday, August 1, 1995

Spirit:

If you live each moment of your life *trying* for love and service to God, we can, and do work with this desire. When, oh when, dear one, will you stop punishing yourself mentally? This in itself distracts from your ability to find peace and recharge your energies. Love and serve all of life each moment of every day with gratitude and humbleness. This is your constant prayer and we hear your every whisper. Meditation heals your being, teaches wisdom, brings peace, supports unconditional love and lets you hear God's advice—this is why it is so important.

Remember to pray for others and never doubt your ability to send healing to those in need. It takes time to truly internalize God's truth, but once time is spent doing this, the end result will be a positive one. Were you not shown the result of healing prayer? Be proud of yourself, and of your progress, my daughter, and more wisdom will be sent to you. Ask, seek, knock with love and patience, and the rose within will unfold in all of its beauty. Peace be with you.

Thursday, August 3, 1995
Diane:

Obstacles are placed in front of us for reasons. It is necessary for me to decide what my priorities are, and then put them in proper order. I pray for help in doing this and to grow in my ability to place others' needs before my own—to love unconditionally and truly feel the distress of others within my own heart. It is so hard for me to know the fine line between compassion of understanding, and compassion to try and help. Sometimes others do not want help. Is this a weakness within them or me, or both? I often fault myself for lacking in compassion and unconditional love, and yet, unwanted help accomplishes very little.

Spirit:

Judge not and you shall not be judged. Remember well, dear one, it is always the intent of the heart which holds the truth. Prayers and honest, heartfelt concern do much good, even though such energy *cannot* be seen with the physical senses. Again remember well, the ego or self-will is a constant enemy of all those in the physical part of life for it feeds on praise, reward and false honesty. Go deep within yourself and align your desires and feelings with spiritual laws. Then, and only then will you begin to sense the truth about yourself. No one else can do this for another; it is the responsibility of each who walks in the physical world. The tragedy is that so few are even aware of their own potential in finding the God force within, and so many are lost because they do not know *where* to look. Perhaps your writings can awaken others as it has awakened you. Move ahead, dear one, and may peace be always with you.

Friday, August 4, 1995
Spirit:

We come with such love, dear one. The first suggestion we bring to you today is to enjoy the freedom of your ability to think with an open mind, for few are truly able to do this. Send all worries and confusion away; these only tangle the beautiful connection you strive to maintain between us. The physical mind tends to categorize everything and neatly stash it away like a computer, failing to enjoy and revel in the beauty of what the information is trying to say to you. We implore you to live with peace and joy as you carefully organize your life to do God's will.

If you do not hear the first time, we will place meaningful information in front of you again. Many times one must reread and further digest the words therein. You, like everyone, have many, many talents—some of which are hidden. It is the desire within which nutures these abilities, plus the time which one is willing to give to perfect the talent.

Continue to grow in your ability to meditate. It is through this ability to relax that we can help you the most. Many times we hear you say, "I must get up early to meditate." Do it, dear one, do it. It is in the energy of your desire that we can and will meet. If we know the specific time and place in advance, much more can be accomplished. Set no preconceived ideas about what can and will happen, but rather come with a grateful heart filled with love. This is the ideal frame of mind.

You live with little fear—is this not a great blessing? Congratulate yourself, dear one, for you have come far, yet push on to overcome self-imposed limitations in your life. So many fail to see the power of self-limitation. They spend their lives empowered within the grip of their own enslavement. Think of your writing as a way to free others from this self-imposed prison. You must fight the battle against the "I can't" syndrome. So much of the goodness and greatness of mankind gets locked into this attitude of "I can't." We will help you to find practical ideas to break through the barriers of this false belief.

You must look back upon your own spiritual growth and outline the steps which were most helpful to you. Each life has tragedy built within it, but the bottom line is how one reacts to such situations. What makes a positive thinker? This too is an important topic to dissect, my dear one.

What can one do in a practical sense to become a positive thinker? Pray for guidance and it shall be there in abundance from many sources.

Continue your search for those beautiful "sprites"—as you choose to call them. Nature spirits have been a lost kingdom to those on the physical plane for eons of time, but those who seek Heavenly Father's heart and his unconditional love will bring this great energy back to power again. The earth is in such need at this time in history. Wrong thinking and wrong action has done great damage to Mother Earth, but resiliency is one of her greatest assets. This too must be addressed in your writings.

We come to calm your thoughts as you continue to prepare yourself to find that special calling which only you can do. Follow your intuition, doing what it tells you to do with faithful perseverance. Lock into the wisdom inherent within your own being, and then *do what it tells you.* So many might hear the calling, but for many different reasons they fail to follow what they hear. Be not one of these lost souls. What you allow within your thoughts tells the truth of what and who you are.

Aloneness is an important part in one's development, so accept this as true progress. *Make* time to be alone, even when physical life demands much. This is a sign of self-mastery. One will not fulfill his destiny without self-mastery, and each day lends itself well to learning its lesson. Again, explore the small ways one can learn from any task, big or small, by the mental attitude applied in its completion. Philosophy helps some, but more practical application will reach many others. Use your capacity for logic as we channel more information to you. As you make that special time for meditation available to us, we can supply much in the way of information to you. God bless you and keep on keeping on. Peace be with you.

Wednesday, August 30, 1995

Diane:

Why is it when our ego gets hurt, we tend to pull back the love which dwells within our heart? Why is this, and what can be done to overcome this frailty?

Spirit:

Remember, dear one, life is a gift and an ongoing process to learn the meaning of love and its power, protection and purpose in all of creation. The ego grows through conditioning; each one watches what goes on around him and these influences are very powerful. The God-self knows only love, but the ego learns the traits of fallen man so easily. To place others first is the meaning of spiritual love, but the ego quickly learns to place "me first," and it matters not what rules one plays by in order to please "me." The more insecure one becomes, the more he must scramble to get what he wants and to prove he is the best. Under these circumstances, the God-self has little room in which to grow, so it becomes imprisoned by the false values of the ego. Only when one begins to honestly look at himself can the spirit spring forth, and this special moment is the rebirth of the God-self and its ability to grow.

This is why writing a journal is of great value, for it forces the issues of the day to be reexamined and one has the opportunity to again face what happened. When one writes, it is necessary to think about one's thoughts with more precision, and usually this leads to a more honest evaluation since it is necessary to relive, at least to a degree, what transpired. It is easier to accept one's transgressions in thought than it is to see them spelled out in words. The God-self knows what is right; the ego must align itself with this truth and look at the unkindness and lack of love which dwells therein. This is not a pleasant task, so many fail to even try. This causes great turmoil in the world.

Start by changing yourself and by living a life of purity and love. The light of love is contagious and all can see it, even if they cannot accept it into their own life at that moment. Remember, love is never wasted and its energy increases the more it is used. Write that book, dear one, and share the gems of truth you are finding. Peace be with you, and remember, all things are possible with God. Believe!

Monday, September 4, 1995

Diane:

There is so much to do and so little time in which to do it. Is this then not the paradox of life itself?

Spirit:

Be careful, dear one, that the enormity of the thought does not paralyze you into a state of non-action. Any move to shower love upon another is a start in the right direction to correct the wrongs of the world. Do you not see that it is the little deeds of a lifetime which in the end make a difference?

Look to Mother Nature for your answers to profound thought for she teaches so much. Is not each grain of sand important in making a beach or a desert? Is not each droplet of water a part of the sea? Is not each leaf upon a tree important for the health and well-being of the whole tree? If we fail to care for each species of life in our kingdom, then do we really care for ourselves? Beauty is in the eyes of the beholder, and the lust for materialism and money has clouded the vision of so many spiritual eyes with the desires of the fallen physical body. Help for all will be gained by the caring of those who see love in the present chaos. A flicker of spiritual light burns within each of God's children, but how often do each of us dim the light of another through our carelessness in not caring enough? It is in the learning of consistency, order and trust that faith is found.

Again, look at the lesson of nature—the sun and moon, the tides, the seasons, the cycles of life. Each is important for the working of the whole and is consistent, dependable and accepted with faith that it will happen as expected. Why can man not do the same within his own being? Emphasize the importance and beauty of nature in your book, dear one. Did God not create all things, first in his mind and then into reality? Did God also not give man the ability to create in thought and bring this into reality as well? Be one who sees this great gift and act upon it. Peace be with you.

Wednesday, September 20, 1995

Diane:

Meditation and journal writing have taken a back seat of late, but this will not remain so. How can those dear ones in spirit help me if I keep the doorway between us almost closed?

Spirit:

We wait for you ever so patiently, dear one, so anguish not over your projected shortcomings, but rather make each experience in your life, no matter how mundane, a true stepping stone to something greater and more meaningful. Is it not wiser to draw every essence out of each moment than to live in regret and gain nothing? Be not one who spends energy on anything but positive thoughts filled with love even for what is unlovable.

Love is the pathway to finding these unique gifts for is not love involved in those activities you enjoy doing? Learn to dwell more upon your own thoughts for they are connected to the reservoir where the *All* originates. Heavenly Father desires to make each of us part of the whole of his creation and to learn its truths and secrets, but it must be done through *your own* efforts and understanding. Each negative thought or aspiration blocks the pathway, so always be on guard. Since you are master of your own being, refuse to allow entrance. It is truly that simple. If, per chance, an unwelcome visitor slips in, immediately change your thoughts to that of love and the unwelcome visitor will leave. Honest, negative feelings must indeed be released from within, but each time you take full control and change their negative hold over your thoughts, love can infiltrate and begin to ease the pain.

Love is *all* positive and it consumes the life of one who gives himself to doing the will of Heavenly Father. Let your inner light radiate forth, spreading love and beauty wherever you go. Peace be with you.

Thursday, September 21, 1995

Diane:

Music is a love in my life, yet why do I not spend more time doing it?

Spirit:

Perhaps, dear one, it is because you have chosen the pathway of doing for others first, and this choice leaves little time for your own desires after completing what must be done in daily living. These precious delights will last forever, so look into eternity for the time in which to do them.

Find the joy hidden within all things, my child. This is the secret to peace and happiness. We are delighted to have you back. Remember that the connection can only grow stronger with a sincere desire to touch, and it will be so. Everything is possible to one who seeks to find answers to the unknown, into the world of faith. Heavenly Father sees into his children's hearts and grants their wishes in his own way and in his own time. This is the difficult lesson to learn, but within it lies peace and all the other fruits of the spirit. Know this and strive always to find yourself in the perfection of his glorious love. Peace be with you always, dear one.

Sunday, October 1, 1995
Diane:

Are there not many times in life when one must move along on faith alone? What is the true meaning of faith?

Spirit:

Faith, dear one, is knowing that God is *always* with you. His light encircles you; his love and power surround and protect you. Wherever you are, God is. As this truth arises from within your own being and penetrates the difficulties of life, you find more peace and joy in daily living. One can roll with the flow much more easily and not get caught in the mire of negative reaction to the vicissitudes of life. It is the thought reaction which causes the most difficulty and pain. Once one takes action through the eyes of faith, problems begin to dissipate and instead are placed into their proper perspective. Faith lets you see beyond the moment, knowing all will work out in God's own time. Faith comforts all who are willing to place their deepest desires into Heavenly Father's hands and wait for the answer to surface from within. They will appear from that faith-filled place where

God dwells. This period of waiting is faith, and it grows stronger with use. We come close to be with you and bring you peace.

Wednesday, October 4, 1995
Diane:

There are many problems in our society today and I pray that somehow these troubles can be addressed and peace will reign among all races. I am beginning to see that much more effort and concentration is needed to love rather than to hate. Hate is a quick reaction to something one does not like or agree with, but it damages the spiritual side of one's being. One cannot change from hate to love easily, but with patience and true examination of the intent of your heart, progress can be made.

Place what you hate into the hands of God or his son, Jesus, to grow in love and peace. This is an important first step, for it grows in power a little more each day. This energy can be used in a positive way to help soothe the many problems of this world. The more intense the positive energy becomes, the greater will be its healing power. Hear, dear Heavenly Father, the intent of my heart to send out only love and help us to heal the world. I know deep within that this is possible, for all things are possible with God. Forgive me for failing to spend more time in heartfelt prayer. It is my lack of self-control to pace myself better, but you know I am working on this fruit of the spirit everyday, and I shall be victorious.

Monday, October 9, 1995

"We look beyond what seems to be reality and behold the possibilities of God's splendor at work! Yes, the best is yet to be!"[51]

"For mortals it is impossible, but not for God; for God all things are possible." *(Mark 10:27)*

Diane:

I'm trying very hard to slow down a bit and listen to the message my body is trying to tell me. My knee has been painful of late, and other parts of my body are stiffer than usual. Somehow I am not in synch with my inner self. Perhaps too much busyness and doing household chores, and not enough prayer, and soaring into the realm of finding and using my unique gifts for the benefit of all.

Obviously I have not found that beautiful spot where my desires match what God wants and needs me to do. We must always remain on guard to chase away the negative thoughts which constantly bombard us. If negativity remains too long and we allow it to begin influencing the mind, illness will show its ugly face somewhere. I know this so well intellectually, but it is of little value to me if I cannot totally believe that all things are possible with God. Help me, dear Heavenly Father, to grow in this ability to find your white light of healing and protection that I may do your will for the remainder of my life. Help me to better organize my time to help others, but not overlook the need to pray, meditate and study within my own life.

It seems a balance must be found for life to flow with a perfect rhythm. I know in my heart of hearts that the ultimate goal each is seeking is the ability to tap into the creativity and power of God's love and goodness. Each day teaches a lesson in how to follow and find this goal. Prayer will keep me centered and meditation will lead the way.

Spirit:

Health is perhaps the reward for listening well, dear one. It is time to quiet your inner being through more meditation and contemplation. Set a time in your daily schedule again to pursue this endeavor, and then watch the results. Each *is* responsible for his own temple where God dwells. One must take the necessary time to find peace among the many forces which pull at each who walks the physical plane. How necessary it is to realign one's purpose! Ask, seek and knock. If you do this, you will be at peace.

Thursday, November 9, 1995
Diane:

There is so much in physical life that one can only conjecture about; then intuition has to play a big part in knowing the truth. Oh, to open the power of my intuitive abilities to seek the truth of Heavenly Father's spiritual laws! How does one do this, dear friends in spirit?

Spirit:

Grow in your ability to trust, dear one. Trust God, trust in yourself and in your ability to find the wisdom buried deep within your own being. All of the answers are there. You must release them through service to others in *all* circumstances. Heavenly Father watches for deep devotion and a total commitment to doing his will. Trust in God, for he is always there. But can God trust you to be always there for his many other children? Each must prove himself worthy, for this unlatches the door to enlightenment. As the trust increases, more spiritual truth enters into the conscious mind. Only those who seek the spiritual pathway with a sincere heart can begin to open the door to such treasure. We will talk of this again. Peace be with you.

Wednesday, November 29, 1995

Diane:

Yesterday marked nine years since Ang passed over. My heart has healed and one day we shall share love and life again. But in the interim there is much we each must accomplish. Time becomes less important in my life, and the secret to joy is appreciating what one is doing at the moment.

I'm again reading *The Miracle of Mindfulness* by Thich Nhat Hanh.[52] To control one's mind through concentration is very important. I am stuck on a plateau in need of a better routine for meditation and I must make the effort to do this.

Printing my writings is also an important step as well. I need that boost of inner confidence to truly complete the job, but Heavenly Father will help me to find this strength within. Of this, I have no doubt. Soon I shall become less occupied with the daily needs of physical life. Yet I am who I am, and helping others is high on my priority list. However, maybe the book will help others as well.

Spirit:

Balance, dear one, balance. We see you implementing spiritual truth in your daily life as naturally as you breathe, and this is great progress. So be grateful as you live a life of prayer. The desire to serve Heavenly Father shines forth from your heart with great brilliance, and we come to tell you this periodically in the form of a pep talk. You must remember to be in control of your thoughts *always*. This is the truest pathway to serving God, for wisdom can travel from within only through pure thought. Love of all things strengthens one's ability to hear the beauty of spiritual laws. Through your love you can and do influence others. Know this and be energized by those who come close to give you courage and love. Peace be with you, dear one.

Sunday, December 10, 1995
Spirit:

Dear one, think and pray for others, and your own concerns will become less. This will help you to continue to cope with problems without a detrimental effect on your own spiritual being. Once you have sent a problem into Heavenly Father's hands you *must* have faith that the perfect solution will be forthcoming in his own time. Each time doubt or negative thoughts are allowed to surface, the positive energy is diminished. Everything works within spiritual laws and you, in physical life, see with such limited vision.

See nothing but good and it shall be so. Feel only love and it shall be so. Remember, dear one, faith is *knowing* without seeing the results. Pursue a life of giving to others without any desire for a return. This is the only answer to finding everlasting joy; unselfish acts of kindness kill the unwanted ego which lives within each. You must be willing to trust your Father's will and let your own will be non-existent. This is the most difficult task to accomplish, but we urge you to climb ever higher upon the spiritual pathway. The more difficult the challenge, the more you must pray, meditate and seek what you already know. This is the truth from God which lies hidden within each of his children. Your task is to open fully to your spirit where God dwells. Pray for wisdom to enter the lives of all people;

the light is there but for the darkness of ignorance. The presence of God watches over you, for wherever you are, he is. Peace be with you always.

Sunday, December 17, 1995
Diane:

There is much to accomplish this week, but I'll take things one at a time and always do my best to enjoy everything. These precious feelings which accompany every activity are the prerequisite to enjoying eternity. Every moment of the now is what we use to build our steps to climb into paradise with Heavenly Father. Anyone can find joy in happy times, but those who desire the truth of enlightenment must find joy and meaning in the moments of sadness, sorrow and pain.

Spirit:

We hear your daily cries for understanding and for doing your Father's will. We come to encourage you to strive for joy and understanding, compassion and love, even in the darkest moments. Only on the wings of positive thought can we build the energy to produce what you desire.

Look beyond earth's shadows and catch a vision with your inner eye; imagine with faith and trust for all things are possible with God. In those many interims of waiting, help those less fortunate than you, always giving of yourself with love, gentleness, kindness and goodness. Forgive those who see with limited vision and pray for them. These simple rules will do much to rid the world of its negativity and all those emotions which cause detrimental results. It is the living spirit within each which kindles and radiates light spreading love and beauty upon this earth.

One must start with himself and the light that shines forth will touch the spirit of another until this force makes the difference. Never be discouraged by outward signs, but rather look more closely for the deeper meaning as you strive to help others that cross your path. We guide and give strength to all, but especially to those who follow the call of service. Step by step we try to ignite the spark of light energy in all of God's children with great love and unending patience.

Can you feel our energy around you? *Know,* and know that you know, that we always stand nearby to comfort and help you, especially your husband, parents, many relatives and friends. Dear one, to be in your aura is an uplifting experience of joy; so many come to be with you. Remember well the power of love. Peace be with you always.

Epilogue

Many years have passed since the last journal entry in this book. Since I put my pen down on December 17, 1995, I haven't felt a call to write regularly as I did during the seven years before that date. When I ask myself why, I don't have a ready answer except to say a certain process has been completed; a certain message delivered. In writing my journal and reading it over and over, my grief at the loss of my husband was lessened, and I found wisdom from within that gave me a new way to live.

Since 1995, my abiding rules of the road remain centered on the fruits of the spirit: love, joy, peace, patience, kindness, goodness, faithfulness, gentleness, and self-control, and I continue to measure all of my thoughts and actions by these words. I still have daily conversations with spirit and Heavenly Father, whose love and light guide me constantly. I continue to pray, meditate, and practice yoga; all disciplines which keep me spiritually grounded. How blessed I am!

One simple prayer also serves me well: *God, help me to know thy grace.* When this prayer first entered my life, I asked, "What is grace? What does it mean?" After a few days, an answer came: Grace is the sacred fulfillment of unconditional love. Yes, I can testify to that. I know I am loved. If I have concerns, answers come to me, and if I feel lost, I am comforted.

My own spiritual climb is indeed one full of grace. I can do nothing alone, through special talent or effort. I must be willing to be quiet, to listen, and to lean on the presence of God and loving spirit.

I find that I can live my life without judging or blaming others, and that is a great relief. I am still being given gifts of hope, joy, and gratitude, and I've learned that if I can love enough, there is nothing to fear. In my eightieth year, I feel young in spirit, and I don't fear death. The spirit world is just another side of life—a magnificent experience that I anticipate with positive expectation. Perhaps this is because the world of spirit no longer seems a world of the unknown. I *know* it's there, waiting for me, just as I know Ang is there, waiting.

How has my experience with journaling helped me in specific, practical ways? I have been able to harness good attributes and experiences from my younger years and integrate them into my present life. Based on my life-long love of gardening, I have developed a rich indoor nursery, which I tend year round. It brings me much daily joy. I studied music in college, and music remains a source of great happiness for me. For many years, I was a kindergarten and nursery school teacher for small children. They taught me how to think like a kid and to be open to the wonder of each moment. My experience with them blesses me whenever I catch a glimpse of sunrise or hear the rain falling on my roof.

As an avid gardener, I spend a great deal of time in my yard. In July 2009, I was bitten by a deer tick. While the test for Lyme Disease was negative, I was infected with a potentially more serious, exotic-sounding disease called Babesiosis, and I landed in the local hospital for six days. I got through my illness well because of my good mental, emotional, and physical condition—all derived from daily practices which I owe largely to my experience in writing my journal.

When my mother came to live with me, she needed much attention, and at times we were both very tired. Because I had learned to turn to God for everything, I simply asked for a little light to come into our situation. The next day, when we were sitting on my deck, a tiny stray kitten jumped on my mother's lap. She loves kittens, and her relationship with Smokey gave her a new lease on life. A precious little light, indeed!

When I was ready to sell my bed and breakfast, I didn't know where to begin. I had a personal acquaintance who was a real estate agent, and she was ready to help. Everything fell into place. I see that constantly in my life today: Everything falls into place if I step back far enough to let God's hand move in my life.

Through journaling, I developed the habit of seeking to do God's will. That practice is a genuine part of me now. I know that I'm here for God, and I'm willing. I still go through hard times, but I always find that if I bring God into any difficult situation, the reward is spiritual growth. I would not be where I am today if I had not gone through the sorrow of losing my husband. My desperation sent me into the center of my being, and God was waiting for me there. Now I can accept whatever comes with an open mind, open eyes, and an open heart.

Would I trade the spiritual growth I have gained for more years with my husband beside me? Probably so. I still miss him immensely. But the growth I have experienced is invaluable, just as my life with Ang was—both deeply good; both richly rewarding. I know God is with me no matter what else is happening. He is with all of us, whether we are fully aware of it or not. The reality is that Ang died many years ago, but I have been blessed by an ongoing sense of his caring presence in spirit and the ongoing love of God. I can only be grateful.

Just to test the waters, I picked up my journal again on September 1, 2003. I was curious to see if spirit would come through again in my writing. Here is the result:

Monday, September 1, 2003

Spirit:

Life is what you yourself make it to be, my little one. I talk to you all the time through your thoughts. It matters not that you do not have profound dreams, for instead you travel through the unknown as you sleep, and your experience is manifested to you as truth and wisdom. How many in life would be overjoyed to say, *I know that I know that I know*. All you need personally is to have confidence in your own intuition to put your journal writings on paper in book form. Is this truth not bubbling up to spring forth?

Conjure up the effort and courage to do it. If only you could see all those who cheer you on, for they know firsthand how important knowledge of the spirit world truly is. Each must find peace, love, faith, joy, patience, goodness, kindness, gentleness and self-control while still in the physical body. Spiritual attributes come from God, our Heavenly Father, and it is up to each human being to live life in accordance with divine will. How else can one find the beauty of creation-heaven? Depth of the soul must be found, or at least acknowledged, while in the body.

Mankind has much to learn and we channel through you dear one, for you take the time to seek, and thus you hear my voice and the voice of all those who help you. Pray often and believe that all will be well, and it shall be so. Walk in peace and love.

Macci
Family Photos

Angelo & Diane Macci

Mr. & Mrs. Macci
August 15, 1954

Angelo & Diane
Through the Years
Mid-60s & 70s

Macci Children & Diane

Sue, Diane, Lee, Angela, John

Macci Grandchildren & Diane

Left to right, top to bottom:
Melissa, Lauren, Taylor, Jennifer, Allyson, Ryan, Diane, Jessica, Matthew, & Kep the dog.

Sources

As I wrote in my journal over a period of seven years, I spontaneously included inspirational writings or sayings from various sources. They are listed below so that readers who choose to do so may find the exact citations related to these words.

---

[1] *The Quiet Mind, The Sayings of White Eagle* by Grace Cooke. The White Eagle Publishing Trust, Liss, Hampshire, England.

[2] *Hands of Light: A Guide to Healing Through the Human Energy Field* by Barbara Ann Brennan. Bantam Books, New York.

[3] *The Quiet Mind, The Sayings of White Eagle* by Grace Cooke. The White Eagle Publishing Trust, Liss, Hampshire, England.

[4] *Scientific Healing Affirmations* by Paramahansa Yogananda. Self-Realization Fellowship, Los Angeles, California.

[5] Eknath Easwaran and F. M. Dostoevsky. Both from *Words to Live By: A Daily Guide to Leading an Exceptional Life* by Eknath Easwaran. Nilgiri Press, Petaluma, California.

[6] *Words to Live By: A Daily Guide to Leading an Exceptional Life* by Eknath Easwaran. Nilgiri Press, Petaluma, California.

[7] *The Quiet Mind, The Sayings of White Eagle* by Grace Cooke. The White Eagle Publishing Trust, Liss, Hampshire, England.

[8] Edward Everett Hale. Source unknown.

[9] *The Prophet* by Kahlil Gibran. Alfred A. Knopf.

[10] *Words to Live By: A Daily Guide to Leading an Exceptional Life* by Eknath Easwaran. Nilgiri Press, Petaluma, California.

[11] *The Quiet Mind, The Sayings of White Eagle* by Grace Cooke. The White Eagle Publishing Trust, Liss, Hampshire, England.

[12] *The Quiet Mind, The Sayings of White Eagle* by Grace Cooke. The White Eagle Publishing Trust, Liss, Hampshire, England.

[13] *The Quiet Mind, The Sayings of White Eagle* by Grace Cooke. The White Eagle Publishing Trust, Liss, Hampshire, England.

[14] *The Quiet Mind, The Sayings of White Eagle* by Grace Cooke. The White Eagle Publishing Trust, Liss, Hampshire, England.

[15] *Words to Live By: A Daily Guide to Leading an Exceptional Life* by Eknath Easwaran. Nilgiri Press, Petaluma, California.

[16] *Words to Live By: A Daily Guide to Leading an Exceptional Life* by Eknath Easwaran. Nilgiri Press, Petaluma, California.

[17] *Edgar Cayce: The Sleeping Prophet* by Jess Stearn. Bantam Books, New York.

[18] *An Angel in My House* by Tobias Palmer. Harpercollins Books.

[19] *Have a Great Day—Every Day* by Norman Vincent Peale. Fleming H. Revell Co.

[20] *Words to Live By: A Daily Guide to Leading an Exceptional Life* by Eknath Easwaran. Nilgiri Press, Petaluma, California.

[21] *The Quiet Mind, The Sayings of White Eagle* by Grace Cooke. The White Eagle Publishing Trust, Liss, Hampshire, England.

[22] Robert Browning. Source unknown.

[23] *Words to Live By: A Daily Guide to Leading an Exceptional Life* by Eknath Easwaran. Nilgiri Press, Petaluma, California.

[24] Henry David Thoreau. Source unknown.

[25] *Bhagavad Gita*. Nilgiri Press, Petaluma, California.

[26] *Words to Live By: A Daily Guide to Leading an Exceptional Life* by Eknath Easwaran. Nilgiri Press, Petaluma, California.

[27] Mother Teresa. Source unknown.

[28] *Have a Great Day,* by Norman Vincent Peale, a Fawcett Columbine Book published by Ballantine Books, New York.

[29] *The Quiet Mind, The Sayings of White Eagle* by Grace Cooke. The White Eagle Publishing Trust, Liss, Hampshire, England.

[30] *The Way of the Disciple,* title of a prayer in *The Quiet Mind, The Sayings of White Eagle* by Grace Cooke. The White Eagle Publishing Trust, Liss, Hampshire, England.

[31] *Words to Live By: A Daily Guide to Leading an Exceptional Life* by Eknath Easwaran. Nilgiri Press, Petaluma, California.

[32] Jalaluddin Rumi, in *Words to Live By: A Daily Guide to Leading an Exceptional Life* by Eknath Easwaran. Nilgiri Press, Petaluma, California.

Sources

[33] *Daily Word.* Unity, Kansas City, Missouri.

[34] *Daily Guideposts,* November 5, 1993.

[35] *The Quiet Mind, The Sayings of White Eagle* by Grace Cooke. The White Eagle Publishing Trust, Liss, Hampshire, England.

[36] *Words to Live By: A Daily Guide to Leading an Exceptional Life* by Eknath Easwaran. Nilgiri Press, Petaluma, California.

[37] *Words to Live By: A Daily Guide to Leading an Exceptional Life* by Eknath Easwaran. Nilgiri Press, Petaluma, California.

[38] *Words to Live By: A Daily Guide to Leading an Exceptional Life* by Eknath Easwaran. Nilgiri Press, Petaluma, California.

[39] *Have a Great Day Every Day* by Norman Vincent Peale. Fleming H. Revell Co.

[40] *Daily Word.* Unity, Kansas City, Missouri.

[41] *Spiritual Enfoldment 4* by White Eagle. The White Eagle Publishing Trust, New Lands, Liss, Hampshire, England.

[42] *It's in Every One of Us*, song by David Pomerantz.

[43] *Daily Word.* Unity, Kansas City, Missouri.

[44] *Unity Magazine,* article by Jan DeVries.

[45] Antoine de Saint Exupery. Source unknown.

[46] *Daily Word.* Unity, Kansas City, Missouri.

[47] *Daily Word.* Unity, Kansas City, Missouri.

[48] *Unity Magazine*, article by Philip White, May 1995.

[49] *Daily Word.* Unity, Kansas City, Missouri.

[50] *The Miracle of Mindfulness* by Thich Nhat Hanh. Beacon Press.

[51] *Daily Word.* Unity, Kansas City, Missouri.

[52] *The Miracle of Mindfulness* by Thich Nhat Hanh. Beacon Press.

Scripture quotations are taken from these sources:
- The Holy Bible, King James Version. Thomas Nelson, Inc.
- The New American Bible. Catholic Bible Publishers, Witchita, Kansas, 1971–72 edition.
- The Holy Bible, New International Version. © 1973, 1978, 1984 by Biblica, Inc.™ Used by permission of Zondervan. All rights reserved worldwide. *www.zondervan.com.*
- 1989 Favorite Bible Quotations Calendar. © 1988, Antioch Publishing Company, Yellow Springs, Ohio.

Phoenix, Arizona

For general inquiries (or to contact author Diane Macci), send an E-mail to *PB@PhilipBurley.com* or write to:

Adventures in Mastery, LLC (AIM)
P.O. Box 43548
Phoenix, AZ 85080

About Adventures in Mastery and Philip Burley

The mission of Adventures in Mastery (AIM) is to provide inspiration, education, and information about the spirit world and finding God within through practices such as prayer, meditation, mindful living, and service. Mastery Press, a division of AIM, publishes books which increase public awareness of the spirit world, universal love, and self-knowledge. Philip Burley, President of AIM, is a publisher, author, speaker, and teacher in the field of meditation and spiritual development whose spiritual senses have been fully open since early childhood. He has served the public as a professional medium and spiritual counselor for three decades.

www.ingramcontent.com/pod-product-compliance
Lightning Source LLC
Chambersburg PA
CBHW020347170426
43200CB00005B/77